7-17-16

To Vivian
with admiration
for all you've
accomplished.

Ben

A Battlefield of Values

A Battlefield of Values

America's Left, Right, and Endangered Center

Stephen D. Burgard and Benjamin J. Hubbard

Foreword by Jack Miles

PRAEGER™

An Imprint of ABC-CLIO, LLC
Santa Barbara, California • Denver, Colorado

Library of Congress Cataloging-in-Publication Data

Names: Burgard, Stephen, author. | Hubbard, Benjamin Jerome, author.
Title: A battlefield of values : America's left, right, and endangered center / Stephen D. Burgard, Benjamin J. Hubbard.
Description: Santa Barbara, California : Praeger, 2016. | Includes bibliographical references and index.
Identifiers: LCCN 2015038600| ISBN 9781440831928 (hardback) | ISBN 9781440831935 (e-book)
Subjects: LCSH: Political culture—United States. | Values—Political aspects—United States. | Right and left (Political science)—United States. | Polarization (Social sciences)—United States. | Identity politics—United States. | Religion and politics—United States. | Christianity and politics—United States. | United States—Politics and government. | United States—Religious life and customs. | BISAC: POLITICAL SCIENCE / Political Process / Political Parties.
Classification: LCC JK1726 .B87 2016 | DDC 320.50973—dc23
LC record available at http://lccn.loc.gov/2015038600

ISBN: 978-1-4408-3192-8
EISBN: 978-1-4408-3193-5

20 19 18 17 16   1 2 3 4 5

This book is also available on the World Wide Web as an eBook.
Visit www.abc-clio.com for details.

Praeger
An Imprint of ABC-CLIO, LLC

ABC-CLIO, LLC
130 Cremona Drive, P.O. Box 1911
Santa Barbara, California 93116-1911

This book is printed on acid-free paper ∞

Manufactured in the United States of America

To Steve's children—Helen, Drew, and Patrick

To Ben's family—Judy, Susan, and David

Contents

Foreword by *Jack Miles*   ix

Preface   xiii

Introduction: America's Divided Heart   xv

Chapter 1   The Religion Factor   1

Chapter 2   What People Think and Believe Religiously   31

Chapter 3   What People Think and Believe Politically   45

Chapter 4   America's Great Debates—Immigration, Gun Rights, and Climate Change   61

Chapter 5   America and the World—Religiosity and the American Character   79

Chapter 6   What Matters to the Right   99

Chapter 7   What Matters to the Left   111

Chapter 8   What Matters to the Center and Why It's Endangered   127

Chapter 9   The New Centrists—Can They Rescue Our Struggling Democracy?   147

Chapter 10 "A Battlefield of Values"—Politics, Culture,
            and Religion in Orange County, California   161

Chapter 11 Besieged Media Go Polar   177

Chapter 12 Chivalry May Be Dead, but What about Civility?   199

Chapter 13 Conclusion—Still Embattled, Still Endangered,
            but Still Hopeful   217

Bibliography   221
Index   223

Foreword

I first met the late Steve Burgard, whose idea it was to write this book, as a disembodied voice coming from a small triangular microphone set on a round conference table at the *Los Angeles Times*. Around this table, I gathered each morning with my fellow members of the *Times*'s editorial board to determine what political positions the newspaper would officially take. We were a liberal crew, but the newspaper was trying at the time (the 1990s) to customize the editorial page of its Orange County edition to appeal to that county's famously conservative readership without cutting the edition loose entirely from the mother ship. Steve, a noticeable step to the right of the rest of us, had been hired to provide what was called for.

At the time, the main Los Angeles editorial page had a Chicano male editor, a black female associate editor, two other black editorial writers, three Jews, two elegantly liberal white-haired Episcopalians, and one Sierra Club conservationist with Greenpeace leanings. There was nary a socialist or communist among us, I hasten to add, contrary to the charge occasionally leveled by an irate subscriber, but we did reflect the liberal tilt of Los Angeles county just as well as we did its ethnic, religious, and social diversity.

Steve—white and white-haired but no limousine liberal—thus had had his work cut out for him from the start. He was in the minority, and he had to advance his minority views as a disembodied voice trying to gain a hearing among nine or so decidedly outspoken liberal opinionators. Little by little, however, he made his way forward, and he did so oftenest with one of the clear strengths of the book before you, the book that he conceived and began, and that Ben Hubbard has now concluded. That strength was the strength of patient, clear, grounded, and above all concise reporting.

Burgard and Hubbard take you well behind the headlines in this book, deep into the sources of the polarization that now so grievously afflicts American political discourse. They pay unique attention, in tracing those sources, to religion. But they would be the last to say that liberals and conservatives are divided by theology alone. Real political, economic, and cultural issues are at stake; and so with malice toward none and charity toward all, as Abe Lincoln would put it, and with their trademark concision, they give us cold-button versions of a tough list of hot-button issues. We've felt the heat. They're here to turn on the light.

If my association with Steve began on the journalism side of my CV, my friendship with Ben began on the religious side. Like me, Ben has taught religious studies. And beyond any claim that I can make for myself, he has been an explorer of the religious geography and sociology of Orange County. I knew both writers separately before I discovered that they had discovered one another. Ben may have been predisposed by temperament and training to an awareness of religious diversity, but he also has an advanced degree in journalism and has taught that subject too. The combination is unusual but pays off in this book in a refined appreciation of how sometimes barely recognized or only half-remembered religious influences can play a large, even a determining role in the shaping of a political philosophy.

Any pair of reporters attempting to offer cold-button versions of their set of hot-button issues while engaging at every point the background issue of polarization would see America as it looks from *where* they happen to write, for every locale offers a slightly different lens through which to view whatever is to be viewed. Orange County turns out to offer a surprisingly fresh and unexpected lens through which to view this key set of common American issues, and most of all the overriding American political handicap of insuperable polarization.

Steve Burgard went on from his success at the *Los Angeles Times* to become director of the School of Journalism at Northeastern University. But as I discovered after I myself ended up on the faculty of the University of California, Irvine, in the heart of Orange County, the County had never quite left Steve. To my initially intrigued surprise, he spent some weeks every year as a journalist in residence with the UCI department of political science, still deeply engaged by this unusual place and the unusual vantage it offered him on a besetting array of national issues. Professionally, he was squarely in the Boston-to-Washington policy-wonk megalopolis. Personally, he had not stopped thinking about Orange County.

Ben Hubbard is now semi-retired from the California State University at Fullerton, also in Orange County, and this book may well prove the first of several from the pen of a man who has found his chosen subject in an unlikely venue that is evolving rapidly demographically and otherwise. Santa Ana, the largest and oldest of the towns that grew together into the exurban conglomerate that is Orange County, is now over 90 percent Hispanic and (when registered) majority Democratic. Yet the old white-evangelical-conservative Orange County lives on in new forms: Orange County is the birthplace, for example, of that powerful new expression of conservative Christianity, the megachurch. (Think of Barack Obama and John McCain meeting in debate at Saddleback Church in 2008, the proceedings moderated by the estimable Rev. Rick Warren.) In what was once the quintessence of white-bread, vanilla-ice-cream America, a microcosm of global religion and global society has suddenly come into existence.

Let me offer a concluding word on the distinct tone in which this book is written, for these two authors demonstrate the solution to the very problem that they have identified. I call their tone gentle cordiality. Such once was the tone in which a fair amount of American political discussion, even strained discussion, took place. But in these latter days, wrath as expressed anonymously online or theatrically on television has become a rehearsed form of entertainment that virtually eclipses thought. Yet if gentle answers are persistent and informed, they can foil even such rehearsed wrath. As the Book of Proverbs puts it (15:1), "A gentle answer turneth away wrath." As for cordiality, the term comes ultimately from the Latin *cor, cordis*, "the heart"; what is cordial is heartfelt. In these pages, Burgard and Hubbard speak gently, from the heart, but with the staying power of carefully marshaled information. Between them, they may, at long last, begin to turn our self-crippling American wrath into the real talk so many of us long to hear again.

—Jack Miles,
Distinguished Professor of English
and Religious Studies,
University of California at Irvine,
Orange County

Preface

I met co-author Steve Burgard in the mid-1990s when I began writing an occasional column on religion for the *Los Angeles Times*/Orange County edition. In fact, it was Steve who recommended to his editors that I be given this opportunity. Over the years we became good friends, and I helped him make the transition from journalism to academia as he became director of the School of Journalism at Northeastern University in 2002. We continued to cooperate on various projects, especially the first and second editions of a book he edited *Faith, Politics and Media in Our Perilous Times* to which I contributed a chapter. At some point in 2012, I lamented to him the increasing polarization in Congress and society in general, and proposed we write a column about this for the *Boston Globe*. He came back with a counterproposal: "Let's write a book about the problem." Thus began the hunt for a publisher and ultimately the green light given us by ABC-CLIO to produce this book. Steve was on his first sabbatical as a research fellow at the Harvard Divinity School when, on October 26, 2014, he succumbed to a serious lung disease at age 66. His death was, of course, a great loss to his family, including his children Helen, Drew, and Patrick, to his colleagues at Northeastern, and to his co-author. I decided the project had to go on in his memory and because we both believed so strongly in the thesis of the book.

Steve had been a superb editor of my work at the *Los Angeles Times* and that editing had continued during the earlier stages of the book. So, in the end, I hope the finished product lives up to his high standards and serves as a fitting memorial to his outstanding work as a journalist and a professor of journalism.

I received a lot of support with this project, this labor of friendship, including especially from my wife Judy who hung in there once again (there were prior books) as I cloistered myself in my upstairs office month after month to finish the work. She both encouraged the project and rode herd on me to meet the due date. My son, David, provided technical support and daughter, Susan, was in my corner rooting for me. Jack Miles, distinguished professor of English and religious studies at UC Irvine, provided encouragement and guidance after Steve's death and graciously agreed to write the Foreword. Retired engineer and good friend Tom Egan read some of the material, especially the chapter on Orange County, and provided wise suggestions and a lot of moral support. Two of my students from California State University, Fullerton, Robert Cortes and Arnold Francisco, read and edited many of the chapters and were very helpful in making the book clearer and more readable. They were one more testimony to how important my students have been to me over a long career in higher education—in fact, how much they have been my life.

Finally, I am grateful to ABC-Clio and my editor Anthony Chiffolo who believed in this project and provided the additional time needed to finish the book after Steve's untimely death, and to project editor Jennifer Crane.

—Benjamin J. Hubbard

Introduction: America's Divided Heart

Americans agree on certain core values such as freedom, opportunity, rule of law, and fairness. After that, it's a race to the poles, as if, to paraphrase the popular book, "The Right Is from Mars; the Left Is from Venus."

You would think that people in the world's most successful democracy would agree more over what's right and what's wrong for the country, but, in fact, we don't. We are caught in a perpetual pendulum that swings right and left over what is right and just.

Division and conflict are not new to American life. However, previously in American history these differences were based more in regional perspectives, in agendas of political parties, or in straightforward disagreements over foreign intervention. Today, we have a structural conflict over values and perspectives built into the very framework of the country that goes to the core of what people believe. It finds expression in strong areas of disagreement on policy matters such as the role of government, reproductive issues, the environment, and immigration.

These variances increasingly are fixed and extreme. We hear conservatives talk about "leftism" as a kind of new secular belief system, where entitlements are a given. On the left, conservatives are dismissed as extremist, nativist, and homophobic.

To find evidence for this, consider the political rhetoric in election seasons on talk radio and cable TV news shows. Just watch where the margins tilt in recent national elections, not simply over the toss-up or battleground states that get media attention. But it happens on a deeper level in our running national discourse in media and in public conversation.

To say that we are polarized is an oversimplification of our national dilemma. We are this way to be sure, but we are so in a wide range of areas where in theory for a functioning democracy there ought to be more common ground. These cover domestic policy, foreign policy, and social and cultural issues.

The news media, the logical choice in a democracy for sorting out differences, are themselves caught up in a new set of competitive circumstances from social media and other economic and cultural forces. These drive them to report increasingly to segmented audiences, and there is evidence that even traditional "legacy" media are ready to abandon traditional norms of objectivity. This means that the institution vested in American democracy with the role of informer and mediator is in fact compromised in that task by its own set of problems.

We are not merely polarized; we are divided with a passion of righteous certainty over issues where our positions arise from differing and deeply held sets of beliefs. People make decisions about where to live based on perceptions of how other people think. In our own anecdotal conversations with students, we find that young people learn early on that there are topics in their own families and circles of friends that essentially are off-limits. (Co-author Ben Hubbard has an introductory lecture in his religion and politics course at Cal State Fullerton on the "undiscussables.") So we are not only divided, but we effectively are training future generations that opportunities may be shrinking for pragmatic and negotiated solutions to differences that were available in earlier times.

Nate Silver, in his 2014 postelection analysis of swing districts for the *New York Times*, found that the swing set is shrinking in size. And despite prognostications about an ascendant ideology, the reality is that a pendulum keeps swinging. The certitude that seemed to emerge about a permanent Republican majority in the Bush era has evaporated. The reelection of President Obama created a kind of self-confidence on the other side that proved to be temporary in the 2014 Republican landslide. Both sides appeared at the beginning of 2013, before and after niceties of inaugural harmony, to dig in; and the digging and intransigence has continued through 2015.

The frustrations of the fiscal cliff[1] debate at the end of 2012 and early 2013 show where hardened positions lead to choices that once seemed so unthinkable that they were proposed as a way to ensure that compromise would be reached. In early 2013, we saw where the unthinkable became possible and even likely.

Everybody wants a better America, but our differences turn out to be informed by powerful sets of *fixed* civic and religious values that take a partisan and inflexible turn and often are in direct conflict in the national arena. The increasing polarization of politics and our national conversation ultimately is based in unyielding sets of beliefs and values. Some of these are religious. Some are civic. Some arise from secular humanistic perspectives.

In many cases, hot-button issues like immigration and gay marriage come down to a collision of identifiable core values. In the case of immigration, for example, initiatives like one in Oakland to provide vulnerable undocumented workers with identification cards that double as debit cards pair off important sets of values against each other. The need for economic justice so that workers don't have to carry cash and risk robbery, essentially a protective safe-path up in the American system, is in collision with the argument that such efforts amount to an amnesty program that weakens efforts to make the immigration laws have teeth. The long legal struggle over gay marriage has been playing out as a national debate between civil rights versus upholding the primacy of a long-standing societal construction for what makes marriage unique. In late June, 2015, as this book was heading to the publisher, the Supreme Court in *Obergefell v. Hodges* ruled 5–4 that same-sex marriage is legal nationwide. Nonetheless, the struggle over gay rights will continue on other issues, for example, whether county clerks opposed to gay marriage will have to issue licenses to gay couples, and whether florists or bakers will be compelled to accommodate.

The battlefield of values has become a vast stage in American life where elections can tip. The ethical high ground is constantly shifting as the people who decide elections weigh competing values, with some emerging, some waning, at any given time. The basis is sometimes religious but also humanist and social-justice based, depending on right or left perspectives.

These conflicts are frustrating and appear beyond resolution, and some of them may be conflicts we will have to live with for generations. There has been a lot of conversation about this polarization, but there is a need to examine where these values come from, how they have been reconciled in the past in a kind of national consensus, and how they are not being reconciled now.

In the final part of the book we explore some areas where there may be glimmers of a national accommodation and even a new values-based American character. These are built on some of our history but also on the confluence of our civic agreements, and the wisdom of spiritual and philosophical traditions that are available to us as resources now more than ever. There is also reason to believe the logjam can be moved over time by education and interdisciplinary work. These lie between areas of science, philosophy, psychology, and religion that long have been isolated provinces.

It's clear that polarization will continue for the foreseeable future. The division in America has been lamented in recent election campaigns, in how people see Washington, and in news coverage itself. That rift will reemerge powerfully as the 2016 presidential race gains momentum.

These conflicts are drawn out in sharp relief in what in effect are constant election cycles. No sooner are we done with one election then handicapping of the next begins, and candidates, voters, and interest groups in primaries are pulled sharply in opposite directions well in advance of primaries and left with middle-ground conflicts to resolve in general elections. Candidates, and the press itself, increasingly have become fragmented to the point where messages are tailored for audiences of the believers. We will explore in Chapter 8 the possibility that the center may be disappearing.

Prior to Chapter 8, we will examine why the "religion factor" still looms large in our national consciousness (Chapter 1); how Americans' core political and religious beliefs affect our current stalemate (Chapters 2 and 3); how this is exemplified in the "great debates" about immigration, gun rights and climate change (Chapter 4); how religious and ethical factors, going back to colonial days, have shaped the nation's character and its foreign policy (Chapter 5); what matters most ideologically to those on the right, left, and center of the political and cultural spectrum (chapters 6–8).

We go on in the succeeding chapters to examine how the political and cultural center—though disillusioned with polarization—might still rescue us from our civic malaise (Chapter 9); what lessons about political and religious dialogue can be gleaned from looking at a specific urban region, Orange County, California (Chapter 10); why the online media revolution offers both promise and peril to our striving for more effective government (Chapter 11); and how the virtues of civility and tough but respectful dialogue might be an elixir for national unity in the midst of our diversity (Chapter 12).

Some of this is not new, as witnessed by the long-running "culture wars" of the 1990s. However, what we have seen in the early twenty-first century suggests there are powerful new forces at work in American life that could permanently influence values-based national coalitions around the things that matter most to women, Latinos, and people who are not religious or are agnostic and unaffiliated with traditional religious groups. A bedrock set of conservative values and principles, while holding sway in many localities, increasingly is challenged as America undergoes profound ethnic change.

Our hope is that this book will both point out the unhealthy chasm of polarization in the nation and also describe with empathy why people of good will can hold such divergent beliefs and values while still ascribing to the motto on our currency: "*e pluribus unum*" ("from many one"). We are attempting, in other words, to describe and appreciate the dearly held values of the left and the right, liberals and conservatives, and help each side realize that the progress of the nation toward "a more perfect union" only happens when we tack to the center. Compromise in politics, and in life generally, will always be difficult and painful. Without it, however, the Constitution would never have been finalized and the long slow path toward justice for more and more Americans would not keep happening. Politics, like life itself, involves "the art of the possible."[2] Civil society can only move forward when the "endangered center" is protected as the locale where all citizens benefit the most.

NOTES

1. Term used to describe Congress's inability in 2012 to reach a compromise on taxes and spending that would have caused great harm to the U.S. economy if not enacted. On January 1, 2013, with the passage of the American Taxpayer Relief Act of 2012, the nation avoided falling over the precipice.

2. "Politics is the art of the possible" is an expression apparently first used by German Chancellor Otto von Bismarck in a newspaper interview in 1867. In an 1884 speech to the German Reichstag, Bismarck expanded on the idea by stating that "politics is not a science, as the professors are apt to suppose. It is an art."

Chapter 1

The Religion Factor

This is a book about the problem of polarization in America and about ways to understand and narrow the great divide between liberals and conservatives and between traditional people of faith and their liberal (and sometimes nonreligious) counterparts. We hope that understanding the complicated relationship between religion and politics in Chapter 1 will provide an entrée into the problem.

Co-author Ben Hubbard opens his college course Religion and Politics in the United States by calling these two vital and emotional areas of life "the undiscussables." They are such touchy subjects that bringing them up, for example, around the dinner table at a Thanksgiving family gathering, is risky. Yet, they need to be discussed. America's great political divide has made it more and more difficult to discuss religion as it relates to politics whether in a small group, a town hall, a state legislature, or the U.S. Congress without the conversation ending in rancor. So we start with a basic principle: *Whether or not you are a believer, religion will have an impact on your world.* This was true when French journalist Alexis de Tocqueville toured our new nation in the 1830s, and it still is. He expressed it this way: "Upon my arrival in the United States it was the religious aspect of the country that first struck my eye. As I prolonged my stay, I perceived the great political consequences that flowed from these new facts."[1] The debates over abortion, contraceptive coverage in Obamacare, climate change, teaching evolution in public schools, school prayer, and gay rights all intersect with the faith factor. We will analyze these topics in detail at various points in this study to help find common ground in a divided nation.

U.S. FOREIGN POLICY AND MISUNDERSTANDING THE FAITH FACTOR

When Ayatollah Khomeini swept into power in Iran in 1979, the State Department was largely unaware of the degree to which Shia Islam saw politics as an extension of religion. So, when 52 State Department workers were taken hostage by Khomeini's fanatical devotees shortly thereafter and held for 444 days, our government and the public were shocked and incredulous.

It also appears that President George W. Bush and his war planners paid scant attention to the sharp divide between majority Shiite Muslims in Iraq and the minority Sunnis when planning the invasion of that country and administering it during the occupation. Former diplomat Peter W. Galbraith in his book *Unintended Consequences: How War in Iraq Strengthened America's Enemies* claims that—two months before the invasion of Iraq—Bush was unaware of the differences between the two sects.[2] Failure to factor in the significant differences between them may have led to miscalculations that helped spark a de facto religious war that is still festering and may yet undo any progress toward democracy in post-2003 Iraq—especially with the massive ongoing threat from the so-called Islamic State or ISIS (Islamic State in Iraq and Syria). Our colleague and distinguished university professor at University of California, Irvine, Jack Miles summed it up this way: "The greatest long-term lessons to be learned from the historic blunder of the second Gulf War must be never again to underestimate the soft power of religious difference to trump the supposedly hard realities of guns and money."[3] To this day, moreover, American foreign-policy still does not seem to grasp the political dimensions of radical Islam and the apocalyptic implications of Shia Islam, especially as manifested by the Islamic State. (We expand upon this point below.)

Although we will discuss U.S. relations with Israel in Chapter 7, it should be clear that our close yet complicated relationship with the state of the Jewish people involves a dense intersection of religion with congressional affairs, international politics, and evangelical Christianity. The troubled relationship between President Barack Obama and Prime Minister Benjamin Netanyahu is a case in point.

THE APOCALYPTIC MIND-SET

All three of the monotheistic religions—Judaism, Christianity, and Islam—have powerful apocalyptic themes in their sacred scriptures that, while minority reports, have become the central focus of religious thinking for some groups throughout history. The power and attraction of the apocalyptic mind-set is rooted in the tragic dimension of human existence, especially humanity's propensity to violence and war. It seems to many believers the world is in a constant state of uncertainty about whether the future will be better than the past and whether some type of final battle, some Armageddon, between supposed forces of good and evil will take place—must take place—in the near future. This mind-set is connected to the Christian belief, as described especially in the book of Revelation, that God's judgment upon wickedness, and the triumphant return of Jesus Christ to defeat Satan and the forces of evil once and for all, is a certainty. Throughout history, some Christians have speculated about when the end would arrive in their lifetimes, even to the point of becoming obsessed with the idea. In 1844, Baptist preacher William Miller predicted that the world would end on October 22 of that year, and many people believed him. Their "great disappointment" would be the first of many such disappointments right down to the present.

The immense popularity of the *Left Behind*[4] series of books about the events surrounding the last days is a testimony to the power of apocalyptic thinking. Thirteen of the 16 books in the series have been bestsellers and had a profound influence on conservative Christians. They describe a series of events beginning with the so-called rapture of Christians into heaven, followed by a brief period of tribulation, then a thousand-year reign of Christ on Earth, and a final battle with Satan before the world ends. Israel has a prominent part in this imaginary scenario: Invaded by Russia, the Jerusalem temple eventually rebuilt, its desecration, and the conversion of Jews to Christianity. And Israel is seen having a pivotal role in the fulfillment of biblical prophecy: Reborn as a state in 1948, the Temple Mount captured in 1967 and perhaps a rebuilt Temple at some point before Christ's return. As we discuss in Chapter 6, evangelical Christian support for Israel is to some extent motivated by this predicted state of events, and it affects U.S. politics. In fact, one of many reasons why conservative Christians are so critical of President Obama is that he is seen as not being sufficiently supportive of Israeli policies. Another theme in the *Left Behind* series is that during the tribulation the world will be governed by a superstate that conservatives equate with the United Nations. This, in turn, might help explain their suspicions about the UN as a world government usurping U.S. sovereignty.

Today, however, it is within the so-called Islamic State/ISIS that apocalyptic thinking might be playing its most decisive role. The disciples of ISIS have returned to the historical roots of Islam, its battle for survival, and its early conquests and found a model for the creation of their own caliphate in Syria and Iraq. And they have found Quranic mandates—interpreted literally for their scorched-earth policies toward nonbelievers (which includes Muslims of a nonfundamentalist worldview). In a powerful essay in *The Atlantic*, "What ISIS Really Wants and How to Stop It," Graeme Wood stresses that Western governments must face the fact that the zealots of the Islamic state are engaged in holy war. As Wood puts it, "If religious ideology doesn't matter much in Washington or Berlin, surely it must be equally irrelevant in Raqqa or Mosul."[5] That this is not the case has only been realized slowly by Western diplomats. As Wood goes on to explain, "For certain true believers—the kind yearning for epic good-versus-evil battles—visions of apocalyptic bloodbaths fulfill a deep psychological need."[6] The true believers of ISIS long for the final battle that might usher in the end of days, and they will fight to the death for their cause. The West needs to take this very seriously.

PRESIDENTIAL POLITICS

In theory (see Article VI of the U.S. Constitution about there being "no religious Test" for public office), a candidate's religious affiliation should be irrelevant to his or her fitness for office. However, presidential politics past and present have inevitably included religious issues. This was especially true in the 2008 race when President Obama and Senator John McCain took part in a Faith Forum on August 16 that year at Pastor Rick Warren's nationally prominent Saddleback Church in Lake Forest, California. The event was unprecedented in a political campaign and may never recur, but it demonstrated that religion matters even in an age of growing secularism.

And there were other religious complications for the two candidates. Obama was skewered by Republicans and the conservative media for his membership in Trinity United Church of Christ in Chicago, headed by the Rev. Dr. Jeremiah Wright whose fiery sermons included a damning indictment of the nation over racial injustice and our addiction to war. Obama disavowed the comments, but was hurt by his close connection to Wright. Ironically, the then-presidential candidate was considered to be a Muslim by at least 12 percent of the public.

McCain was hurt, though less seriously, by an endorsement from evangelical pastor John Hagee who had made controversial statements about the providential nature of the Holocaust for the creation of the State of Israel. Despite Hagee's later disavowal of the comments, the senator quickly distanced himself from the preacher.

In the 2012 presidential contest, the religion angle was much more prominent in the primary season, especially with Republican candidate and conservative Roman Catholic, Rick Santorum. The former Pennsylvania senator railed against hedonism, abortion, and contraception, calling the latter practice "unnatural." In the general election both Obama and former Massachusetts governor Mitt Romney had reasons for putting religion on the back burner—the president because of his Muslim and Kenyan roots via his father and his opponent because of widespread misunderstanding and distrust of his membership in the Church of Jesus Christ of Latter-day Saints (Mormons).

Whether a religion angle will affect the 2016 presidential race remains to be seen; but it might, and values issues, so closely tied to one's religious beliefs, will surely emerge. This will certainly be the case for former Arkansas governor and Southern Baptist minister Mike Huckabee, who is reprising his 2012 run, and perhaps even more so if Senator Ted Cruz (R-TX) emerges as the Republican nominee. Cruz's father, Rafael, is a charismatic preacher; and the senator himself helped write the brief that persuaded the Supreme Court to approve a monument of the Ten Commandments outside the Texas state capitol in Austin.[7] Wisconsin Governor Scott Walker's father is a retired Baptist preacher, and the governor attends an evangelical nondenominational church. Like Cruz and Huckabee, his values are deeply conservative. Former Senator Rick Santorum, another candidate in 2012, is back in the race and still disputes global warming. Though a Roman Catholic, Santorum thinks Pope Francis, who is deeply concerned about climate change, should leave science to the scientists—despite the pope's having an advanced degree in chemistry. Former Florida governor Jeb Bush is a convert from the Episcopal Church to Catholicism (he, like Santorum, would be the second Catholic president, if elected). Although devout, he does not usually discuss his faith publicly. Despite being a social conservative, Bush parts company with the right wing of his party on immigration (his wife is Mexican American).

No matter who ends up winning the Republican nomination, the abortion debate will be a factor in 2016, as will the struggles over gay marriage, immigration, and climate change. Religion-related issues will be waiting in the wings and may come center stage—especially in primary season.

GOD IN THE WHITE HOUSE IN THE TWENTIETH CENTURY

Faith has always been a factor in presidential elections and the presidency itself. John F. Kennedy's struggle to convince the electorate that his Catholicism would not hinder his ability to govern without taking orders from the pope was a milestone moment for Catholicism in America. (Today, by contrast, Vice President Joe Biden, House Speaker John Boehner, and six Supreme Court justices are of that faith). But Jimmy Carter, the first professedly "born again" chief executive, put faith in the White House into a new focus. Despite this, Carter felt strongly that the press never took his religious convictions—and their impact on his policies—seriously enough. For example, his conviction that the Abrahamic faiths had a deep connection, and a profound desire to make peace, inspired his efforts to complete the Camp David Peace Accords between Egypt and Israel in 1979 despite huge obstacles.

Carter's successor, Ronald Reagan, during his first term flirted with apocalyptic thinking—the intense concern about when the world will end that is still a major issue for evangelical Christians, as noted above. In 1971, he told California state senator James Mills that, "For the first time ever, everything is in place for the battle of Armageddon and the second coming of Christ."[8] This was in line with his description of the Soviet Union as the "evil empire." Ironically, such thinking helped motivate Reagan to up the ante in the arms race with the USSR and contributed to its collapse.[9]

CONTROVERSIES OVER THE CROSS

Religious symbols are customarily placed on the graves of service members who have died in combat—crosses for Christians, Stars of David for Jews, and so on. However, controversies have arisen when a cross is placed exclusively on public land. In 1934, a cross was erected in the Mojave Desert on Sunrise Rock to honor those killed in World War I and was maintained by volunteers. However, in 1994, the site became part of the Mojave Land Reserve, an area of 1.6 million acres administered by the National Park Service. Then in 1999, Frank Buono brought the cross to the attention of the American Civil Liberties Union, which asked that the cross be removed because it violated the Establishment Clause of the First Amendment. In October 2000, the Park service—based on a lower court ruling—informed the ACLU that the cross would be removed within a few months. Ultimately, the case was appealed to the Supreme Court which ruled 5–4 in *Salazar v Buono* (2010) that Congress had acted correctly when it tried to transfer the land surrounding the cross to veterans groups. The high court then sent the case back to the U.S. district court where Judge Robert Timlin ruled the Park Service should transfer the one-acre parcel where the cross would reside to the Veterans of Foreign Wars post in Barstow in exchange for five acres of land donated to the Park Service. On Veterans Day, 2012, a group of one hundred people dedicated a new seven-foot cross and plaque on sunrise rock where it stands today. It was a convoluted compromise, but a compromise nonetheless.

A second cross controversy is at least as significant, and a resolution is close but not certain. A cross was first erected on Mount Soledad in San Diego in 1913. The present one (47-feet high) was erected in 1954 and became a memorial to honor veterans of the Korean War. Then, starting in the early 1990s, plaques honoring veterans have been placed on walls that surround the base of the cross. Because it is on city property, the ACLU brought suit to remove it. A protracted legal battle ensued in which some federal judges viewed the cross as a war memorial, while others saw it as a large visible symbol of Christianity on public land. The case finally reached the Supreme Court in 2014, but it refused to issue a ruling and sent the dispute back for another review by the Ninth Circuit Court because one additional appeal had not been heard. In the meantime, Congress on December 12, 2014, tucked a provision into the National Defense Authorization Bill that allows the cross and the thirty-six hundred adjacent plaques to be acquired by the Mount Soledad Memorial Association. It will then begin talks with the U.S. secretary of defense on how to bring about the land transfer, including the very crucial price tag. ACLU lawyer David Loy, representing the Jewish War Veterans Association, said the congressional authorization "might moot the case and it might not."[10] We may not have seen the end of this complex First Amendment litigation, but a final resolution now seems more likely.

A third cross controversy intersecting with church–state issues resulted from a surprising discovery at the site of the 9/11 attack. In the midst of the debris of Six World Trade Center, an intact crossbeam emerged, apparently originating from the north tower. Workmen with access to the site began using the cross as a shrine, leaving messages on it or praying in front of it. It eventually ended up at St. Peter's Church, which faces the World Trade Center site; but in July 2011, after a short ceremony of blessing, the cross was returned to ground zero, placed in the National September 11 Memorial and Museum. Most visitors to the site have found the cross to be very inspirational, and the Jewish Anti-Defamation League issued a statement of full support for inclusion of the "metal beams in the shape of the cross" found at ground zero. The American Atheists organization filed suit for removal of the cross, but in July 2014 (which turned out to be a monumental time for church–state court decisions) the Second U.S. Circuit Court of Appeal ruled that—because it was a symbol of hope and historical in nature—the steel beams did not deliberately discriminate against atheists.[11]

PRESIDENT GEORGE W. BUSH'S FAITH-BASED INITIATIVE

Religious organizations in America have been an immense source of philanthropy since colonial times, for example, Catholic Charities, the American Friends Service Committee, the Salvation Army, Bread for the World, and Habitat for Humanity. When he became president, Mr. Bush sought to expand on an idea he had implemented in Texas while governor: that government would fund charitable work by churches, mosques, temples, and synagogues as long as the money was not used for direct religious purposes, especially proselytizing. So, by executive order, Bush established in 2001 the White House Office of Faith-Based and Community Initiatives. In 2005, for example, the Office distributed more than $2.2 billion in competitive social service grants to faith-based organizations (FBOs). Because of First Amendment considerations, several stipulations were placed upon religious organizations seeking this funding:

- These groups must not use government funds in support of specifically religious activities such as prayer, religious instruction, or conversionary efforts;
- Whatever inherently religious activities might be offered by an organization must be separated in time or place from those services receiving federal help; and
- FBOs may not discriminate on the basis of religion when providing social services.

President Obama renamed the program the White House Office of Faith-Based and Neighborhood Partnerships and created an advisory council of religious and secular leaders and scholars from diverse backgrounds.

Both the American Civil Liberties Union and Americans United for the Separation of Church and State have disputed the constitutionality of the faith-based program. They have argued that government grants would go to supporters of the Bush or Obama administrations or to minority pastors who committed their support to one or the other of the chief executives. In 2007, the Supreme Court in *Hein v. Freedom from Religion Foundation* ruled 5–4 that executive orders may not be challenged on the basis of the First Amendment's Establishment Clause if the plaintiffs' only claim to legal standing is that they are taxpayers. Americans United was not persuaded, however, and argued that there is little, if any, evidence to show that FBOs provide services more effectively than government or secular agencies. So another debate at the intersection of religion and the politics vis-à-vis the First Amendment will continue, as America works through its implications.

There are others: the words "in God we trust" on our currency, the phrase "under God" in the Pledge of Allegiance, the opening of sessions of Congress with prayer, and—to bring the debate to its most recent juncture—the May 2014 Supreme Court decision in *Town of Greece v. Galloway*. In yet another 5–4 decision, the Court ruled that Greece, New York, may permit volunteer chaplains to open each city council session with a prayer even though they are almost exclusively Christian in content. The plaintiffs, Susan Galloway and Linda Stephens, had argued that the prayers amounted to a governmental endorsement of Christianity. Writing for the court majority, Justice Anthony Kennedy noted that "to hold the invocations must be non-sectarian would force the legislatures sponsoring prayers and the courts deciding these cases to act as supervisors and censors of religious speech." He cautioned, however, that it would be unconstitutional to use legislative prayers as a pretext to condemn or attempt to convert those who are not members of a particular faith.

The preceding discussion of the fine line between governmental neutrality and endorsement of religion—what the First Amendment calls "an establishment of religion"—brings to mind the wise comments of Ninth Circuit Court of Appeals Justice John T. Noonan Jr. in his masterful study *The Lustre of Our Country: The American Experience of Religious Freedom.* Noonan notes that the religious matrix of our nation, even though it has no official faith, makes it necessary for judicious compromises to be made so that both religion and nonreligion might thrive and not face misunderstanding or persecution.

MISCALCULATIONS OVER ARTIFICIAL CONTRACEPTION

President Obama's most important legislative accomplishment in his first term was the Patient Protection and Affordable Care Act ("ACA," sometimes called Obamacare), but it has been hugely controversial. Among other problems, he and his administration miscalculated how much the Act's mandating of comprehensive birth control coverage would offend the Roman Catholic hierarchy. True, Catholic women use artificial contraceptives about as often as the general population. And the mandate did not apply to employees of officially Catholic organizations such as diocesan headquarters. However, Catholic teaching on the practice has been clear since Pope Paul the Sixth issued his 1968 encyclical "Of Human Life" prohibiting artificial contraception.[12] The ACA rules meant that women working for Catholic hospitals and universities were entitled to contraceptive coverage, which prompted the bishops' complaint that they were paying for an immoral practice.

The president and then-Secretary of Health and Human Services Kathleen Sebelius fashioned a compromise whereby insurance companies would pay separately for the coverage. Despite this, the hierarchy, joined by the evangelical CEOs of Hobby Lobby Stores, Inc., and Conestoga Wood Specialties Corp., challenged the decision. While Catholic teaching opposes all forms of artificial birth control, the two corporations specifically opposed two types of contraception: the intrauterine device (IUD) and the morning-after pill (Plan B or Ella). These two methods are thought to be abortifacients (a drug or device that induces an abortion) because, according to some medical experts, they may keep a fertilized egg or zygote from being implanted in a woman's uterus.

In a very controversial June 2014 decision, the Supreme Court ruled 5–4 in *Burwell v. Hobby Lobby Stores, Inc.* and *Conestoga Wood Specialties Corp. v. Burwell* that, because the two corporations are privately held—that is, there is no essential difference between the business and its owners—they cannot be required to provide contraceptive coverage to their employees. In her dissenting opinion, Justice Ruth Bader Ginsburg stated that "until this litigation, no decision of this court recognized a for-profit corporation's qualification for religious exemption from a generally applicable law."[13] The apparent solution both for Catholic institutions such as universities, and for the employees of Hobby Lobby and Conestoga, is for the Obama administration, via the ACA, to provide contraceptive coverage that is distinct and unrelated to these entities. What makes the ruling unique is the high court's interpretation that corporations, at least privately held ones, have religious liberty rights akin to those of individuals under the 1993 Religious Freedom Restoration Act and the First Amendment. Once again, the religion factor profoundly influenced politics and personal behavior. And this will probably not be the end of the matter. As University of California, Irvine, law school dean Erwin Chemerinsky opines, "Despite all the claims that its holding was narrow, the Supreme Court's decision is the broadest in American history in providing corporations the ability to claim an exemption to a law based on the religious beliefs of their owners."[14]

THE CIVIL WAR OVER ABORTION

No national issue involving religion and politics has been as divisive and apparently irreconcilable as that over the legal right to an abortion. The debate has led to the murder of several abortion providers, to clinic bombings, and to acts of civil disobedience by groups such as Operation Rescue (now known as Operation Save America).

By 1900, abortion was illegal in at least some circumstance throughout the country. Thirty states prohibited it outright (except to save a woman's life, as in the case of uterine cancer or an ectopic pregnancy); 20 others allowed the procedure under certain circumstances (for example, rape or incest).

Then in 1973, the Supreme Court set aside all of these laws in *Roe v. Wade*, probably the court's most controversial decision in more than a century. It set up a trimester system of state interest in a fetus's life in accord with its increasing viability. Thus, states could not prohibit abortions early in a pregnancy but could impose increasing restrictions or complete bans as the fetus approached viability. In 1992, the high court in *Planned Parenthood v. Casey*, while upholding *Roe*, replaced the trimester system with that of viability, whenever that occurred, to define a state's right to trump a woman's autonomy. States now had the right to regulate abortions as long as they did not write laws that imposed an "undue burden" on the woman seeking one. In 2007, the Court ruled that partial-birth abortions, a procedure in which fetuses with gross abnormalities were aborted late in a pregnancy, were illegal. In June 2014, the Supreme Court ruled unanimously that a Massachusetts law mandating a 35-foot distance between abortion protesters and women entering a family-planning clinic was unconstitutional. The court did note that these women must be accorded some degree of personal space, and they left that determination up to the states.

The state's right to limit some abortions and a woman's right to choose are now on more of an equal footing.[15] However, many conservative state legislatures have found ways to make procuring an abortion difficult by requiring, for example, that a woman undergo counseling, verification, and testing procedures lasting several hours. Hence, in 87 percent of U.S. counties, there are no abortion providers. In Arkansas, and North and South Dakota, there is just one clinic doing the procedure. In Mississippi, the one remaining abortion clinic was set to close because the law required its practitioner to have admitting privileges at the local hospital, which none of the hospitals would grant. However, the Fifth Circuit Court of Appeals ruled in July 2014 that the law "imposes an undue burden on a woman's right to choose abortion."

Texas in 2013 passed a bill requiring abortion providers to make hospital-grade improvements to their facilities. On appeal, a federal district judge blocked the law, but a three-judge panel of the Fifth Circuit Court of Appeals sided with Texas. Then in October 2014, the Supreme Court issued a stay of that ruling while appeals proceed. Stay tuned—it's complicated and it's not over. For now, the pro-choice side is holding its own overall in the judicial war but is losing the battle on the ground in many states.

That is the legal situation, and the religious landscape is just as contentious. The Roman Catholic, Evangelical Christian, and LDS/Mormon Churches line up in virtually complete opposition to abortion, while Jewish[16] and liberal Protestant groups are generally pro-choice. The public is torn with 47 percent pro-choice in a May 2014 Gallup survey, 46 pro-life. However, support for abortion has declined in the past 20 years from a high of 56 percent in 1995.

Although both the pro-choice and pro-life movements have always sought the support of religious bodies, there is actually very little in the scriptures of Judaism and Christianity to buttress the arguments of either side. Exodus 21:22–23 describes an incident in which two men are fighting and a pregnant woman in the melee miscarries. The assailant must pay her husband damages for the death of the fetus; but, if the woman herself dies, he is subject to capital punishment. So a clear distinction is made between fetal life and human life. The Talmud, a massive legal commentary on the Hebrew Bible/Old Testament, states in Tractate *Oholot*, 7, 6:

If a woman has [life-threatening] difficulty in childbirth, the embryo within her must be dismembered limb by limb [if necessary], because her life takes precedence over its life.

For Judaism, then, feticide is not homicide and the mother's life takes primacy. A fetus is not human until it starts breathing:

Then the LORD God formed man from the dust of the ground, and breathed into his nostrils the breath of life; and man became a living being. (Genesis 2:7)[17]

In the case of Christianity, the New Testament offers no guidance on the morality of abortion. Both St. Augustine (who lived from AD 354–430) and St. Thomas Aquinas (1225–1274) did not consider the fetus to be a human person at least during the first trimester of its existence. In 1869, however, the Roman Catholic Church took the position that ensoulment begins at conception. Conservative Protestants took about a century to join the pro-life camp. As late as 1971, the Southern Baptist Convention agreed in a joint resolution:

We call upon Southern Baptists to work for legislation that will allow the possibility of abortion under such conditions as rape, incest, clear evidence of fetal deformity, and carefully ascertained evidence of the likelihood of damage to the emotional, mental, and physical health of the mother.[18]

However, by 1980, the Rev. Jerry Falwell declared that "the bible clearly teaches that life begins at conception." Falwell's Moral Majority organization saw the antiabortion position as aligning with the tide of conservatism resulting from the election of President Reagan that year.

It might be easy for liberals to see Falwell's decision as politically convenient. But he and everyone else agree that a fetus is a living being entitled to the respect for life accorded to all creatures from butterflies to whales to humans. The grand theological question is whether embryonic and fetal life is human life, whether a fetus is a person, whether feticide is homicide.

There might never be an answer to this question satisfying all religious groups, and women in need would continue to seek abortions even if *Roe* were overturned and many states outlawed the procedure completely. In the decades prior to *Roe*, as many as one million illegal abortions were performed annually in the United States with five thousand women dying and many rendered sterile as a result.[19] Perhaps pro-choice and pro-life groups could at least agree that the conditions conducive to unwanted pregnancies—poverty, crime-ridden neighborhoods, hopelessness—should be addressed. For example, the abortion rate for African American women (with much higher poverty rates) is three-and-one-half times than that of whites. It is a sad irony that the work of Planned Parenthood (only 3 percent of whose work involves abortion) has prevented millions of unintended pregnancies and consequently thousands of abortions. Yet, conservative Christians, especially the Roman Catholic leadership, condemn the organization unequivocally. Finally, 92 percent of all abortions are performed in the first trimester when the fetus does not possess a functioning brain and hence cannot experience pain. It seems hard to equate abortions at this stage with capital murder.

RELIGION'S GAY RIGHTS DILEMMA

While religious bodies eventually lined up clearly on one side or the other of the abortion struggle, this was not the case with the battle for lesbian, gay, bisexual, and transgender rights. Nonetheless, in contrast to the abortion battle, there *were* a few scriptural passages condemning homosexual acts. These texts, combined with widespread misunderstanding of the nature of homosexuality, resulted in near-universal condemnation of gay sex by the monotheistic faiths until the 1960s. Correspondingly, the American Psychiatric Association considered homosexuality a mental disorder until 1973.

The principal Hebrew Bible texts cited by those religions who consider homosexual acts sinful are Leviticus 18:22 and 20:13 both of which condemn sexual acts between men as "an abomination" (lesbianism is not mentioned anywhere). In Genesis 19:4–11, the men of Sodom demand that Lot release his two male visitors so that they might "know" (sodomize) the pair. The visitors turn out to be angels who blind the Sodomites.

In the New Testament, the key scripture is in the Letter to the Romans 1:26–27. There, St. Paul speaks of men and women exchanging "natural intercourse" with shameless acts and receiving the due penalty for their actions (presumably venereal diseases).[20] For conservative Christians and Jews—in fact for almost all believers until the 1970s—these texts, along with widespread societal misunderstanding and prejudice about the nature of homosexuality, all but ended the discussion.

In the more than 40 years since then, psychiatric attitudes about homosexuality began to change, and liberal Jewish and Christian scholars have reevaluated the scriptures just summarized. There is now widespread consensus among them that the ancient Israelites who penned the Levitical texts had little understanding of gayness as a genetic predisposition, and that the real sin of the Sodomites was their desire to humiliate the strangers—xenophobia in the extreme. In Romans, Paul may have been reacting to gay and lesbian prostitution and the widespread sexual abuse of young boys by older men in the Greco-Roman world (a practice that both contemporary straight and gay individuals condemn).

For conservatives, however, such explanations are dismissed: the Bible is God's revealed word and is unequivocal. Moreover, gay sex is considered unnatural by most conservatives. Also, while the great majority of LGBT community members (92 percent) feel that society has grown more accepting in the past decade, acceptance of gays and lesbians by members of various religious groups varies widely. On the question of whether homosexuality should be (a) accepted, (b) discouraged, or (c) neither/both/don't know, the assessment by the general public is favorable by 60, 31, and 8 percent, respectively; by Roman Catholics 71, 20, and 9 percent; liberal Protestants 65, 26, and 9 percent; Jews 79, 15, and 6 percent; but for white evangelical Christians the assessment is negative by 30, 59, and 11 percent; and by Mormons 26, 65, and 9 percent.[21] A poll released in June 2014 by the First Amendment Center indicates that 61 percent of respondents agree that the government should require religiously affiliated groups receiving government funding to provide health care benefits to same-sex partners of employees—even when the religious groups oppose same-sex marriage.

Further, 54 percent of the public agrees a business offering wedding services to the public should be obligated to serve same-sex couples, even if the business owner objects to gay marriage on religious grounds.[22] This matter came to a head in late March 2015, when the Indiana Legislature passed its own version of the federal Religious Freedom Restoration Act (Indiana Senate Enrolled Act 101) that prevents state and local governments from enacting legislation that would "extensively burden" a person's exercise of his or her religion. The problem with the act is that "person" includes "a partnership, a limited liability company, a corporation, a company, a firm, a society, a joint-stock company, and unincorporated association, or another entity" if any such organization claims its practices are compelled or limited by a religious belief. Consequently, to use a common example, a bakery could refuse to make a wedding cake for a gay couple. There was an immediate and stunning reaction to the law from the business community nationwide, in Indiana, and from the NCAA whose headquarters are in Indianapolis. Indiana Governor Mike Pence was put on the defensive and persuaded the legislature to amend the law so that refusal of a public company to serve members of the LGBT community was not permissible. The same turnaround happened within days in Arkansas when it passed a similar law. In the lyrics of Bob Dylan, "The times they are a-changin.'"

Though most members of liberal Protestant churches favor gay rights, the churches themselves have agonized over the matter and have lost some conservative members in the process. Currently, Conservative, Reform and Reconstructionist Jews, the Society of Friends (Quakers), the United Church of Christ, the Evangelical Lutheran Church in America, and Unitarian Universalists approve of gay marriage; and the Presbyterian Church USA concurred in June 2014, subject to ratification by its regional presbyteries. The American Baptists (so-called northern Baptists), Methodists, and Episcopalians will *bless* but not officiate at gay weddings. However, all of these liberal churches accept LGBT members.

In 2013, the Methodists suspended Rev. Frank Schaefer after he performed a same-sex marriage for his gay son. He was reinstated but then defrocked after he refused to promise he would not perform another such marriage. But in June 2014, the defrocking was overturned on appeal. Nonetheless, the church's overall oppositional stance on gay marriages remains, at least for now.

In California, the epic legal battle over Proposition 8, which declared marriage legal only between a man and a woman, was massively supported and funded by the LDS/Mormon Church and American Catholic bishops. On the other side, the Episcopal Church, most Jewish organizations, and the Unitarian Universalists strongly opposed the proposition. It was passed by voters with a 52–48 margin that stunned the liberal-leaning California electorate. However, the Ninth Circuit Court of Appeals ruled Proposition 8 unconstitutional in 2010 resulting in an appeal to the Supreme Court. In 2013 (*Hollingsworth v. Perry*), the high court ruled that the plaintiffs did not have standing to bring the case and Proposition 8 was overturned. In a conjoined case (*United States v. Windsor*), the court ruled that portions of the Defense of Marriage Act were unconstitutional and would no longer be enforced by the federal government.

Two distinguished attorneys, Theodore Olson and David Boies, teamed up to wage the legal contest that ultimately led to the Supreme Court's epic 2013 decision. Mr. Olson, President George W. Bush's former solicitor general, argued in *Bush v. Gore* (2000) that the Florida recount in the disputed election should be halted. Mr. Boies represented former vice president Al Gore, arguing that the recount should continue. Yet, in this case, a conservative and a liberal made common cause in the pursuit of fairness and equity for the LGBT community. Their partnership might serve as a parable for the way persons with sharply different political and religious views

(Olson is pro-life, Boies pro-choice) can join forces when the cause of justice overrides a sectarian dispute.

Then, on June 26, 2015, the high court ruled 5–4 in *Obergefell v. Hodges* that gay marriage was now legal in all 50 states, bringing to a close this contentious legal struggle. Nonetheless, conservatives will work around the margins as best they can to preserve the rights of those opposed on moral grounds to gay marriage, for example, the owners of small businesses refusing to accommodate gay customers and municipal judges unwilling to perform gay ceremonies.

There is a fascinating irony in the painful but gradual evolution of religious attitudes toward the LGBT community. While everyone from President Obama to the Supreme Court now approve of gay marriage, Americans' attitudes on the morality of therapeutic abortion have evolved to some degree in the opposite direction—toward greater caution and conservatism.

What is important, we think, is for people on all sides in these emotional religio-political debates to appreciate the very real issues at stake— in particular, the meaning of personhood and the nature of marriage. People need to listen carefully to the reasoning of the other side; because, in so doing, they may come to realize the complexity of the issues and at least appreciate how intelligent and ethical individuals can assess them so differently. Basic stances may not change, but hopefully they will be more informed and one's opponents no longer caricatured and even demonized.

EVOLUTION VERSUS CREATION SCIENCE

Then there is the nearly century-long debate over teaching evolution in public schools. In 1925, science teacher John Scopes stood trial in Dayton, Tennessee, for agreeing to do so. Though Scopes was convicted (later overturned on a technicality), the so-called Monkey Trial alienated conservative Christians and deepened the divide with their liberal counterparts. Since then, the Supreme Court[23] and a federal district court[24] have overturned state laws granting equal time to the teaching of creationism or intelligent design (ID) in schools alongside evolution. After the decision against their position in *Edwards v. Aguillard* (1987), creationists attempted to decouple their theory from theology by maintaining that nature was so complex it demanded an intelligent designer. However, the scientific community and the courts have not agreed.

Still, the struggle continues as creationists use every strategy possible to give their option a hearing in public schools. Science education standards in

Louisiana, Tennessee, and Texas, for example, permit public school teachers to present "alternatives" to evolution. In 2008, Louisiana passed its Science Education Act that allows teachers "to use supplemental textbooks and other instructional material to help students understand, analyze, critique, and review scientific theories in an objective manner," especially regarding "evolution, the origins of life, global warming and human cloning."[25]

Conservatives in these and other states received help and encouragement from the Discovery Institute, a Seattle-based, nonprofit think tank dedicated to giving intelligent design equal time alongside evolution, and calling it "a theory in crisis." Its main goal is to teach the controversy, while maintaining that ID deserves the same degree of scientific investigation as evolution. However, both the decision in *Kitzmiller v. Dover Area School District* (2005) and the position of the American Academy for the Advancement of Science make it clear that ID is really a theologically based concept desperately posing as hard science.

The 2006 documentary, "A Flock of Dodos: The Evolution–Intelligent Design Circus," is an enlightening and humorous attempt to explain the controversy and point out the foibles on each side—dismissive scientists in one camp, stubborn creationists in the other. The film ultimately sides with evolution, but gives its opponents a fair hearing. In some respects the film parallels the approach taken in a course offered for many years by Professor James Hoffman at California State University in Fullerton (where co-author Ben Hubbard teaches), "Evolution and Creationism." The course in the Liberal Studies Department is rigorously scientific but sympathetic to the religious and sociological dynamics that attract people to creationism/intelligent design. A parallel approach is used in some senior high school social studies classes but not in the science lab.

Unfortunately, religious conservatives can't seem to leave this matter alone. As noted above during the discussion of evolution and creation science, Louisiana in 2008 passed the Louisiana Science Education Act, which claimed to empower teachers, principals, and other school administrators to hold "open and objective" discussion of scientific theories, including but not limited to, evolution, the origins of life, global warming, and human cloning. Once again, creationism is attempting to slip into science education through the back door. Attempts to overturn the law have so far been unsuccessful. And in Tennessee, where the whole fight began, the legislature in 2012 passed a law authorizing school officials to help students think critically about "scientific subjects that may cause debate and disputation, including, but not limited to, biological evolution, the chemical origins of life, global warming and human cloning."

Despite the judicial rulings and the almost universal opinion of the scientific community, 46 percent of Americans (in a 2012 Gallup poll) reject evolution and believe that God created humans in their present form at one time within the last ten thousand years.[26] One might conclude that such people are intellectual dunces or Bible-pounding fundamentalists. Yet, doing so overlooks the deeply felt reasons for their opposition to the idea. If mankind is descended from lower life-forms, what about being created in the "image and likeness of God" (Genesis 1:27)? And what about natural selection, which conservative believers sometimes equate with atheism, Nazi-era "survival of the fittest," eugenics, and even genocide? Finally, though evolution is much closer to a law—like gravity—than a theory, as with all science it needs to be improved upon and is still a work in progress.

The point is not that creation science and intelligent design are real biology, but that the religious sensibilities of millions of Americans must be viewed empathetically if a respectful dialogue is to occur. That dialogue might win over conservative believers—who are very similar to political conservatives—to at least give evolution, with God as its catalyst, a fair hearing. (And evolutionists should be open-minded to creationists who may have insights about nature and the human spirit that are worth hearing by skeptical scientists.) Otherwise, the great divide in American political and cultural life has another reason to keep widening.

These considerations of the evolution–creationism debate and the long struggles over abortion and gay rights are meant to serve as a paradigm for the approach taken in this book to the many passionately debated topics we are discussing. While complete neutrality is never possible, our hope is that the attempt to look with balance and empathy at these opposing viewpoints will prove enlightening.

READIN', WRITIN', 'RITHMATIC...AND RELIGION?

The previous discussion of the evolution–creation science debate segues into a related issue: prayer in public schools. Several Supreme Court decisions in the post–World War II era have removed sectarian religious instruction, prayer, and Bible reading from the nation's public schools. The first, *McCollum v. Board of Education* (1948), outlawed religious instruction by ministers, priests, and rabbis from being conducted during the school day on school property. (However, the high court did declare as constitutional "released time" [*Zorach v. Clauson*, 1952], which permits students to leave the school campus during the school day for religious instruction elsewhere.) Then in 1985, the court also found unconstitutional the practice of "shared time" during which secular teachers would instruct students in English, math, science, and so on, while parochial teachers provided religious instruction on school property.

But the most far-reaching and controversial decisions were *Engle v. Vitale* (1962), and *Abingdon v. Schempp* and *Murray v. Curlett* (1963). The former outlawed a generic school prayer that New York State's Board of Regents had mandated to be recited in all public school classrooms at the start of the school day. The latter conjoint decision outlawed the recitation of the Lord's Prayer and devotional Bible reading in the schools. In a side comment to the ruling, Justice Tom Clark did note "that one's education is not complete without a study of comparative religion or the history of religion and its relationship to the advancement of civilization."[27] Consequently, at many high schools nationwide a course in the world's religions is offered as an elective.

Upset by this decision, 20 states by 1984 had laws permitting a moment of silence at the start of each school day, only to have the Supreme Court in *Wallace v. Joffrey* (1985) find even this procedure in violation of the First Amendment. Undaunted, many states fine-tuned the moment-of-silence concept and either required—or made optional—the practice, and this time it was upheld. A U.S. district court in Virginia and the Fourth Circuit Court of Appeals[28] upheld the Virginia version of the moment of silence. As long as the moment is genuinely neutral and does not encourage prayer over other quiet, contemplative activities, it is permissible. Although it may be dancing on the line between church and state, the current situation strikes us as a reasonable accommodation. Public schools need not be religion-free zones, and the moment of silence makes prayer completely optional as long as teachers also maintain a discreet silence and neither encourage nor discourage whatever thoughts a student might want to entertain. In fact, President Bill Clinton issued a series of guidelines that made individual prayer permissible before school and at lunch and other school break times. Clinton's directive also permitted so-called group prayer at the flag-pole before the start of classes and use of the school for religious or Bible clubs as long as secular clubs (science, chess, etc.) were also allowed.

On another sensitive front, David Green, founder and CEO of Hobby Lobby (also see "Miscalculations over Artificial Contraception," above), was the driving force behind a proposal made to the Mustang, Oklahoma, school board for a four-year public high school elective on the history and impact of the Bible. However, the church–state watchdog group Americans United along with the ACLU and the Freedom from Religion Foundation challenged the fundamentalist orientation of the course, and in November 2014, the school district decided to cancel it. Green has stated publicly that the class would teach the doctrine of biblical inerrancy which calls into question his claim that the course would be taught academically and objectively. Mark Chancey, who teaches religious studies at Southern Methodist University, reviewed the curriculum for the liberal Texas Freedom Network and detected "the presence of frequent errors and extensive sectarian bias"[29] in the curriculum. This may not be the last attempt by Green and others with his fundamentalist convictions to try getting such a course into a public high school. Green, in fact, is building a Museum of the Bible in Washington, DC, and might eventually use this as a catalyst to propose his curriculum to other public schools around the country. However, Americans United and similar groups will be ready, armed with their conviction that the First Amendment's Establishment Clause must be safeguarded.

In sum, many well-intentioned people simply cannot accept the idea of public schools as religion-free zones. They look around at contemporary society with its plague of drugs, violence, and sexually explicit material in the media and online and feel something must be done to protect children. Yet, this is primarily the task of the home, religious institutions, and voluntary organizations such as the Boy Scouts and Girl Scouts. The First Amendment does not allow it to be otherwise. However, public schools may teach character education, "a national movement creating schools that inculcate ethical, responsible and caring young people by modeling and teaching good character through emphasis on universal values that we all share." These core ethical values include caring, honesty, fairness, responsibility, and respect for self and others.[30] Moreover, academically based courses on the religions of the world—some of which are already incorporated in sixth and seventh grade world civilization curricula—have the potential to improve the religious literacy of America's children and have a salutary effect on their moral compass. Of course, college courses on the religions of the world and other aspects of religion and culture play an important role in increasing the nation's religious literacy and a spirit of respect and tolerance in our multicultural society.

ISLAM AND ISLAMISM

The terror attacks of September 11, 2001, precipitated a national debate about the nature of Islam and its place in American life that is still in play today. In particular, was it possible to distinguish terror in the name of Islam from a dynamic, worldwide faith with 1.4 billion adherents that has made signal contributions to civilization, especially in its first millennium? This situation has influenced many scholars and media professionals to use "Islamism" to denote a highly politicized and fundamentalist form of the religion. "Islamism" is often linked to jihadism,[31] the conviction that holy war and even suicide terror are justified to protect and further Islam.

There have been numerous hate crimes committed against Muslims, Arabs, and Sikhs (sometimes taken to be Muslim) since 9/11 (160 in 2010, for example),[32] with the number actually increasing in recent years. A principal reason for the uptick has been the continuation of extremely lethal terror attacks by jihadists or Muslim extremists in London, Madrid, Jerusalem, Bali, Bombay, Paris (with the slaughter of the editorial staff of the satirical French magazine *Charlie Hebdo* in January 2015), and elsewhere. For many people there is a close link between Islam and terror. Moreover, the Muslim Middle East is in turmoil, with the "Arab Spring" morphing into an Arab winter. Tunisia, Libya, and Egypt have all been through political upheavals, Lebanon is a powder keg with a history of religious strife, Syria is gripped by civil war, and Iraq is battling for its soul (as already noted). In the midst of this turmoil, Islamic extremists such as Al Qaeda, the Islamic State, and Boko Haram (i.e., "no western education") in Nigeria continue to sow chaos and extreme violence, and to besmirch authentic Islam (see discussion above, "The Apocalyptic Mind-Set").

Additionally, attacks against European Jews, especially in France, serve to cast all Muslims in a bad light. Consequently, while 41 percent of Americans had a favorable opinion of Islam in 2005 (versus 36 percent unfavorable), that number had dropped to 30 percent in 2010 (versus 38 percent unfavorable).[33] One of the ironies of the negative reactions to Islamism is that the people who suffer most from this plague are Muslims themselves in countries like Pakistan, Syria, Iraq, Somalia, Sudan, Kenya, and the Central African Republic. We must keep the big picture in focus to adequately assess Islam in the modern world.

ISLAM AT GROUND ZERO

Perhaps the most serious and emotional debate over Islam in America has centered around the proposal to build a Muslim community center and museum, including a mosque, very near—though not within sight—of ground zero and the National September 11 Memorial Museum. Despite rather pro forma approvals by various levels of New York City government, in 2010 Pamela Geller, president of the American Freedom Defense Initiative, mounted a scathing attack on the project, including ads on NYC buses that indicted Islamic radicalism. By contrast, then-mayor Michael Bloomberg vigorously defended the community center. Many Americans, though, including the relatives of 9/11 survivors, objected to the plan, citing its close proximity to ground zero. Today, plans for a scaled-down version of the original building are still on the drawing board, but funding remains uncertain.

However, another contentious issue has emerged over a seven-minute film, "The Rise of Al Qaeda," shown in the Memorial Museum. Although most visitors and scholars consider the overall treatment of Islam there as balanced and informative, the film's juxtaposition of Al Qaeda with Islam and terrorism offends many Muslims, such as Sheikh Mostafa Elazabawy, imam of Masjid (mosque) Manhattan. In sum, it is clear that Islam's place in American society will continue to spark controversy and to divide those who see it as another respected faith in the country's religious mosaic and others who are just not comfortable with a religion so often linked to violence. It is hoped that education and tolerance—along with professional contacts between, for example, Muslim physicians and engineers and their Jewish and Christian counterparts—will make Islam a more welcomed faith.

THE ROOTS OF FUNDAMENTALISM

In the nineteenth century, European, especially German, biblical scholarship was making significant advances in the scientific examination of texts, using literary analysis, history, archaeology, and other methods. They discovered that, for example, there were parallels to the flood account of Genesis 7–9 in the earlier Babylonian flood story, the *Epic of Gilgamesh;* and that the account of Jesus's virginal birth (Matthew 1:18–25 and Luke 1:26–38) has echoes in the miraculous birth legends of numerous ancient figures such as Asclepius, Romulus, Alexander the Great, and Emperor Augustus.

Many traditional biblical scholars and clergy in America were becoming more and more alarmed at the implications of this scholarship. Hence, between 1910 and 1915, biblical scholars at Princeton Seminary, with financial support from Lyman and Milton Stewart, founders of Union Oil (Unocal), published in pamphlet style a set of "Fundamentals" or core beliefs that defended the literal truth of the entire Bible and laid down other basic beliefs that all Protestant believers should accept. These included Jesus's divinity, his virgin birth, his death as atonement for the sins of humankind, his bodily resurrection and physical return, his miracles, and the literal truth and reliability of every word of scripture, usually referred to as biblical inerrancy.

This last fundamental—that the Bible is without error in all respects, religious, historical, and scientific—really encompasses the others. It has become the hallmark of conservative-evangelical Christianity. It massively affects the views of such believers on evolution, gay marriage, and abortion. As long as so-called higher biblical criticism is either completely disdained or employed only on the margins, the divide between conservative and liberal Protestants will remain significant. However, not all evangelicals are strict literalists, and a growing movement of moderate conservatives has emerged over the past 30 years. A prime example is the position taken by the highly regarded Fuller Theological Seminary in Pasadena, California. Here, biblical criticism is used judiciously with core fundamentals such as Jesus's virgin birth, miracles, atoning death, and resurrection still accepted. However, at nearby Biola Seminary in La Mirada, California (cofounded by Lyman Stewart), inerrancy still reigns largely unchallenged, though even here biblical scholarship is making modest inroads. Overall, strict biblical literalism is on the wane yet still remains strong in schools such as Biola, most Southern Baptist and Missouri Synod Lutheran seminaries, and at Bob Jones University in South Carolina.

FUNDAMENTALISM IN NON-CHRISTIAN FAITHS

Though "fundamentalism" originated as a Protestant Christian term, in the past 40 years its meaning has broadened to include very conservative religious movements in other traditions. Thus, scholars and the media speak of Islamic fundamentalism, Jewish fundamentalism, and so on. The Iranian Revolution of 1978, when that nation became a theocracy, brought even more attention to the subject. In the late 1980s, a group of religious studies scholars, led by the distinguished historian of religion Martin Marty, began the Fundamentalism Project, which produced a major study, *Fundamentalism Observed*.[34] It created a profile of worldwide fundamentalism including the following features:

1. An extreme, "us-versus-them" mentality that is unwilling to compromise with moderates within one's own faith and finds other religions totally lacking in truth.
2. A defensive mentality that sees the outside world as massed against the true believers and trying to destroy them and their values and that condemns certain nations or individuals, for example, America, the "Great Satan," and Israel, the "Little Satan," as Iran's religious leaders put it. Al Qaeda, Hezbollah, Hamas, Boko Haram, and the Islamic State (the current Islamist attempt to create a caliphate in Syria and Iraq) all share this worldview.
3. A literal reading of scriptures allowing for interpretations only on the basis of other passages in the sacred text (for example, Bible or Quran) and not on the basis of outside scholarly sources.
4. A missionary zeal that seeks to bring new believers into the fold, sometimes forcibly.
5. A desire to bring the state under the control of the fundamentalist religious community so that a theocracy results (as in Iran).

6. A dominant role for men in all spheres of life such that the role of women is largely domestic.
7. A sense that the world is in a state of crisis, or that "the end is near," and that the true believers will play a dominant role in the events of the end times.
8. A sophisticated use of the tools, but not the values, of modernity—especially the press, Internet, and social media—in achieving its aims.

An important distinction must be made between (a) fundamentalism and (b) extremism or violent fanaticism. The fundamentalist worldview might trigger acts of violence, for example, the assassination of abortion provider Dr. George Tiller while ushering at his church in Wichita, Kansas, in 2009, or numerous instances of terror in the name of God, as with suicide-terror jihadists who believe they are agents of the Almighty. But fundamentalism in North America and Western Europe is usually ideological and political, and acts of violence are comparatively rare. Tragically, violence linked to fundamentalism has become frequent in the Muslim world.

Fundamentalism and religious absolutism are also manifest in disparagement of less orthodox members of a particular faith. In both Israel and the United States the Haredi, a type of ultra-Orthodox Jews, have little respect even for modern Orthodox Jews and complete disdain for the Reform Jewish movement. In Saudi Arabia, the Salafi[35] sect takes an extremely literalist view of the Quran and considers moderate Muslims to be heretics. Unfortunately, this brand of Islam has significantly influenced American mosques, especially through Salafi publications and financial support of such mosques by the Saudi government. American Muslims overall are considerably more moderate (and financially successful) than those in Europe and the Arab Muslim world.[36] But they are drawn toward conservatism by Salafism whose tenets include extreme opposition to the existence of the State of Israel. The Sunni–Shiite tensions manifested today in Iraq, Syria, Lebanon, Yemen, and elsewhere are energized by this kind of intolerance.

In parts of Africa, a de facto religious war is raging between Christians and Muslims. This is especially true in Nigeria and the Central African Republic. In Egypt, Coptic Christians have felt the wrath of extremist Muslims in the wake of the recent turmoil there. Muslims have experienced the hatred of extremist Hindus in India during the past 30–40 years with the rise of the BJP Hindu nationalist party, and in Burma/Myanmar where the Islamic Rohingya ethnic group suffers extreme persecution.

These conflicts spring in part from the truth claims of many faiths. Is Judaism a complete, fulfilling faith or does Christianity supersede it? Is Christianity the one, true religion or does Islam add another dimension of truth? The answer to these and similar questions depends on personal religious convictions often springing from childhood and geography—not on debates or arguments. It appears that religious freedom is the only realistic response to the mystery of religious difference.

The world is, and will remain, extremely diverse religiously, with thousands of branches and subbranches within Christianity alone. The human community desperately needs to eradicate intolerance, hatred and violence between faiths, and even within the same faith family, in this new century. That will require that freedom of conscience and respect for believers of all faiths—and no supernatural faith—become paramount.

DOES RELIGION CAUSE WARS?

The discussion thus far of the religion factor might lead the reader to conclude that religion is principally a cause of communal tension and conflict worldwide. In fact, co-author Ben Hubbard, after his field of study became known, has occasionally heard a new acquaintance comment that "religion has been the greatest cause of wars in human history." He has then had to diplomatically point out that by far the greatest source of human misery and slaughter, for example in the twentieth century, was totalitarian ideologies such as Soviet communism, Nazism, and Maoism.

Granted, religion has sometimes either sparked or abetted violence and war or remained largely silent in the face of tragedies such as the Holocaust. But, on the other side, religion throughout history has been the single greatest source of philanthropy and the alleviation of human suffering. The worldwide Catholic organization, Caritas International, and its affiliate, Catholic Charities USA, Church World Service (affiliated with National Council of Churches of Christ), Lutheran World Service, American Jewish World Service, the Mennonite Central Committee, and the American Friends Service Committee (Quakers) are among a host of religious groups providing ongoing charitable work. Moreover, religion provides hope, community, meaning, and morality to billions of people. It has also been at the forefront of justice issues, such as the abolition of slavery, opposition to modern warfare, and advocacy for the poor and oppressed.

CAN THE WORLD'S DIVERSE FAITHS COOPERATE FOR THE COMMON GOOD?

The concept of genuine interreligious or interfaith dialogue did not emerge until a remarkable event in 1893, the Columbian Exposition in Chicago. Its focus was science, technology, and the arts—certainly not the religions of the world. However, in 1891 a group of visionary Chicago clergyman sent invitations to religious leaders from many nations to come to the fair and give the religions of the world their own exposition. Though there were some dissenters, the response was overwhelmingly positive. One of those who declined, however, was the Anglican Archbishop of Canterbury who wrote, "The Christian religion is the one religion. I do not understand how that religion can be regarded as a member of a Parliament of Religions without assuming the equality of the other intended members and the parity of . . . their claims."[37] That dissent is still central to the unwillingness of most conservative and evangelical (Protestant) Christians to participate in the now-worldwide interfaith movement.

The Parliament consisted of papers read by scholars of faiths East and West, including the Hindu monk Swami Vivekananda who took the conference and the country by storm. His mantra, that religious bigotry and fanaticism have caused untold human suffering, has continued to inspire the interfaith movement.

Though there were efforts to reprise the Parliament, obstacles intervened, especially the two world wars. But, as the centennial of the event drew near, another group of Chicago visionaries launched the 1993 Parliament, again in Chicago, with eight thousand attendees. A 1999 Parliament followed in Cape Town, South Africa, in Barcelona, Spain (2004), and in Melbourne, Australia (2009). A 2015 event will be held October 15–19, 2015, in Salt Lake City. Each of the past meetings has stressed some aspect of a global ethic through caring for the Earth, assisting indigenous and impoverished people, and eliminating religiously motivated conflicts.

A second interreligious movement emerged in the 1990s at the instigation of Episcopal Bishop William Swing of San Francisco—the United Religions Initiative, inspired in part by the fiftieth anniversary celebration of the United Nations' founding in 1945 in that city. It has over 400 cooperation circles in 72 countries, each of which must have members from a least three faiths. It has initiated peace-building efforts in northern Uganda, Ethiopia, and elsewhere.

Many cities across the nation now have some sort of interfaith council to promote cooperation and tolerance. (In Chapter 11, we will look specifically at interfaith activities in a specific locale, Orange County, California.) The result of these organizations at all levels has been an immense growth in interreligious education, understanding, and cooperation. Nevertheless, the question remains: Can this movement really change hearts, challenge corrupt governments, and reduce violence between members of different faiths? And does the unwillingness of conservative religious leaders to participate in the work hamper its credibility?

For conservative Christians and other fundamentalists there is one true faith. So dialogue with untrue beliefs is considered a sellout, an implicit recognition that other religions are authentic. However, for the foreseeable future, there will be many religious traditions worldwide that inspire love of neighbor, justice, and compassion. That includes—besides the over two billion Christians worldwide—1.4 billion Muslims, 900 million Hindus, 350 million Buddhists, 24 million Sikhs, 14 million Jews, 7 million Baha'i Faith members, and several million followers of other traditions (Zoroastrianism, Shinto, Daoism, Animist, Wicca, et al.). Surely, we think, to understand these traditions and cooperate with them to repair a broken world is what the Infinite Source of Existence desires, however one understands the Divine or Absolute. There are also perhaps one billion people with no formally religious beliefs. They, too, deserve absolute respect, understanding, and protection from discrimination.

CONCLUSION

Religion, like politics, ethnicity, and nationalism is a complex reality having the potential for great good, considerable evil, and, especially in America, a presence that must be factored into the realms of politics and culture. Put another way, government officials, the media, health providers, attorneys, and academics ignore religion at their peril. Our hope is that this discussion of religion's constant intertwining with politics, law, morality, and culture—and the need for compromise in resolving significant differences in how people feel about these issues—will make clear that a morality of accommodation is indispensable to the practical business of making society work amid very real differences between conservatives and liberals. Some people will be put off by the phrase "a morality of accommodation." This should not be taken to mean abandoning one's beliefs or moral principles, but rather accepting the reality that in a highly pluralistic society there will be profound differences at times between the left and the right, Democrats and Republicans, believers and nonbelievers. We think that, by understanding and appreciating opposing viewpoints on the issues discussed in this book, we can make progress as a society in the pursuit of "a more perfect union."

NOTES

1. *Democracy in America* (Trans. Harvey C. Mansfield and Delba Winthrop). Chicago: University of Chicago Press, 2000, p. 282.

2. www.rawstory.com/news/2006/ambassador_claims_shortly_before_invasion_Bush_0

3. "Lessons from Iraq: Religion and the Journalism of International Relations" chapter 3, p. 45, in Stephen Burgard (ed.) *Faith, Politics and Press in Our Perilous Times*. Dubuque, IA: Kendall Hunt Publishing Co., 2010.

4. The series consists of 16 books by Tim LaHaye and Jerry B. Jenkins (Tyndale House, 1995–2007). Four films based on the books have also been produced.

5. *The Atlantic*, March, 2015, p. 82.

6. Ibid., p. 87.

7. *Van Orden v. Perry*, 2005. An enlightening portrait of Cruz is Jeffery Toobin's "The Absolutist," *The New Yorker*, June 30, 2014, 35–45.

8. James Mills, "The Serious Implications of a 1971 Conversation with Ronald Reagan." *San Diego Magazine*, August (1985): 140–44.

9. On the religious dimension of the administrations of Kennedy, Carter, and Reagan, see Randall Balmer, *God in the White House—A History*. New York: HarperCollins, 2008.

10. Retrieved June 19, 2014.

11. http://en.wikipedia.org/wiki/World_Trade_Center_cross. Retrieved August 3, 2014.

12. The Church does permit so-called natural family planning (NFP) that involves avoidance of intercourse during a woman's fertile period, often coupled with the tracking of her basal body temperature and cervical mucus to pinpoint fertile and infertile periods. The complexity of the method has resulted in only about 4 percent of Catholic women utilizing NFP, even though it has a quite high success rate in avoiding conception.

13. As quoted in the *Los Angeles Times*, "Contraceptive Ruling a Win for Conservatives," July 1, 2014, p. A10.

14. "On Hobby Lobby," *Los Angeles Times*, July 1, 2014, p. A15.

15. http://en.wikipedia.org/wiki/Abortion_in_the_United_States.   Retrieved June 19, 2014.

16. Orthodox Judaism permits abortion only in limited circumstances, though it is mandated if the mother's life is in danger. Muslim scholars forbid the procedure after 120 days, and a minority say only the mother's health or rape are legitimate grounds.

17. All scriptural quotations are from *The New Revised Standard Version* of the Bible (1989).

18. Quoted in Jonathan Dudley, "How Evangelicals Decided That Life Begins at Conception," www.Huffingtonpost.com/jonathan-dudley/how-evangelicals-decided-that-life-begins-at-conception_b_2072716.html.

19. "The Impact of Illegal Abortion." www.ourbodiesourselves.org/health-info/impact-of-illegal-abortion/03/23/2014.

20. The First Letter of Paul to the Corinthians (6:9) and the Letter of Jude (1:7) both briefly condemn sodomy.

21. Bruce Drake, "How LGBT Adults See Society and How the Public Sees Them." www.pewresearch.org/fact-tank/2013/06/25/how-lgbt-adults-see-society-and-how-the-public-sees-them.

22. Charles C. Haynes, "In New Poll, Marriage Equality Beats Religious Objections." www.firstamendmentcenter.org/in-new-poll-marriage-equality-beats-religious-objections/.

23. *Edwards v. Aguillard*, 1987.

24. *Kitzmiller v. Dover Area School District*, 2005.

25. www.slate.com/articles/health_and_science/2014/01/creationism-in_public_schools_mapped_where_tax_money_supports_alternatives.html. In June 2014, the United Kingdom banned the teaching of creationism as a scientific theory in its public schools.

26. About a third of respondents believe humans evolved but with God's guidance, while 15 percent accept evolution with no divine involvement. www.gallup.com/poll/155003/Hold-Creationist-View-Human-Origins.aspx.

27. This aside by Justice Clark helped provide a rationale for the founding of departments of comparative religion or religious studies at public universities in the 1960s, many of which now include such departments.

28. *Brown v. Gilmore*, 2001.

29. "Out of Gas in Mustang," *Church and State*, January, 2015, p. 4.

30. Charles C. Haynes and Oliver Thomas, *Finding Common Ground: A First Amendment Guide to Religion and Public Schools*. Nashville: First Amendment Center, 2007, p. 155.

31. The term "jihad" primarily means a holy struggle for righteous conduct, but its secondary meaning is military struggle for the cause of Islam.

32. www.splcenter.org/get-informed/browse-informed/browse-all-issues/2012/spring/FBI-dramatic-spike-in-hate-crimes-targeting-muslims.

33. www.pewforum.org/2010/08/24/public-remains-conflicted-over-Islam/.

34. Chicago: University of Chicago Press, 1991. See also Gabriel Almond, R. Scott Appleby, and Emanuel Sivan, *Strong Religion: The Rise of Fundamentalisms around the World*. Chicago: University of Chicago Press, 2003.

35. Salafism is sometimes equated with Wahhabism, though some Salafists reject the connection. Both movements are ultraconservative and very influential in Arab Muslim states, especially Saudi Arabia, Qatar, and the United Arab Emirates.

36. Jen'nan Ghazal Read, "The Diversity of the New Immigrant Religious Population," in Stephen Burgard (ed.), *Faith, Politics and Media in Our Perilous Times*. Dubuque, IA: Kendall Hunt, 2013, pp. 130–34.

37. Quoted in John Henry Barrows (ed.), *The World's Parliament of Religions*, Vol. I, p. 22. Chicago: The Parliament Publishing Company, 1893.

Chapter 2

What People Think and Believe Religiously

The country's "I'm right; you're wrong" impasse arises from a conflict that has grown more serious. Too many not only hew to what they believe; they have lost the energy, interest, and commitment to find common ground.

This has happened in the face of two phenomena that ought to argue the other way, for more familiarity with other points of view and for more ease at reaching compromise on differences.

The first contradiction is that technology and globalization ostensibly have provided a new digital transnational arena in which the fluency in ideas and perspectives ought to be easier, not harder. When we hear that the world has shrunk and that the conventions of the nation-state have eroded in favor of global perspectives, this is what we're talking about. There is no area where more information is available now in contrast to what was available in the past than in the areas of religion and values. Yet we often hear that globalization can have an unsettling effect, even with its new wonders and possibilities.

There are many marvels in the digital age and the possibilities are undiminished, no doubt. However, this information revolution with its smaller world also is producing and contributing to a kind of underlying malaise. It arises from economic stagnation, the inability to improve standard of living because of the migration of jobs across the nations, and even the divisions between haves and have nots that are considered part of the overall American national problem nowadays.[1] An irony of the information age is that we are finding that as the world shrinks, we are in some ways becoming more, not less, parochial. A Pew study finds that people want to live only around those who agree with them and would be unhappy if family members married across the partisan divide and that there is self-segregation going on all over.[2]

Moreover, alongside whatever new religious understanding we may have, zealots now have a new platform to have their parochial concerns magnified to global importance by social media. In some cases, the attention going their way has allowed them to tee up a profound hatred of the United States, and specifically its democratic norms and values. These extreme views are incompatible with core religious values in the world's major religions as understood by rational people.

Second is the underlying set of policy concerns rooted in religious consciousness that runs through our national life as discussed in the preceding chapter. If we are a religious people, the notion that being centered in faith and values concerns ought to be a confidence builder, not a source of anxiety or alarm about the fraying social fabric. If we have all these people who are informed by religious sensibilities, then even the most commonsense notions of the toleration inherent in religiosity ought to grant our people a common assurance that other points of view will be respected. We know this despite having ample evidence that religious conflict runs very deeply in human history. However, respect for other views is an intrinsic expectation in a democratic experience that has been up and running for several centuries. One should be able to assume that the adherent of another faith also has a civic education and has been inculcated with the importance of respect for other perspectives. The result is that religion and democracy together have powerful norms to make people more inclusive.

There is something wrong in the picture if piety, indifference, or even hostility to religion in the end makes us narrower in our thinking and less tolerant of others. This ought to go without saying, but the divisions are so sharp today that we literally are compelled to go back to basics. A dominant critique of religion in our political culture is that it is more a hindrance than a help. Certainly, liberals and agnostics, armed with the skepticism of science and the excesses of some religious conservatives, are only too willing to remind us of this. This is because religious fanaticism has the potential to produce narrow-minded and uncompromising perspectives. This happens where the true believer gets locked in to a doctrinal position on some religious-based issue and becomes unmovable on political politics and intractable on public-policy positions.

Now the critics of religion are not its therapists. For some of them, it may be easier to just dismiss faith-based perspectives. This, it turns out, is a key division point that blocks our ability to arrive at meaningful consensus on a range of perspectives and issues. However, unless one is completely cynical about religion, and there are critics who truly do find it malevolent, then the stated values of toleration and inclusion that many religions advance at minimum ought to provide a basic expectation for how religious people engage the world.

Also, if the secular world has shrunk because of technology, the American religious landscape itself potentially has become more familiar and intimate. This is because there now are so many religious denominations and ideas out there to choose from. This ought to mean that people are driven by the sheer force of religious logic to consider that some of their own ideas match up with others, while other perspectives do not. There are reasons why this in fact is not happening, or at least not to a sufficient degree to really help us out. There will be more on this in Chapter 10.

Certainly the American political tradition has sufficient experience in accommodation, which stands in marked contrast to the political, social class, or religious fragmentation that exists in other countries even today. Some of this still exists and we will meet some of those people. However, for the American democratic experiment to continue working, citizens need the ability to reconcile conflicting sets of deeply felt positions.

TWO GAPS: POLITICS AND BELIEFS

We have a fundamental problem in this young century. The tools for a multi-religious understanding are in place and actually have been mobilized in important past moments since the tides of immigration forever changed the American landscape in the late twentieth century. However, we still haven't done the work necessary to bridge the doctrinal and ideological divides that in many cases are indefensible in the twenty-first century.

It appears that we have two parallel conflict arenas in religion and values coexisting within the hearts and minds of Americans. One of them, the continuation of what has been called the culture war, essentially has the country in a vice grip of stubborn conflict and righteous rectitude over who possesses the moral high ground. It pits the religious right against the secular left. The second is subtle but in some ways promising, and it arises out of the assets available to us by new immigration that took place in the late 1960s, bringing new religions values and perspectives to our shore and potentially changing forever the nature of religion in public life in the United States. A decade-and-a-half into a new century, we have fallen short of mobilizing its potential and this new religious wisdom has not really taken sufficient root to help us through our impasses. We will have more to say about both as we go forward.

Some people are simply giving up. It is far easier to retreat to comfort zones and blame the other side without doing the work. We will look at indications from polling that this is actually what's happening. In fact, what strikes us as significant is that nobody bothers much to explain what the normative values are that underlie so many stated assumptions and positions. In many cases, you actually have to go to the trouble to mine the origins of these beliefs to see where they come from.

Nor should we find great comfort in the new "nones" (religiously unaffiliated Americans; see Chapter 9) or the ascendancy of secularism as a panacea. We are not talking here so much about the important principle of separation of church and state, but rather this notion that a religion-based sensibility is simply one choice among many. With this is a suggestion that the country might be better off tabling the religious values in public life question entirely and opting for a kind of public agnosticism. On the other side, there are, for example, Catholics pressuring the relatively new pope not to compromise on doctrine. There always has been a tension between conflicting perspectives, but the chasm seems especially perilous in the current environment.

POLAR NATION

This is a remarkable time when our deep divisions are made plain on several levels. We see them in the cool findings of survey research, and in the hot spectacle of people arguing publicly about why they are right and the other side is wrong. There is plenty of evidence that we are well into a prolonged period of national intransigence.

Anecdotal evidence of a nation sharply divided runs like a river through the 24-hour online and legacy news reports, print, broadcast, and vast blog world. This torrent of news from the battlefield on political, cultural, and religious outlooks exacts a price, if even only to wear us down and confirm the cynical views of "the other" found in the national polls. Over time, events have a way of reinforcing the divisions. At the same time, examining and dissecting individual conflicts can have value for revealing the assumptions on which these beliefs are based. Some controversies in the news have embedded in them elements that reveal how and why our national conversation is not hitting on the right cylinders and resolving differences.

This is not to diminish the heartfelt nature of the principles being espoused on the poles. In fact, at the core of deep divisions are important values in a democratic society that come into collision. Moreover, the nature of our society is such that many conflicts play out in the news media or come to the public's attention through the courts, this democracy's place of choice to resolve differences through the rule of law. The alternative is a society where dissent and controversy are suppressed.

The argumentation going on in what's been called "the public square" is only part of the story. In principle, it's healthy that the country has a robust if testy array of conflicts over things people hold dear. It's the inability to resolve them and even hear what the other side is saying that is distressing. The resulting stalemate has the effect of producing lingering bitterness or discouragement at even trying to bridge important gaps. The partisans playing in our national sandbox have arrived at a level of disapproval of each other that is alarming.

The animosity that partisans harbor for those who venture different values-based perspectives is on full display on a range of issues. At times it may seem that we get nowhere. If this seems a harsh assessment, we will consider some items. First, one in which a liberal columnist defended a political adversary on the right in the face of outrageous and even heartless criticism from his own rabid supporters. The second involved intolerance for a position on gay marriage that led to a Silicon Valley executive being run out of town. Finally, a discussion of how the Hobby Lobby Supreme Court case decision in 2014 touched every conceivable nerve and may have demonstrated some flawed assumptions and a rush to judgment.

The first two are examples of passionately held beliefs run amok in full public view. In both cases, prominent media figures, skilled at argumentation, jumped into the fray to argue for sanity. There was an unusual aspect to their engagement. They did so, not to advance the causes with which they normally are allied. Rather, they were appalled to see the mistreatment of targets of scorn on the *other* side of their positions. There may be no better way to grasp how bad things have become than to see reasonable partisans cry foul about what's happening across the aisle, and to mobilize their advocacy and editorial skills in the interest of decency and fairness. In effect, the effort was to try to right the listing ship of civil conversation. Stories arising out of two issues follow, filled with the passion and rectitude of our times: immigration and gay marriage.

TEDDY BEARS AT THE BORDER

Viewers watching cable network news programs in early July of 2014 saw a steady flow of news reports arising from an emergency at the border brought on by a flood of immigrant children from Central America. This conflict pitted the concerns conservatives have with secure borders against the concerns of liberal immigration reform activists, and, in this case especially, faith-based human rights advocates. It was not unusual to see cutaways from congressional anti-immigrant speechifying to scenes from just inside the border, where immigrant toddlers could be seen falling asleep on the shoulders of adult companions carrying them into detention centers. It was at this time that Sarah Palin called for the impeachment of President Obama, declaring that opening the borders was a deliberate White House strategy. Writing on the conservative website Breitbart, she said, "This is his fundamental transformation of America. It's the only promise he has kept."[3]

As complicated as resolving the nation's immigrant crisis is, there is a stark symbolism in the sight of exhausted children that reaches across political lines and touches our basic humanity. You might be led to the conclusion that there are partisans on the right who think, "We have met the enemy, and it is the world's kids."

If we set the border passion aside for a moment, we have two colliding sets of values, both at least credible in the abstract and rooted in established national ambitions and norms. On the one hand is the United States' long tradition of welcoming immigrants to what after all is an immigrant nation, and to providing a sanctuary. The other is the need to preserve the integrity of national borders, to protect our people from terrorists, and to control and manage immigration in a way that ensures the continuation of civic cohesion and the survival of an American identity.

But here is an example of where a national priority, secure borders to uphold law and order and ultimately to advance civic unity, was taken to the absurd. The potential consequences of putting politics first are severe enough to raise questions about the priorities and core values of anti-immigration activists and politicians.

The columnist E. J. Dionne Jr., a national bellwether of sanity, provided a snapshot of how absurdly locked-in the "antis" on the right had become on this issue. In a *Washington Post* column, writing in part from his grounding in a progressive Catholic point of view, he came to the defense on humanistic grounds of someone on the other side, the media conservative and talk show host Glenn Beck. Beck, who rarely finds a spotlight he doesn't like, didn't like this particular one. His supporters were all over him and he cringed at the thought that this was damaging to his career. His offense? He was scorned by his usual flag-waving constituency for the gesture of bringing teddy bears, toys, and supplies to provide comfort for some of the Central American children brought inside the border. Beck had stuck his neck out to give some kids a little joy, and, when the anti-immigration corner normally in his camp hollered, Dionne was appalled. He concluded, "It's one more sign of how the crisis at our border has brought out the very worst in our political system and a degree of plain nastiness that we should not be proud of as a nation."[4]

A PRICE FOR POLITICAL SPEECH

Righteousness taken to the extreme is not the province of partisans on any one side of the nation's ongoing social and cultural battles. In another response, the restoration of civil discourse became the goal. The British author, editor, and blogger Andrew Sullivan is openly gay, and he is married, which obviously counts for something when a public intellectual enters any charged discussion of gay marriage. While self-described as conservative, and no left-winger, Sullivan also has advocated positions consistent with the liberal or progressive positions. In this instance, he felt compelled to speak out, and not on the side one generally might imagine of a gay activist issue. First some background.

A breathtaking tide of support for gay marriage swept the country in the wake of a Massachusetts Supreme Court decision and, in 2004, the state's issuance of marriage licenses to same sex couples. This movement represented a reversal of national sentiment, which began gradually with a wide split in favor of opponents in 1996, with an uptick in support to 2000, and then gradually meeting with roughly even support around 2011. From there, it has been almost all a race to the support side, with younger generations leading the charge. "For the group born between 1980 and 2000, often referred to as 'millennials,' the amount of support was overwhelming by the year 2014, with a full 68% supporting gay marriage."[5]

The polling has taken place against the backdrop of a battle in the courts centered in large part on the equal protection clause of the Fourteenth Amendment. On this justification, too, the movement in popular support for gay marriage was pronounced. A *Washington Post*–ABC News poll in March 2014 found that 50 percent of respondents believed there was a constitutional right to gay marriage. Significantly, when constitutional questions were set aside to focus only on support, the split was 59 percent in support of same-sex marriage, with 34 percent opposed.[6]

The courts at the time were marching state by state in step with changing sentiment in overturning ballot initiatives or local measures outlawing same sex unions. By the summer of 2014, conservative Utah joined a collection of states reversing local bans. These rulings took place also in the context of the U.S. Supreme Court decisions in 2013 that struck down part of the Defense of Marriage Act, in favor of allowing married same-sex couples access to federal benefits and, separately, allowing such marriages to take place in California.

This legal and cultural change was accompanied by some predictable conflicts, providing ample fodder for talk show hosts and for some spectacular conflicts over such mundane but celebratory things as wedding cakes.

Ordinary citizens and big-name public intellectuals, like Sullivan, entered into the fray.

One case in Colorado involved a refusal by the owner of a bakery to provide a cake to a same-sex couple.[7] Here in one bakery was a classic collision of two titanic values or goals: religious freedom and antidiscrimination. The owner of the firm, when ordered to provide a cake, was unrepentant and unmoved. He instead vowed to enforce his own kind of equality of customer treatment. He told CBS Denver that he would still provide for gays in settings other than marriage, but henceforth he would not make wedding cakes for anybody, whatever their orientation.[8]

Sullivan was moved to cry foul by the dismissal in 2014 of Mozilla's chief executive because he earlier had made a political contribution to California's Proposition 8, the 2008 initiative that defined marriage as being between one man and one woman. Brendan Eich had been on the job only a matter of weeks when the company's board began to feel the heat. OkCupid, a dating service that could be accessed through Mozilla's Firefox software, asked people to find another way onto its site, and for a time posted a strongly worded letter of disapproval. Some software developers said they no longer would create apps for the company.[9]

Eich resisted pressure to renounce his donation and argued that his position did not arise from any impulse to discriminate; he said he always tried to adopt an inclusive approach in his business work. He believed that a diverse environment would produce the best results in the new Internet world.[10] It became clear in this debate that, regardless of any subtle distinctions Eich may have tried to raise, Mozilla's board became increasingly uncomfortable about how the company would be perceived if he stayed on.

At the same time, if Eich's position was stated correctly, he was sent packing not because of evidence he discriminated against gays or gay married couples, or even proof that he harbored ill will. It simply was for what he believed about the institution of marriage, separate from his work life. If that's true, perception aside, the company was saying that there were political views that until very recently were majoritarian views and were now considered unacceptable. A political contribution, in effect political speech, to advance those views was unacceptable for continued employment.

A put-off Sullivan delivered a post for his blog, *The Dish*, under the telling headline, "The Hounding of a Heretic." In a passage that got attention in news accounts, he wrote, "The whole episode disgusts me—as it should disgust anyone interested in a tolerant and diverse society. If this is the gay rights movement today—hounding our opponents with a fanaticism more like the religious right than anyone else—then count me out."[11]

Despite Sullivan's prominence in media, he does not appear to have received much coverage from some major editorial pages that cheered the continuing reversal of barriers to gay marriage, and by long traditions have been committed to free speech. The *New York Times* covered the Mozilla issue in its news columns and, on the editorial page the same year, welcomed a U.S. Court of Appeals decision regarding reversal of a Utah ban, noting, "All in all, this has been a year of extraordinary progress on same-sex marriage."[12] However, its editorials' space passed on Mozilla and left the issue of Sullivan's witch hunt complaint to others. A blogger made passing reference to the ugliness, before settling on a line that Mozilla and Eich should have known that he didn't belong working there in the first place.[13] The *Los Angeles Times,* a major newspaper in the state where the Proposition 8 controversy had raged, in September 2014 called on the U.S. Supreme Court to uphold gay marriage, but it also deferred to a blogger to address the Sullivan issue: "Gay Rights 'Anti-Bullying Activists': The Biggest Bullies of Them All."[14]

Media are one aspect of the Mozilla controversy to illustrate that the rush to judgment and willingness to overlook important concerns runs deeply in the national culture and conversation. Here is an example of how editorial boards may contribute to the climate. Case by case, incident by incident, a national impasse hardens and a set of assumptions settles into the infrastructure of our common life about where key players stand and will remain. This is significant in the case of prestigious legacy news organizations like the *New York Times* and the *Los Angeles Times*, because much of the polarization in other media is attributable to a digital and commercial revolution, the changes in platforms, or business and market positioning strategies. What major news outlets are selling in the Wild West of the global Internet is their tradition of standards, independence, and credibility. It may be that the boards decide against wading into a controversy on grounds that they have made their major policy pronouncements already. If true, however, this would not account for the selective editorial scolding and praising that goes on daily on all manner of people and events in the news.

During his five minutes in the spotlight, Eich said enough to suggest he wasn't a bigot and was motivated on a principle about what marriage was as a social construction that was widely shared in conservative intellectual circles. While the tide of court cases on the side of approving gay marriage as a basic civil right approached a tsunami, a federal judge in Louisiana asked some pesky questions about who would have to be allowed to marry in the future and concluded, "This court is powerless to be indifferent to the unknown and possibly imprudent consequences of such a decision."[15] The upshot of editorial silence in exploring a fuller discussion invited in a case like this has a reinforcing effect. It confirms the notion that partisans should be assured that the major media won't disturb them on either side; they won't be pleasantly surprised or uncomfortably prodded to rethink fixed views.

LESSONS FROM THE HOBBY LOBBY CASE

The squall over the U.S. Supreme Court decision in *Burwell v. Hobby Lobby Stores*, a case in 2014 involving Obamacare and contraceptives, provided a rare window into many dimensions of our predicament. It is significant because so many players in the current impasse had a role or were heard from: the legislature, the presidency, the judiciary, the ideological camps and the advocacy groups, and the media. We could see on full display the larger question of how deeply religion plays into the fabric of American life. Moreover, it is an example of how the partisans have their positions for restatement at the ready, and where by contrast the particulars may be far more complex. These may bring into a play an entire range of personal and political views, and they may be set in the context of both the legislative process and the unfolding of First Amendment case law on religion.

The politicization of reproductive rights is a long story. Its power to reappear was summarized by Gail Collins, the *New York Times* columnist. As the midterm congressional elections arrived in 2014, she poked fun at the notion that Republicans had discovered women's rights. Her column reminded readers that only a few years earlier a GOP Senate candidate had suggested that a woman who had been raped couldn't get pregnant. She noted that the effort to ascribe personhood to any manner of fertilized egg had fallen flat and that suddenly Republican candidates faced with a glaring gender gap were finding ways to champion the benefits of *birth control*, even if one candidate couldn't bring himself to utter those two words without an assist from his audience.[16]

In *Hobby Lobby*, a divided Supreme Court found that a privately held corporation with religious objections could not be compelled to provide contraceptive coverage for employees under Obamacare. This set off a howl of protest in support of Justice Ruth Bader Ginsburg's dissent that the door would be open to all manner of religious exemption claims by corporations. It's hard to say, of course, what claims might actually follow, but the decision also may well have been narrower than feared. The church and state constitutional law expert Robert Tuttle of George Washington University pointed out that the nonprofits already had the exemption, so this was an extension, not the creation of a new area. He suggested that it would be hard for larger corporations to argue as convincingly as the small Hobby Lobby company management did from a faith-based perspective. If he's correct, here an instance where alarm buttons are at the ready whenever the Supreme Court speaks, regardless of how narrow the scope of an opinion may be. Meanwhile, as liberals were concerned about the overreach of religion, there was concern on the other side of the debate. At the time of the debate, there already was litigation in the works from Little Sisters of the Poor, a Catholic charity organization, and hundreds of other religiously affiliated nonprofits. The objection was even to having the insurance company handle directly the contraceptive requests of nonprofit employees.[17]

The Hobby Lobby case demonstrated how two powerful values-based advocacy groups, those alarmed about any hint of restriction on reproductive rights and those given to the narrowest interpretation of when human life begins, are poised to advance fixed arguments in the courts of law and the court of public opinion. This is at the core a case about the free exercise clause of the First Amendment, and what it means to whom at what point in time. It had received a political boost from Congress in its nearly unanimous 1993 passage of the Religious Freedom Restoration Act. This was a "feel good" piece of legislation at the time, enjoying bipartisan support, because it was designed as a kind of course correction for an earlier Supreme Court decision that denied Native Americans the use of peyote in their religious ceremonies. But ceremonial peyote for Native Americans is a different matter from a case that opens a sensitive area of long conflict about reproduction, privacy, and when life begins. A perhaps unintended consequence was that the legislation had planted a skirmish in a time capsule to be opened by the Hobby Lobby case.

For those unhappy with the Hobby Lobby decision, even if it is as narrow as Tuttle suggests, a larger question is raised. What did liberals think they were voting for in the Religious Freedom Restoration Act? Apparently the answer is that religion is a good thing to stand up for and a feel good thing to vote for politically. However, a larger question of "for whom" matters once a law is put to the test. The law could not have been clearer that Congress enacted legislation that specifically prohibits putting an undue burden on the exercise of religion. Moreover, Justice Anthony Kennedy's concurring opinion broke it down to its simplest element. Why could the executive branch not do what it had done for the other religious providers?[18] The answer has to be that it had a predisposition not to accommodate, rather than the intention of the 1993 legislation, which was to restore a predisposition to accommodate.

At the same time, one has to ask whether some religious conservative voices in this case might be calling this issue of distancing or purity of position too close to the line. If, as the court pointed out, especially in Kennedy's concurring opinion, an accommodation had been made to provide arm's length on contraception for the nonprofit provider, which could be extended to a small faith-based company board, then why press the issue? It is not as if the question of contraception for Catholics is new. Nor are the theological questions about when life begins entirely clear to any thoughtful and moral person, even if there are institutional positions.

This is a case that demonstrates that for things to work in a diverse society, partisans need to take a deep breath, take stock of what they are getting through policy choices or court decisions, and rethink what they can live with. For some, this will be asking too much. For the rest of society, a failure to find a common ground that accommodates key perspectives only serves to contribute to our impasse. Hobby Lobby illustrates that for its flaws, the system of judicial review is set up to work by finding the best possible resolution within the constitutional framework. However, the partisan battlefield is filled with fixed positions.

We are left with a profound question beyond the particulars about whether to make a pragmatic legal accommodation. Why can't we bridge the divide about basic legal facts and have a conversation based at least in what the reality of birth control methods is? Otherwise we are locked in a "my reality versus your reality" conundrum. Other questions: Do we have to respect beliefs that are proven to be ungrounded? Is insufficient attention being given to the profound question of when life begins?

Whatever the answers, we know the extent of our differences. The value of survey research is that it catapults us out of the realm of case or anecdote and into something like an accurate portrait of collective points of view, assuming that such things as sample size and margin of error receive proper attention. In June 2014, the Pew Research Center for People and the Press released an important study, *Political Polarization in the American Public.* It provided an overarching portrait of a nation politically divided at a very basic level and how this was influencing important things in American life. These findings were supported by other studies and, in a most dramatic way, by the companion torrent of news coming out of the poles.

The essential findings were summarized nicely by the subhead of the study: "How Increasing Ideological Uniformity and Partisan Antipathy Affect Politics, Compromise and Everyday Life." The study puts a dent in the notion that there is much of anything by way of overlap between the two main political parties nowadays and makes clear that gaps have grown considerably over a 20-year period.

We used to hear about liberal Republicans, of the Nelson Rockefeller stripe, and blue collar or Reagan Democrats. Of groups such as these, we might think: Well, there is a common perspective in there somewhere between constituencies in the major parties. There appears to be much less room to work with today. The Pew study finds that 92 percent of Republicans are to the right of the median Democrat, and 94 percent of Democrats are left of median Republicans.[19]

In other words, since 1994 just about everybody in either party has drifted much farther right or much farther left than the people remaining in the center group of the other party. Beyond this is a more daunting finding. Partisanship has turned to animosity and a sense that the other side is actually harmful for the country. This sentiment has profound implications for how people in the major parties line up and even live and socialize. The study finds, "People on the right and left also are more likely to say it is important to them to live in a place where most people share their political views, though again, that desire is more widespread on the right (50 percent) than on the left (35 percent)." They simply don't trust the other side and want little to do with them.[20]

The study does find that these views are not shared by most Americans but injects a discouraging and cautionary note that people in the center tend to be disengaged from the political process. So if the study is correct, the politically active and committed people in the major parties keep to themselves, don't want to talk to the other side, and have drifted to more hardened positions. These data are significant when it comes down to the political disputes that emerge in the ebb and flow of our national life.

Some big picture considerations are in order here: There are two sets of ideological fissures, one political and cultural, the other resulting from religious doctrine and philosophy of life. The two have become intertwined but actually are separate. We will make the point throughout this book in various ways that moderates on the left and right must summon the political courage to save the "endangered center" from extinction. We will see in Chapter 12 that groups such as No Labels are making a start at closing the great divide, but more brave politicians, media mavericks, business leaders, academics, and concerned patriots must face facts: We are an ideologically alienated nation desperate for a cure for our malaise.

NOTES

1. Nouriel Roubini, chairman of Roubini Global Economics and professor of economics at the Stern School of Business, New York University, discussed aspects of a "new nationalism" in "Economic Insecurity and the Rise of Nationalism," theguardian.com, June 2, 2014.

2. "Polarization Is Dividing American Society, Not Just Politics" Nate Cohn, *New York Times*, June 12, 2014.

3. "Exclusive—Sarah Palin: It's Time to Impeach President Obama," Sarah Palin, *Breitbart*, July 8, 2014.

4. "Bordering on Heartless," E. J. Dionne Jr., *Washington Post*, July 13, 2014.

5. "Gay Marriage," Pew Research Center, February 23, 2014.

6. "Support for Same-Sex Marriage Hits New High; Half Say Constitution Guarantees Right," Peyton M. Craighill and Scott Clement, *Washington Post*, March 5, 2014.

7. "Colo. Gay Discrimination Alleged Over Wedding Cake," Ivan Moreno, AP story in *Yahoo!News*, June 6, 2013.

8. "Masterpiece Cakeshop's Jack Phillips Vows to Stop Making Wedding Cakes Altogether after Court Rules in Favor of Gay Couple," Curtis M. Wong, *Huffington Post*, June 3, 2014

9. "Mozilla's Chief Felled by View on Gay Unions," Nick Bilton and Noam Cohen, *New York Times*, April 3, 2014.

10. Ibid.

11. "The Hounding of a Heretic," Andrew Sullivan, *The Dish*, April 3, 2014.

12. "A Milestone for Same Sex Marriage," Editorial, *New York Times*, June 27, 2014.

13. "The Campaign against Mozilla's Brendan Eich," Vikas Bajas, *New York Times*, April 4, 2014.

14. "Gay Rights 'Anti-Bullying' Activists: The Biggest Bullies of Them All," Charlotte Allen, *Los Angeles Times*, April 7, 2014.

15. "Federal Judge, Bucking Trend, Affirms Ban on Same-Sex Marriages in Louisiana," Campbell Robertson, *New York Times*, September 3, 2014.

16. "Passion for the Pill," Gail Collins, *New York Times*, September 5, 2014.

17. "The Hobby Lobby Impact: A Q&A." David Masci's interview with Robert Tuttle, Berz Research Professor of Law and Religion, George Washington University. www.PewResearchCenter.org/fact-tank/2014/07/02/the-hobby-lobby-impact-a-qa

18. Kennedy, A. concurring, *Burwell v. Hobby Lobby Stores*, http://www.supremecourt.gov/opinions/13pdf/13-354_olp1.pdf, June 30, 2014.

19. *Political Polarization in the American Public*, Pew Research Center.

20. Ibid.

Chapter 3

What People Think and Believe Politically

We have seen how values perspectives lie at the root of many of our divisions and will return in a subsequent chapter to look at three of the big controversial issues in our time. First, in this chapter we take the plunge at the level of philosophy of life and beliefs, both religious and secular. This is to explore assumptions that inform people's responses to a wider range of conflicts. Later, we'll consider common sets of attitudes and values on the right and left and look into how we may have fallen into patterns of predictable thinking. We had a hint of this in Chapter 2, where the reactions of partisans were poised and ready for response to news events.

RELIGIOUS VERSUS SECULAR OUTLOOKS

When we talk about core personal beliefs, we approach sensitive and cherished ground. This terrain has to do with either religious sensibility or secular outlook, not just political perspectives. In our view, there is not enough examining going on of what these core beliefs really say when matched against each other, because there may be glimmers of accommodation awaiting—and that makes ideologues uncomfortable. What we do know is that there is a sharp division between people who want religion to play an important role in public life and those who don't, and that division seems to fall along party lines. Some of these divisions were outlined in a

Pew Research Religion and Public Life poll just before the midterm elections in 2014.[1] The polling suggests a separation between those who would like to see religious perspectives more prominently at play in politics and public life and those who want more separation and tend to a more secular disposition. This is a big, basic difference in our people.

Our fractured public discourse acknowledges that people believe this or that. However it leaves everybody off in their separate corners, mostly to talk to each other. This is important, because if people remain immovable in their ideologies, there are consequences beyond just the question of getting along. An important piece is the journey from those fundamental "what-we-believe" things back into the political arena. In a healthy environment, there might be room for accommodation. It's there where the differences find expression in an electorate that has become fixed and predictable. The *New York Times*' Nate Cohn has written in the political sphere about the manufacturing of "ideologically consistent candidates," and we'll discuss later in the chapter what some observers have concluded.[2]

In the arenas of beliefs, social and cultural attitudes, and political behavior, our divide has settled into something broad and deep. We don't know whether this is serious enough for the long term to produce a completely balkanized country. The country has had other instances in its history when the whole democratic experiment could have flown apart. Mindful that sectarian and regional ideology have a role in our past conflicts, we'll explore that possibility. We know for certain that signs of our divisions are everywhere; perhaps most memorably evident in recent election cycles in this young century in those colorful television set maps of the voting-conservative red states and voting-liberal blue states. We've seen it down on the ground in the strategies of campaigns, as happened in the 2004 presidential election. The George W. Bush campaign targeted the "values voter" and tried to convince Catholics that Senator John Kerry was out of step with his own faith.[3] Kerry later acknowledged being tone deaf as a presidential candidate to faith considerations. As such, he became part of an ongoing Democratic reckoning with underestimating the importance of religion.

One of our concerns had to do with the irony of having assets that turn to liabilities. Americans have what might be called "habits of citizenship" built into our national DNA. This appears to be failing us today or is even producing unintended negative results. What are they? They can be found in these big areas of civic life and religion, and as such are basic. We are participants in a democratic experiment, which is a condition either of birth or of choice. This carries an expectation of our collective willingness to work with our differences, either to accept or to mediate. This is true for believer and nonbeliever alike; it's a qualification of citizenship.

Our assumptions and what we do about them matter on all levels in the democratic experiment, not just with respect to our values and religion. For much of what happens, such as filing signed tax statements or sharing the road with bicycles, is dependent at the outset on our voluntary cooperation, absent the watchful eye of enforcers. As a religious people, a characteristic observed by de Tocqueville early in our national experience and evident in polling today, we have universal values that ought to make religiosity an added tool for aiding in getting along and for making conflict resolution an active and willful process.

So here are big questions for us that are a running theme in this book. Why isn't it working? Are we willing to do the work with the resources both civic and religious at our disposal? We'll talk about the first question here, and in more detail about civility as a greatly underemployed tonic in Chapter 12.

Suffice it to say for now that this has to do with our attitudes and the effort we're willing to make with democracy's fellow travelers. The agnostics and atheists value many of the same things religious people do, especially where humanistic and spiritual values intersect. This is some of what we have in mind when we talk about glimmers of accommodation. They are clear about the parts of organized religion they find odious, and then they chart out a set of values that actually line up with the things religious people say are important about how to live. This ought to be a boon, not a liability, in a diverse society. Few are talking much about that. We are challenged by both our secular (civic) and belief commitments to make an effort across the aisle to sort these things out. It is this work that isn't getting done, and a root explanation for our current impasse.

Moreover, rather than assuming that the two are hopelessly at odds on the big picture, how about daring to look under the hood to examine statements and beliefs about the core of human spirituality? When we look at what people say they think, there's a mosaic of notions; it's not all black and white in this world of individual seekers and achievers trying out a vast supermarket of ideas for self-improvement and self-realization. Some of these, as we'll see in the discussion that follows, seem wildly at odds on the surface, but underneath have hints of agreement. Too many of us just see the chasm.

"GOD AWAITS OUR DISCOVERY"

The title of this section is posited as a discussion opener to bridge two worlds. There are two interpretations possible, a deliberate double entendre having to do with the division between our national camps. One on the right is rooted in religious belief; the other on the left is secular. This double meaning in a single phrase will, we hope, prove pertinent when applied to questions raised in a *New York Times* Op-Ed column about religious conviction versus profound skepticism. The debate is about whether organized religion is a help or a hindrance and is central to the ongoing culture war. The column, written in the summer of 2014 by regular columnist Frank Bruni, was about the prominent atheist Sam Harris and an experience he conveyed in a new book from a visit to the Holy Land. It helps explain our "what-we-believe-at-the-core" impasse while at the same time, unintentionally, pointing to areas where we may be miscommunicating.[4] First, here's some background.

In a traditional religious context, if it were said of a seeker that God awaits his or her discovery, it's generally clear what would be meant. The person arrives at a religious commitment through some measure of self-effort, and the divine entity, in whatever form we believe it to be, is listening for that knock on the door. We know also that in the Christian tradition there is a concept of grace, which is thought to be less a product of personal effort and more like a favorable wind. Yet even in this understanding, there is the notion that grace or divine feedback to the individual has some connection to the degree of individual effort. This connection between initiative and the serendipitous benefit of grace is found also in the Hindu tradition, which is now available to Americans along with the other religious concepts of the world. Swami Bramananda was a great teacher of monks of the Ramakrishna Order who were dispatched to explain the East to the West at the turn of the twentieth century. They met up with celebrity intellectuals such as Aldous Huxley and Christopher Isherwood in making Vedic scripture accessible to Westerners. Bramananda made a point of affirming that a meaningful relationship with the divine, whatever our religious disposition or belief tradition, is there for the taking for those willing to make an effort. This doesn't just mean that initiative by the individual automatically produces good results in return. But there is a suggestion that a lack of initiative leaves the individual in a kind of existential stalemate, a boat floating in the vast sea of life with its sails down.[5]

To nonbelievers, the notion that "God is simply waiting for us to check in" may be a curiosity, but in the social and cultural battles it also will be a puzzle. The distinction has significance for a new group getting the attention of pollsters and political observers in the camp of agnostics, atheists, and "nones," as they are called by survey researchers in this area; that is, they are not affiliated with any religious group or doctrine. If we were to posit the same proposal for them, namely, "God awaits our discovery," a different meaning would spring up at the opposite end of the "ultimate beliefs" chart. It introduces the notion of the individual at the center of all things, not as recipient of insight or grace, but as *the* verifier of what's plausible or makes rational sense.

For this group, finding or affirming God would be more a process of validation starting without any preconception or expectation, rather than acceptance as the endgame of a spiritual quest. It has significance to the outlook on spirituality particular to these times. It's actually a substantial historic shift of emphasis, comparable on an inner psychological level to the Copernican astronomical model that rattled the established order in the sixteenth century. It gives priority to the individual's skeptical disposition in a scientific age. It says to believers, "We have no proof, and proof is what we would need to sign on." Atheism and agnosticism are not new, by any means. This emerging camp, however, increasingly has become significant as a loose and diverse bloc with a vocal interest in our politics and common affairs. Some evidence for this can be found in a study by the Pew Research Center's Religion and Public Life Project, which reported that the no-religion group was made up of one-fifth of all adults, one-third of people under 30, and was growing.[6]

From this shifting perspective, religion, so central a locus of authority in much of modern history, now itself is more widely under cross-examination. To put it another way, a God concept in the modern person-centric universe will have to pass a series of tests, or we the individuals may affirm disbelief, or simply withhold conclusion. It may be that God cannot be proved at all through the scientific method. If that's the case, so be it, says this segment of the population. For many serious thinkers in this group, nothing is assumed. The challenge for any religious perspective in winning over these skeptics is intensified by what might be termed "the phenomenon of God's invisibility."

WE DON'T SEE, BUT WE'RE RIGHT

The God-invisibility factor may go unrecognized in such a conversation, although it is perhaps *the* underlying assumption in modern conversations about religion, and the starting point for existential disagreement. That is, the phenomena of the universe are observable and subject to verification and analysis through scientific method. But if God is true, one thing that can be said—to the frustration of just about everybody—is that we don't see evidence. Most thoughtful people, either believers or nonbelievers, would acknowledge this. What we have is the testimony of mystics, the scriptures, flights of inspiration in the passages of poets and romantics, and in that sticking point of sticking points, the pronouncements of religious authorities. On the nonbeliever side, we find a disposition to raise questions, to doubt rather than to take up doctrine, and to take aim at shibboleths. Believers think that not seeing God makes life worth the struggle;

nonbelievers think nothing is proven, at least not yet, without some kind of public appearance. A Supreme Being awaits verification in the same manner as life on distant planets. Renowned astrophysicist Stephen Hawking has not found such verification and stated in a September 7, 2010, interview on ABC news that "one can't prove that God doesn't exist, but science makes God unnecessary."[7] Meanwhile, what the skeptics do see coming out of religion is by contrast all too visible, and obnoxiously and dangerously so. Much of how religion plays out on the global stage or in domestic politics is regarded as being at the root of what ails the world.

Can there be a more fundamental division at the starting point of how our beliefs and assumptions create separate camps? This helps explain why it is that the religious American views the world through the lens of faith and teaching, and the unaffiliated are skeptical or want religion out of public life entirely. If we can get to the root of this seemingly irreconcilable certitude at the poles, does this in some way help explain how our collective conversation is misfiring?

One normally does not expect answers, or even such vetting on the Op-Ed pages of the *New York Times*, or, for that matter, any of the major legacy outlets. This kind of big-picture discussion generally is left to books, conferences, and specialty media outlets, even if the *Times* has claimed in its celebrated charge that it offers us *all* the news fit to print. This is so for a host of reasons, among them the mission of a worldly and secular media enterprise, the spheres of interest of columnists and contributors, and the practical limitations of space for articles typically written without direct relevance to the day's news. The newspaper has a strong and influential stable of columnists, and it's not hard to find examples of their references to religion in the news. However, this particular Bruni column was different, and more in the vein of a big-think feature to be found in the *Times* online in a moderated series called the Stone; indeed the Notre Dame philosophy professor Gary Gutting goes deep with Bruni's subject, Mr. Harris, on the nature of consciousness in one of these interviews that appeared after the column.[8]

It turns out that the column didn't just fall out of the sky. The book provided what's called a "news peg," a term for the elements of relevance and timeliness that make something worthy of coverage and also the attention of opinion writers. Harris had just published it with the intriguing title, *Waking Up*. Bruni dug out an anecdote midway through the book that illustrated what he called a "chicken-or-egg question." It's of particular importance as we examine core beliefs that seem starkly at odds. Harris told of walking the shore of the Sea of Galilee on terrain associated with Jesus, and described a moment when a feeling of transcendental calm came over him. For Bruni, Harris's experience captured an important sentiment in expressing how atheists and agnostics feel nowadays about religion. The book, he said, "caught my eye because it's so entirely of this moment, so keenly in touch with the growing number of Americans who are willing to say that they do not find the succor they crave, or a truth that makes sense to them, in organized religion."[9]

Bruni writes, "The question is this: Which comes first, the faith or the feeling of transcendence? . . . Mightn't religion be piggybacking on the pre-existing condition of spirituality, a lexicon grafted onto it, a narrative constructed to explain states of consciousness that have nothing to do with any covenant or creed?" The columnist clearly believes organized religion is a sacred cow. Here was an opening to advance the idea that religion, as we have come to see it in the public square, is something different from what's important in human spirituality. Harris, for his part, confirms in the column that there was no conversion whatsoever for him, by saying that any association with a Christian experience would be "a prejudiced, willed one."[10]

Harris by this time had become a poster person for the rational nonbeliever. According to his website, he is a cofounder and the CEO of Project Reason, a nonprofit foundation "devoted to spreading scientific knowledge and secular values in society." In fact, the Project Reason website takes direct aim at religion because of a kind of exempt status; it's seen as getting a pass from the scrutiny and self-examination that other disciplines are subjected to. At the same time, it's regarded as a troublemaker.

The site explains:

While Project Reason is devoted to fostering critical thinking generally, we believe that religious ideas require a special focus. Both science and the arts are built upon cultures of vigorous self-criticism; religious discourse is not. As a result, religious dogmatism still reigns unchallenged in almost every society on earth—dividing humanity from itself, inflaming conflict, preventing wise public policy, and diverting scarce resources. One of the primary goals of Project Reason is to change this increasingly unhealthy status quo.[11]

His perspective is clear. We return now to our double entendre. For secular thinkers like Harris, we can say "God awaits our discovery" and mean something different from what the religious person has in mind for the getting-to-know-you relationship between humanity and any divine essence. But the complexity and diversity of religious thinking in our pluralistic age matters greatly.

For some religious people, Harris's feeling of transcendence wouldn't be a surprise at all, and they might not try to fit it into a doctrinal slot. "The varieties of religious experience," as Harvard psychologist William James termed them at the turn of the twentieth century, are in a big tent. People in the spiritual communities, both institutional and informal, have been talking about what these experiences may or may not mean for a long time. It might be strange for them to think that Bruni's ordering of which came first, the experience or the religion, was a necessary exercise. Rather, they would interpret Harris's experience differently. It could confirm that structure, imagery, and scriptural interpretation in organized religion exist to help us understand things that are very difficult to understand, especially given the "phenomenon of God's invisibility."

Feelings of calm in a holy place are nothing out of the ordinary for believers. But if spirituality only gains credence when affirmed by skeptics, then it comes down to whether God is something we encounter, or whether the concept of a divinity has something to prove to us. We should consider how ironic this is—that people ostensibly at odds in divided camps, secular versus religious, actually are discussing for their own internal audiences the meaning of the very same experiences. This is one reason why religion and an outlook informed by skepticism in our time is both simple and complicated.

Now back to that Pew poll and what conclusions it draws about the "nones," and what this suggests about people like Harris: "This large and growing group of Americans is less religious than the public at large on many conventional measures, including frequency of attendance at religious services and the degree of importance they attach to religion in their lives."[12]

A new survey by the Pew Research Center's Forum on Religion and Public Life, conducted jointly with the PBS television program *Religion and Ethics Newsweekly*, finds that many of the country's 46 million unaffiliated adults are religious or spiritual in some way. Two-thirds of them say they believe in God (68 percent). More than half say they often feel a deep connection with nature and the Earth (58 percent), while more than one-third classify themselves as "spiritual" but not "religious" (37 percent), and one-in-five (21 percent) say they pray every day. In addition, most religiously unaffiliated Americans think that churches and other religious institutions benefit society by strengthening community bonds and aiding the poor. "With few exceptions, though, the unaffiliated say they are *not* looking for a religion that would be right for them. Overwhelmingly, they think that religious organizations are too concerned with money and power, too focused on rules and too involved in politics."[13]

Harris, when viewed in this survey's framework as atheist, is not a complete fit within the Pew profile, but he has key characteristics. The unaffiliated are a broad group, and by his own words he can be placed among the Pew respondents as one variation on a new kind of seeker. He had his transcendent moment and is one of those who "feel a deep connection with nature and the earth" but is open to some kind of deeper experience. He clearly meets another classification of this group, a feeling that religion is concerned with the wrong things.

The divisions are deep between those who emphasize the importance of doctrine in their lives and the new restive seekers of spirituality in whatever form it feels comfortable. The separate camps are significant especially to the degree that they have created suspicion, finger pointing, and disrespect in the larger political, social, and cultural areas. At the same time, something important is going on in our collective ether. Some of our traditional thinking about what is and what is not important within belief systems is undergoing a transformation as new perspectives come to us from across the globe.

OUR PREDICTABLE PATTERNS

Where do we find larger evidence of the fixed stars in people's minds and how they play out in politics and voting patterns? One place is the work of Nate Cohn, who covers polling and policy for a regular *New York Times* content feature, The Upshot. He wrote before the midterm elections in 2014 that the Democrats could forget about trying to win a majority in the House of Representatives.[14] He dismissed gerrymandering as a fully satisfactory explanation and suggested, "The country is increasingly divided between liberal cities and close-in suburbs, on one hand, and conservative exurbs and rural areas, on the other. Even in red states, the counties containing the large cities—like Dallas, Atlanta, St. Louis, and Birmingham—lean Democratic."[15]

The geographical assembly of like-minded metropolitan voters thus has changed electoral politics. It's done so on the basis of compatibility of outlook for city people on the one hand, and others in the suburbs and rural areas on the other. With respect to the Republican lock on the house, it has peeled off presidential politics from the congressional races, because an overload of Democratic votes in a metropolitan area for president effectively wastes potential House votes. It means nothing in suburban and rural areas that have their own districts. Cohn notes that in earlier periods, a national Democratic candidate with an urban constituency would have to be concerned with alienating rural and Southern voters on social and cultural issues. Certainly this was how Franklin D. Roosevelt built his New Deal coalitions in hard times. However, in presidential politics now, it is possible to assemble unabashedly a coalition of voters in urban areas around support for such controversial issues as gay and reproductive rights. Cohn observes that assembling an ideological collection of compatible voters paid dividends in 2012 for President Obama "but ensured cataclysmic losses in formerly Democratic stretches of West Texas and West Virginia, where restrictions on gun ownership and mining, and support for gay marriage and immigration reform, are deeply unpopular."[16]

Some of the values that have drawn together these geographical blocks of voters arise out of religious convictions and some do not. For example, the debate over guns, as we shall see in the next chapter, has its own dynamics having to do with individual rights, public safety, and interpretations of the Constitution. Others, such as reproduction, are traceable directly to points of view arising from theological and religious perspectives, such as when human life begins, in conflict with privacy rights. What we are finding is that having like-minded voters living in proximity and sharing cultural and religion-based views is a geocultural reality today that has consequences for the nation's political dynamic.

As for the religion factor, the question of whether the Democrats have lost the battle for the hearts and minds of the electorate has been much debated. Another Pew Research Religion and Public Life study took note of the 2004 presidential election history, and went further. It found that the Democrats in general had ceded conservative Christians to the Republican Party because of liberal stands on social issues. That by itself was unsurprising, given all the attention paid to the GOP's evangelical base. However, a second and deeper problem was raised, that the Democrats were being perceived as unfriendly to religion.

The study concluded:

Democrats may have had a problem in recent elections, in other words, not just because their policy prescriptions were rejected by conservative Christians, but also because a large portion of the electorate who may be sympathetic to Democratic positions was nevertheless turned off by a perceived hostility on the part of the Party toward religion, which most Americans see as a positive force with an important public role to fill.[17]

The Pew religion poll eight years later before the midterm election of 2014 found support for a more active, faith-based voice in social and political issues at 49 percent, up from the same period in 2010. Nearly three-quarters thought religion was losing influence in public affairs, and the people who thought this was a good thing were divided. But while as might be expected the percentage wanting a stronger role for religion was concentrated in the traditional Republican base, there were a significant number of Democrat-leaning respondents, 42 percent, who wanted this, too.[18]

Indeed, by the midterm election in 2014, liberal religious perspectives were more forcefully being heard in the areas of immigration, economic fairness, and environmental issues. In a Senate race in Virginia, Democratic incumbent candidate Mark Warner (who was narrowly reelected) counter-attacked when confronted by his Republican challenger on social and cultural grounds. According to the *New York Times*, Warner during a debate had the extreme label turned back on him. "When Mr. Warner attacked his views on abortion, contraception and same-sex marriage, Mr. Gillespie used his Catholic faith as a shield. My religious views, really, Senator, should not be at issue here," he said.[19]

THE GREAT IDEAS DIVIDE

By midsummer of the 2014 congressional midterm year, confidence in Washington had reached a new low. The inability of the institution to reach agreement on key issues related to immigration reform and economic matters brought things to a halt as a hapless and pilloried Congress left town.[20] At the heart of the impasse were core values and partisan perspectives that seem to have become unsolvable and permanently in collision.

Then came the election itself in November when Republicans increased their numbers in the House and took control of the Senate by a significant margin (54 to 46). The president, knowing that the House was even less likely to pass the Senate's immigration bill, responded by issuing an executive order that will permit as many as four million undocumented persons—most of whom are the parents of U.S. citizens—to remain in the country for about three years. Republicans have reacted vehemently to what they see as a usurpation of Congress's role, and payback in the 2015 congressional session was inevitable.

The Democrats see the Republicans as having abandoned compassion and commitment to the notion that the government has a role in helping current and future citizens through difficult economic times. In a *Washington Post* article, Heather Cox Richardson, a Boston College history professor, traced the party's retreat from a progressive-era concern with how government could level the playing field for citizens against special interests. She noted that by mid-twentieth century, the consummate military leader, Dwight Eisenhower, was arguing as a Republican president that the nation should not choose armaments over the need for schools, hospitals, and roads.[21]

That has changed. In the Tea Party era, one can still find traces of the original Republican notion that creating opportunity without the stranglehold of government bureaucracies is a driving principle of philosophy to benefit everybody. But the idea that creating more equitable circumstances is good for all economic classes now is of little interest to many in the current Republican fold. Abiding mistrust of government has come in its place, along with a sense that opportunity and success, through the creation of wealth by elites, will find its way to the benefit of those all up and down the economic ladder—President Reagan's "trickle-down" economics reprised.

If we take Richardson's explanation as a view of the right gone astray from the left, the measure of how far apart the perspectives are can be found in what conservative intellectuals have to say about what's wrong with America. It's a completely different assessment of our national condition. From this vantage point, the problem is that the beneficiaries of the free enterprise system have lost their way, not that Republicans have given up on making life better for ordinary citizens beyond the circle of the rich and powerful. It is the liberals who have morphed, mired in a sense of entitlement and political correctness, and led to abandon the values of hard work, thrift, and gratification deferral. Dinesh D'Souza, the controversial commentator, offers a spirited argument that it is liberals "who rely on government seizure and bureaucratic conquest to achieve their goals and increase their power." The quote comes from a sympathetic column written by the National Review Online correspondent John Fund, in which the author recommends D'Souza's film *America* as "the perfect film to take the family to on a Fourth of July."[22]

At an earlier Republican Leadership Conference in New Orleans, the Republicans showed their own internal divisions over the purity of conservative ideals and appeals to religion. *Duck Dynasty*'s Phil Robertson, caught up previously in controversy over remarks about homosexuality, made a direct appeal for the advancement of a Christian nation. It was left to the former Mississippi Governor Haley Barbour to remind delegates that there was a swath of Americans out there who were not in the evangelical base and would need a broad and pragmatic appeal that, at the end of the day, would determine the outcome of elections. "I hope we will not let purity be the enemy of victory," Barbour was quoted as saying.[23]

The conflict over deeply held beliefs and public policy has skewed any attempt to bridge divisions in perspectives, even as it has proved an obstacle in crafting election strategies. We will take up the question of ideological predispositions on climate change as one example of the great impasse in the next chapter. For the moment, we focus on divisions on the deep level of belief and values systems. For example, obsession with the environment has led one leading conservative commentator and radio talk show host, Dennis Prager, to identify "leftism" as nothing less than a new religion. He has written that it amounts to a fundamental repudiation of core Western values and the adoption in their place of a pagan outlook: "This is the antithesis of the Judeo-Christian view of the world that has dominated Western civilization for all of the West's history. The Judeo-Christian worldview is that man is at the center of the universe; nature was therefore

created for man. Nature has no intrinsic worth other than man's appreciation and (moral) use of it."[24]

It's evident how far into the core so many current controversies go. The
New York Times' Brendan Nyhan offered insight into how beliefs inform
the attitudes and positions of people who, as members of the scientific
community, are aware of the full range of factual complexity. The passions
that bring people into the public arena to advance their values-based
views also can be an inhibiting factor for going public with positions that
might run counter to what they believe. They are, he finds, disinclined to
advocate positions that are in conflict. He suggests that "we need to try to
break the association between identity and factual beliefs on high-profile
issues."[25]

DEPTH OF OUR DIFFERENCES

Our divisions not only are deep enough to inhibit us from setting aside
core points of view. They contribute to a stalemate that some think threatens the functioning of democracy and its mission as the best idea for organizing human affairs. Moreover, there is a psychological component that
reinforces the depth of our differences, often to the core of our beings and
at the level of genetic codes, as we will discuss further in Chapter 12.

The microworld of inner beliefs extends to the macroworld of our
most broad organizing themes. The journalist and commentator David
Brooks argues that we have lost the power of the big binding narrative for
democracy. This is in part because in the post–Cold War era, everybody
has retreated into libertarianism and small-minded positions. If he's right,
then our restless contentiousness is not just about like-thinking partisans
living and working in close proximity with people who do not stir themselves to talk with anybody who disagrees. The big rallying ideas for the
democratic experiment, combining capitalism as the best alternative to
central state planning, with a faith-based vision that eschews godless
totalitarianism, today are a weakened link for our collective enterprise.
In what he terms "a spiritual recession," Brooks argues "if America isn't a
champion of universal democracy, what is the country for? A great inheri-
tance is being squandered; a 200-year-old language is being left by the side
of the road."[26]

This cloudy assessment of an America on the spiritual ropes is shared
by leading public intellectuals and commentators. The author Gary Wills
has written that "small-think" has now managed to capture the soul of
the modern Republican Party, to the point where the majority can be
held hostage in disregard of laws and rules by a vocal minority. Without

the nerve to stand up to them, even party leaders are in the clutches of a kind of "neo-secessionism."[27] Even short of a Civil War–type split, this would exemplify a retreat from big unifying beliefs referred to by Brooks as antidotes to sectarian or political self-interest. Writing in the *Atlantic*, the authors David Sirota and Zaid Jilani conclude that there really are two Americas represented in the House of Representatives, neither party having incentive or cause to please anyone beyond narrow constituencies.[28]

Francis Fukuyama, assessing this malaise in *Foreign Affairs*, sees many of America's political institutions becoming increasingly dysfunctional. This has resulted, he thinks, from "a combination of intellectual rigidity and the power of entrenched political actors" that keeps these institutions from being reformed. And the situation is unlikely to change "without a major shock to the political order."[29]

If we are not chastened by these observations, there is the psychological and even biological component. The psychologist Diane Halpern, a former president of the American Psychological Association, says Congress has been acting like a dysfunctional family, exhibiting such qualities as "my side bias," and is an institution in need of therapy.[30] Thomas B. Edsall, a commentator on trends in American politics, has explored the work of psychologists who argue that we may be hardwired to believe the way we do based on our genes. He concludes, "They may not lend themselves to rational debate and compromise."[31] In fact, these trends have begun to cause the two major parties to, in effect, hate the other side and see them not as competitors but as evildoers. Writing in the Daily Beast, Michael Tomasky opines that Democrats should write off the South: "Forget about the whole fetid place. Write it off. Let the GOP have it and turn it into a Free-Market Jesus Paradise. The Democrats don't need it anyway."[32] Not the most encouraging thought as we conclude a discussion on our belief-based divisions. We'll have more to say later about our predispositions and the choices available to us.

NOTES

1. "Public Sees Religion's Influence Waning: Growing Appetite for Religion in Politics." Pew Research Religion and Public Life Project, September 22, 2014.

2. "Polarization Is Dividing American Society, Not Just Politics," Nate Cohn, The Upshot, nytimes.com, June 14, 2014.

3. "GOP Urges Catholics to Shun Kerry," Michael Kranish, *Boston Globe*, September 26, 2004.

4. "Between Godliness and Godlessness," Frank Bruni, Sunday Review, *New York Times*, August 30, 2014. SR3.

5. Prabhavananda, *The Eternal Companion*, Vedanta Press, 1960.

6. "Nones on the Rise," Pew Research Center's Religion and Public Life Project, October 9, 2012.

7. www.ABC   news.go.com/GMA/Stephen-Hawking-science-makes-God-unnecessary/story?id=11571150.

8. "Sam Harris's Vanishing Self," *The Stone,* Opinionator, *New York Times*, September 7, 2014, http://opinionator.blogs.nytimes.com/.

9. Bruni, op. cit.

10. Ibid.

11. "About Project Reason." www.project-reason.org/.

12. Pew, ibid.

13. Pew Research Center's Religion and Public Life Project, op. cit.

14. "Why Democrats Can't Win the House," Nate Cohn, "Midterm Calculus," The Upshot, *New York Times*, September 6, 2014, http://www.nytimes.com/upshot/.

15. Cohn, op. cit. See a further discussion of this big geopolitical sorting out in Chapter 12.

16. Ibid.

17. "Do the Democrats Have a 'God Problem'?" Gregory A. Smith, Pew Forum on Religion and Public Life and Peyton M. Craighill, Pew Research Center for the People and the Press, http://www.pewforum.org/2006/07/06/do-the-democrats-have-a-god-problem/.

18. Pew Research Religion and Public Life Project, op. cit.

19. "Democrats Put Cultural Issues in Their Quiver," Jonathan Martin, *New York Times*, September 15, 2014.

20. "Congress Off for the Exits, but Few Cheer," Jonathan Weisman and Ashley Parker, *New York Times*, August 1, 2014.

21. "How the GOP Stopped Caring about You," Heather Cox Richardson, *Washington Post,* September 19, 2014.

22. "D'Souza's America," John Fund, National Review Online, June 29, 2014.

23. "At Republican Leadership Conference, the Struggle over the GOP's Future Continues," Dan Balz, *Washington Post*, May 31, 2014.

24. "Judaism, Christianity, Environmentalism," Dennis Prager, April 1, 2014. http://www.dennisprager.com/judaism-christianity-environmentalism/. Accessed September 22, 2014.

25. "When Beliefs and Facts Collide," Brendan Nyhan, The Upshot, nytimes.com, July 5, 2014. Accessed September 22, 2014.

26. "Is America Losing Faith in Universal Democracy?" David Brooks, *New York Times*, June 26, 2014.

27. "Back Door Secession," Gary Wills, *New York Review of Books*, October 9, 2013.

28. "There Really Are Two Americas: Republistan and Democravia," David Sirota and Zaid Jilani, *The Atlantic*, November 8, 2013.

29. "America in Decay (the Sources of Political Dysfunction)," *Foreign Affairs*, 93, 5 (September/October, 2014), p. 10.

30. "Our Government Is Broken" Diane Halpern at TEDxClaremontColleges, http://tedxtalks.ted.com/video/Our-Government-is-Broken-Diane. Accessed September 22, 2014.

31. "How Much Do Our Genes Influence Our Political Beliefs?" Thomas B. Edsall, *New York Times*, July 8, 2014. See further discussion of this issue in Chapter 12.

32. www.thedailybeast.com/articles/2014/12/08/dems-it-s-time-to-dump -dixie.html.

Chapter 4

America's Great Debates—Immigration, Gun Rights, and Climate Change

The discussion to follow of these three great debates is meant to be illustrative, not exhaustive. While books and dozens of refereed journal articles have been written on all three, our primary intention is to show that intelligent, well-intentioned persons have been talking, even screaming, past one another on these issues for too long. We have tried to present some hopefully middle-of-the-road observations that might break down barriers between immovable objects and irresistible forces, as the old song puts it, about other emotional topics.

PART I: IMMIGRATION

"You shall not oppress a resident alien; you know the heart of an alien, for you were aliens in the land of Egypt." (Exodus 23:9)

"I was a stranger and you welcomed me." (Matthew 25:35)

"Give me your tired, your poor, / Your huddled masses yearning to breathe free, / The wretched refuse of your teeming shore. / Send these, the homeless, tempest-tost to me, / I lift my lamp beside the golden door." (Emma Lazarus, "The New Colossus")

In earlier chapters, we discussed the moral and cultural battles surrounding abortion rights, gay rights, and the teaching of evolution in public schools among other topics with a direct connection to religion. The current chapter focuses on the highly emotional issues of immigration (Part I), gun rights (Part II), and climate change (Part III). Here, the religion factor is not directly relevant. However, there are profound ethical dimensions to these issues.

Three years ago, a Latino student in Ben Hubbard's Religion and Politics class at Cal State Fullerton lingered afterward, looking anxious and a bit depressed. Ben had been discussing immigration and suspected this issue was on the student's mind. So he invited him back to his office to discuss his situation. Jorge (not his real name) was brought to America from Mexico at the age of two and has been here ever since. He is a bright and successful student but also an illegal alien, or undocumented person, and therefore unable to obtain legal employment and have a successful future in this country. (He is among several thousand such students in California colleges and universities alone.) Fortunately, within a few months of our conversation, President Obama issued an executive order, the Deferred Action for Childhood Arrivals (DACA), that offers temporary status—and the ability to seek legal employment—to some children who arrived here before 2007. Jorge has now graduated and is employed legally. However DACA is a temporary fix for a small segment of the undocumented population.

The Senate Immigration Bill

In June 2013, the Senate passed a comprehensive immigration act[1] that included very stringent requirements for border security that must be achieved within 10 years before anyone here illegally can obtain a permanent-resident green card. Among the requirements is a doubling in the number of border patrol agents to at least thirty-eight thousand, the completion of seven hundred miles of pedestrian fencing along the southern border, and a complex surveillance system. The estimated 11–12 million people living here illegally could obtain "registered provisional immigrant status" six months after enactment of the bill; but these individuals would have had to arrive in the United States prior to December 31, 2011, and maintained continuous physical presence here. They would need to be free of felony convictions, learn English, and pay a $500 fine. After ten years in this status, the immigrants could seek a green card, while those brought to the country as youths could get the green card after five years along with immediate citizenship. There are various provisions for highly skilled workers, as well as for low-skilled workers (e.g., up to two hundred thousand such persons yearly for jobs in construction, hospitality, long-term care, etc.). In addition, a new agricultural worker visa program would replace the existing one, whereby individuals here illegally—but who have worked in the industry at least two years—could qualify in five more years for a green card if they stay in the harvesting industry. Finally, the bill would mandate that within four years all employers must implement an e-verify program to electronically determine their workers' legal status.

However, the House of Representatives did not pass a parallel bill, and so the country remains stuck in immigration limbo. This is the case despite polls showing that a high percentage of Americans favor allowing illegal immigrants to stay in the country (71 percent in a 2013 Pew Center poll).[2] Another 2013 Pew Center poll indicated (by a 77 percent majority) that increased border security must be part of any new immigration legislation.

Not only is a comprehensive immigration bill unlikely to pass into law anytime soon, the so-called DREAM Act (Development, Relief, and Education for Alien Minors) has been kicking around Congress for 13 years. The bill would provide the potential for permanent residency to certain alien immigrants of good character who have graduated from U.S. high schools, arrived in this country before age 16, and lived here continuously for at least five years prior to the law's enactment. If they were to complete two years in the military or at least two years in a four-year university, they would obtain temporary residency for a six-year period. During that time, if they acquired a university degree, or completed at least two years of college, or served in the military for at least two years and were honorably discharged, they would qualify for the coveted green card. Fifteen states have enacted a version of the Dream Act that grants undocumented students in-state tuition rates and financial aid.

So "Nero fiddles while Rome burns." Instead of getting a handle on an admittedly complex and emotional issue, Congress—especially the Republican-controlled House—continues to be swayed by its most conservative, Tea Party members. With congressional elections on the horizon in September 2014, a wary President Obama heeded the concerns of nervous Democrats in competitive races and postponed a promised executive order on immigration reform until after the election. However, the order, Deferred Action for Parents of Americans, has been blocked by court orders (see further discussion in Chapter 6). And so we continue to stagger from crisis to crisis, as with the next issue to be discussed.

A New Crisis: Children at the Border

Between October 2013 and the summer of 2014, an estimated sixty thousand children and teenagers from El Salvador, Guatemala, and Nicaragua attempted to cross the U.S.–Mexico border in Texas, most of them fleeing the poverty and drug-fueled violence of their home countries. This flood of humanity has overwhelmed the Border Patrol, the Immigration and Naturalization Service, and the Department of Health and Human Services that must care for the children while awaiting a hearing. Unlike illegal migrants from Mexico who, because of treaty arrangements, can be apprehended and quickly returned to that country, the migrants from other Central American countries must, by treaty, be handled differently. This includes deportation hearings to determine whether they have a legitimate fear of returning to their home countries. Because the INS is already overwhelmed with cases, hearings take more than a year during which the migrants are usually sent to live with relatives already in the country (and some will simply not return for their hearings and live in the shadows, always fearing deportation). In July, 2014, so many children needed to be housed in South Texas that some were bussed to government facilities in Murrieta, California, where they were met by a group of about a hundred protesters. These people represent the sizable anti-immigrant movement in California and throughout the country, such as NumbersUSA.[3] They believe that—because America already takes in about a million legal immigrants every year—we should not permit tens of thousands of undocumented migrants to settle here and add to the millions already in the country. They argue that some illegals may be terrorists or drug runners, that they are taking jobs from American citizens, that they may be bringing with them communicable diseases, and that they are straining our social network and to some extent altering the nation's culture. In Santa Ana, California, for example, Spanish is the first language of about 75 percent of the population, and it is the unofficial second language of California and much of the country.

Seeking a Middle Ground

Supporters of immigration reform argue that this nation of immigrants must adopt a more reasonable posture toward migrants who simply want a better life for themselves and their children as they flee horrid conditions in their home countries. Americans are very conflicted on this issue. We are a nation of immigrants, but we are also a nation of laws. Jagdish Bhagwati and Francisco Rivea-Batiz, writing in *Foreign Affairs*, argue that a valuable approach might be to let states compete for immigrant labor. When Alabama, Arizona, Georgia, and South Carolina began legislatively harassing undocumented laborers in recent years, they saw their agricultural and construction workforce dry up and move to more welcoming states. As they write:

As this dynamic plays out, states will begin to compete for illegal immigrants who will then face less harassment and be able to better integrate into their communities . . . A race to the top in the treatment of illegal immigrants is a viable path to reform that would greatly advance human rights in the United States.[4]

The religious community, especially the Roman Catholic Church, which has a large Hispanic constituency in this country, has for many years urged Congress to pass compassionate legislation that both protected our borders and kept them open for legal immigration, along with a fair resolution for these undocumented people. Jewish and liberal Protestant groups in general share these sentiments. Somewhat surprisingly, evangelical Protestants are also very much in favor of compassionate immigration reform. On June 12, 2012, a group of nearly 150 evangelical leaders signed an "evangelical statement of principles for immigration reform" that called for a bipartisan solution on immigration reform based on six principles:

1. Respect the God-given dignity of every person.
2. Protect the unity of the immediate family.
3. Respect the rule of law.
4. Guarantee secure national borders.
5. Ensure fairness to taxpayers.
6. Establish a path to legal status and/or citizenship for those who qualify and who wish to become permanent residents.[5]

Then, in summer 2014, the Sanctuary Movement was rebirthed. In the early 1980s as terrible civil strife raged in Central America, thousands of refugees fled to the United States seeking asylum. At one point, over five hundred churches and synagogues housed refugees and cared for their physical needs. A new organization Groundswell has now enlisted over one hundred congregations to assist the undocumented in various ways. As one participating congregation stated:

Just because Congress has failed to act does not mean that people of faith should also stand idle . . . Scriptures call us to care for the widow and the orphan, but it is time that we act sooner and prevent the creation of widows and orphans through our broken immigration system.[6]

So there is essential unanimity among religious groups in America for a compassionate, balanced, and workable immigration policy. But, as with so many emotional issues, the minority rules. Congress members in conservative states become beholden to ultraconservative Tea Party constituents for fear of losing their seats to candidates on the far right.

In some respects, the poster boy for immigration reform is José Antonio Vargas who was brought to the United States from the Philippines at age 12 but was not informed until 16 that he was undocumented. He went on to graduate from college and become a journalist and was part of a Pulitzer Prize–winning team at the *Washington Post*. In 2011 he wrote a powerful essay about his plight in the *New York Times Sunday Magazine*. Although he won another journalism award for his work, he lost his job, because his undocumented status was now public knowledge. Then in 2013 he produced "Documented: A Film by an Undocumented American" which aired on CNN in summer 2014 and chronicled his case. Ironically, even if the DREAM act were passed by Congress, Vargas would not qualify—he is just over the age-31 cut-off for dreamers. So the immigration wars continue and millions of José Vargas's remain in legal and existential limbo.

PART II: GUN RIGHTS

The United States is a country born from revolutionary conflict, preserved by further conflict (War of 1812), locked in brotherly/internecine conflict (Civil War), stretched to the Pacific in the Indian Wars, and massively increased in size by yet another conflict (Mexican–American War). It moved toward an empire with the Spanish–American War, was transformed into a superpower by World Wars I and II, chastened in conflict by the Korean Conflict and even more so the Vietnam War, and embroiled further in combat by the Gulf War and the Iraq and Afghanistan invasions. There were good wars and bad wars in this chronicle of combat, but our country clearly knows the power of weaponry. There is also the nation's long history of using handguns, shotguns, and rifles for sporting, hunting, and collecting purposes. And our culture is steeped in gunplay from classic Western movies to all manner of television dramas. Weaponry is an important part of American culture, and that is not going to change.

Interpreting the Second Amendment

Along with our gun culture, the Second Amendment to the Constitution guarantees the right of Americans to own guns:

A well regulated Militia, being necessary to the security of a free State, the right of the people to keep and bear Arms, shall not be infringed.

The meaning has been endlessly debated and interpreted. One school of thought argues that the founders intended for citizens to have the right to defend themselves against a tyrannical central government. However, the classical position had always been that the right to bear arms was not an inherent prerogative of citizenship but rather one that derived from service in the militia. When James Madison wrote the Second Amendment in 1789, he wanted to allay the fears of the states regarding a standing army. So the amendment was his attempt to respond to these fears by assuring that national defense would reside in the states and in militias, not at the federal level in a professional army. (One wonders what he would think about the evolution of a standing army as it now exists.)

For most of our nation's history, it was assumed that states could put restrictions on who could own a gun, what type of weapons were permissible and even whether handguns could be prohibited outright in a given municipality. Washington, DC, plagued with gun-related violence, passed an ordinance that outlawed handgun possession by private citizens altogether. However, in *District of Columbia v. Heller* (2008), the Supreme Court ruled 5–4 that the DC law was unconstitutional. Justice Antonin Scalia did note in the ruling that some restrictions on gun use would pass muster.[7] Because the District of Columbia is a federal enclave, not a state, the *Heller* ruling applied only there. But the 2010 ruling, *McDonald v. Chicago*, extended it to the states and became the first high court ruling to declare that the Second Amendment protects an individual right to keep and bear arms for self-defense.

An Emotional Debate

The debate over gun rights remains highly emotional and contentious because of the huge toll in human lives caused by handguns and other weapons, including the terrible massacres at Columbine, Aurora, Virginia Tech, Newtown, Marysville, Roseburg, and many other locales. We pay a high price for the right of individual gun ownership:

- Americans possess at least 300 million weapons of various kinds, a number equal to the population.
- There are about thirty-two thousand gun deaths per year in America, 60 percent of which are suicides, 3 percent accidental deaths, and the remaining 34 percent acts of homicide (a bit over eleven thousand and at least 30 per day).
- New data compiled by the Centers for Disease Control and Prevention's National Center for Injury Prevention and Control indicate that in 14 states gun deaths now exceed vehicle deaths. While a variety of safety features put in place by auto manufacturers and numerous

federal and state regulations to improve car safety have reduced the automobile death rate by 43 percent, gun deaths continue to increase. The firearms industry is one of the least-regulated businesses in the country.[8]

- American children are 11 times more likely to be shot than children in other developed countries.
- For every time a gun is used for self-defense in the home, there are 7 assaults or murders, 11 suicide attempts, and 4 accidents with a weapon.[9]
- Every 30 minutes, an American child is shot and killed or injured by a gun.
- Gun homicides are proportionately much higher in the United States than in any developed nation. For example, in 2010 there were two hundred of these homicides in Canada with a population one-tenth that of America. If Canada had our population, that nation might have experienced two thousand deaths but not eleven thousand.

Organizations such as the National Rifle Association (NRA) point out that, in large metropolitan areas, from 65 percent to 80 percent of gun homicides are gang-related, and most of these victims are young persons of color. But don't these children and adolescents have the same right to life as those in affluent suburbs?

The Brady Act

During the attempted assassination of President Ronald Reagan on March 30, 1981, his press secretary Jim Brady was seriously wounded and left partially paralyzed for life. (He died on August 4, 2014.) This tragedy led eventually to the passing of the Brady Handgun Violence Prevention Act in 1993. The Brady Act requires that background checks be conducted on individuals before a firearm may be purchased from a federally licensed dealer, manufacturer, or importer. If a potential purchaser is cleared by the National Instant Criminal Background Check System, that person may obtain the firearm. In addition, the Act prohibits certain individuals from transporting weapons through interstate or foreign commerce or from receiving any firearm if the individual:

- Has been convicted in any court of a crime requiring imprisonment of more than a year;
- Is a fugitive from justice;
- Unlawfully uses or is addicted to any controlled substance;

- Is unlawfully in the United States;
- Has been discharged from the armed forces under dishonorable conditions;
- Is subject to a court order restraining the person from harassing, stalking, or threatening an intimate partner or child of such partner; or
- Has been convicted in any court of a misdemeanor crime of domestic violence.

Currently, 92 percent of the background checks are completed while the FBI is on the phone with a gun dealer. The Brady Act has worked reasonably well, for example, by blocking 1.9 million attempted firearm purchases from 1994 through 2009, 70 percent of which cases affected felons and fugitives from justice. However, there is a serious loophole in the legislation: Firearms purchases at gun shows and those between private individuals are not subject to the law (and as many as 40 percent of all legal gun sales involved private sellers without a background check).

In 2009, both the House and Senate considered legislation aimed at closing the loophole. The stricter Senate version would have required gun show operators to report sales to the attorney general within 10 days. The Brady Campaign to Prevent Gun Violence, the leading proponent of restrictions on the sale and use of weaponry, strongly advocated for the bill. (A recent national poll found that 92 percent of the public favored a universal background check, while 7 percent were opposed.)[10] On the other side, the National Rifle Association fought against it, arguing that such legislation would impose severe red-tape restrictions with the aim of closing down gun shows. The Brady Campaign and the NRA have been locked in an ideological struggle ever since passage of the Brady Act.

A detailed study by www.Factcheck.org concluded that it is impossible to determine if gun ownership deters crime or increases it. Crime rates have decreased significantly in recent years, but experts attribute this largely to the end of the crack cocaine epidemic (and probably the aging of the population). The study also noted that laws permitting concealed carry of handguns have a negligible effect on crime because of the modest percentage of the population that seeks a concealed carry permit. (However, this may be changing as more and more states pass concealed carry laws. According to the federal government, by 2011 eight million people had concealed carry permits and the number continues to rise. See John Lott's research, below.) Most concealed carry permit applications come from people who are relatively low risk either for crime perpetration or victimization, are generally older, higher income, rural, and white. The study quotes University of Maryland criminology professor Charles F. Wellford: "If there were no guns, the lethality of crimes would be less. You can't have a drive-by knifing." Wellford noted that on the same day as the Newtown massacre an attacker with a knife at an elementary school in China wounded 22 children and 1 adult, but no one was killed—different weapon, different result.[11]

The NRA's position

Although the Factcheck.org analysis is persuasive, there is another way of approaching the issue. The Cato Institute argues,[12] from a common-sense perspective, that gun ownership is surely a deterrent to crime in some cases. In fact, a study by Gun Owners of America maintains that guns are used at least 1.5 million times annually for self-defense.[13] But, when a felony is deterred or prevented, crime statistics are usually not compiled. John Lott, president of the Crime Prevention Research Center, in his book *More Guns, Less Crime—Understanding Crime and Gun Control Laws*[14] has provided perhaps the most convincing yet controversial case for concealed-carry handguns as an essential tool for crime prevention.

Allowing citizens to carry concealed handguns reduces violent crimes, and the reductions coincide very closely with the number of concealed-handgun permits issued. Mass shootings in public places are reduced when law-abiding citizens are allowed to carry concealed handguns.

Lott's findings are impossible to dismiss, yet there is a tragic irony about why more guns may result in less crime. Beginning in the 1960s with the inner-city riots in Newark, Detroit, Los Angeles/Watts, and elsewhere, thousands of handguns were stolen from gun stores; and so began the tragic proliferation of handguns in America. In fact, most handguns used by criminals are either stolen or illegally obtained. So we are faced with a great irony: Guns are ubiquitous, people fear being victims of gun crimes,[15] and so they purchase handguns for protection. In turn, with guns every-where, gun suicides and fatal gun accidents increase.

The debate rages on, with Congress members fearful that any attempts to put restrictions on guns, for example, outlawing so-called assault weap-ons or limiting the size of ammunition magazines to ten bullets, might seal their fate in the next election.[16] In 2014, for example, the NRA and its subsidiary, the Institute for Legislative Action, spent $3,360,000 lobbying Congress.[17]

Yet, there is much to commend the weapons training programs of the NRA:

- In 1956, the organization became the only national trainer of law enforcement officers when it introduced the NRA Police Firearms

Instructor Certification Program. Today, there are more than ten thousand NRA-certified police and security firearms instructors.

- The NRA's fifty-five thousand certified instructor's now train about seven hundred fifty thousand private gun owners per year.
- Since the establishment of the Eddie Eagle Gun Safety Program in 1988, more than 21 million prekindergarten to sixth grade children have learned that, if they see a firearm in an unsupervised situation, they should "Stop. Don't touch. Leave the area. Tell an adult."
- Over the past seven years "Refuse to Be a Victim" seminars have helped more than fifteen thousand women and men develop their own personal safety plan using common-sense strategies.

The NRA's four million members are by and large law-abiding citizens who sincerely believe that weapons make our nation safer and are important for hunting and recreational purposes.

Wayne La Pierre, executive director of the NRA, and Dan Gross of the Brady Campaign need to talk over lunch and be in regular contact. If they did, they might find at least some areas of agreement, for example, that crime, fueled by drug wars in our inner cities, is a blight on the nation needing to be more seriously addressed. They might also agree that the mental health system in this country is terribly inadequate and allows many mentally ill persons to acquire guns and go on murderous rampages. And they might concur that law enforcement could do more to prevent the illegal sale of so many handguns to criminals. But the chasm is still wide: while the public favors stricter nationwide gun control laws by 52–43 percent, they think the NRA better reflects their views on guns than President Obama by 46–43 percent.[18]

There is a bright spot for those who favor greater gun safety. Since the Newtown massacre, nine states have made significant changes to gun laws, while only four have appreciably weakened them. Consequently, more than half of all Americans now live in a state with stricter gun control laws than before that tragedy.[19] California, for example, has passed a law (Assembly Bill 1014) that permits police and sheriffs to confiscate the weapons of disturbed individuals who might pose a threat to themselves and others. The first-of-its-kind law establishes a process for obtaining a restraining order from a court to temporarily limit access to firearms when there are warning signs that someone is at risk of causing a firearm injury or death to him- or herself or others.

Outside of the United Nations building in New York City stands a sculpture inspired by the words of prophet Isaiah about beating swords into plowshares (Isaiah 2:4). It is a huge handgun with the barrel twisted into a knot. Only a messianic age will bring the prophet's vision to reality; in the meantime, conservatives and liberals must come together to make a reduction, at least, in the carnage on our streets.

PART III: CLIMATE CHANGE

Perhaps no contentious issue produces as much contradictory evidence as the raging debate over global warming and climate change. Did average global temperatures actually rise during the first decade of the twenty-first century or decline? Is the amount of ice in Antarctica increasing or decreasing? Are the fluctuations in global temperature and climate part of cyclical patterns that have occurred throughout the planet's history or are they an anomaly never before seen?

The Scientific Consensus

There will always be legitimate debates, disagreements, and reevaluations in the field of climate science. Though we write as nonscientists, we are aware this is how science works under the principle of falsifiability: When new data arrives and calls into question earlier theories, science reevaluates and improves upon its findings. For many years, there has been a growing consensus among scientists worldwide that the Earth is warming, and a principal reason is human activity with a resultant increase in heat-trapping carbon dioxide (CO_2). This is the view of the Environmental Protection Agency—based on findings from both the National Oceanic and Atmospheric Administration and the National Aeronautics and Space Agency. On its website, the EPA summarizes what it considers basic facts about climate change:

- The years 2005 and 2010 were the warmest on record. Sea levels are rising, oceans warming and becoming more acidic, and icecaps melting.
- Because there has been no significant increase in solar energy in the past 50 years, man-made activity has to be the main cause of global warming.
- Global average temperatures have increased 1.4°F in the past 100 years, and scientists project a 2 to 12°F increase by 2100. This will mean lower crop yields, more intense rainfall, and more droughts, among other problems.
- CO_2 levels in the atmosphere are higher than at any time in the past eight hundred thousand years. The climate is expected to change faster than at any time in human history.

The United Nations Intergovernmental Panel on Climate Change (IPCC) essentially agrees with these findings.

The Skeptics

Although some 97 percent of climate scientists agree that man-made activity is the main cause of global warming, the views of the naysayers are important in this debate. A climate change conference sponsored by the Heartland Institute in 2012 concluded that natural climate cycles have turned from warming to cooling, that global temperatures have been declining for more than 10 years and are expected to continue this way for another two decades or more. One speaker at the conference, professor emeritus of geology Don Easterbrook of Western Washington University, actually predicted a 20-year cooling trend. Peter Ferarra who reported on the Heartland Conference, commented on predictions by the IPCC about global warming: "Was that based on climate science, or political science to scare the public into accepting costly anti-industrial regulations and taxes?"[20]

Ironically, when it comes to "political science," Heartland is an ideologically conservative-libertarian organization, once funded by the likes of Charles and David Koch of Koch Industries and other industrialists who oppose environmental legislation. Between 2008 and 2014, Heartland sponsored nine international conferences on climate change, which brought together hundreds of global warming skeptics. In itself, an organization challenging the consensus on climate change might be healthy, but the Institute has had its integrity called into question by some of its tactics. For example, in 2012 it sponsored a digital billboard campaign in the Chicago area with a photo of "the Unabomber" Ted Kaczynski stating, "I still believe in global warming do you?" The tactic caused a furor even among some climate change skeptics, and led to a loss of corporate funding and board resignations. On the website of the 2014 conference, the distinguished Dutch film director and animator, Paul Driessen, had a centerpiece quotation:

I am heartened by the knowledge that we here gathered today will fight on—for honest science, affordable energy, accountable government, and better lives for billions of people—and against the dark forces of climate fanaticism. I also know we are being joined by more and more countries, as they increasingly understand the true nature of ideological conflict.[21]

Despite what the best current science indicates about the dangers of climate change, the nation is locked in a highly politicized, emotional, and divisive debate. What follows is a brief point–counterpoint on the intensity and complexity of the climate debate. The American Meteorological Society summarizes its position as follows:

There is unequivocal evidence that Earth's lower atmosphere, ocean and land surface are warming; sea level is rising; and snow cover, mountain glaciers, and Arctic sea ice are shrinking. The dominant cause of the warming since the 1950s is human activities. This scientific finding is based on a large and persuasive body of research. The observed warming will be irreversible for many years into the future, and even larger temperature increases will occur as greenhouse gases continue to accumulate in the atmosphere. Avoiding this future warming will require a large and rapid reduction in global greenhouse gas emissions.[22]

But, of course, the debate does not end there. Writing in *Forbes Magazine* online, environmental writer James Taylor reports on a survey of the American Meteorological Society in which just 52 percent of the eighteen hundred respondents answered "yes" to whether global warming is mainly caused by human activity. Another 48 percent either questioned whether global warming is happening or would not ascribe human activity as the primary cause.[23] In a later post, Taylor reports on the development by National Oceanic and Atmospheric Administration (NOAA) of the U.S. Climate Reference Network that collects temperature data more scientifically than the old network and has been in operation for about 10 years. It indicates that between January 2005 and April 2014, U.S. temperatures have actually cooled by 0.4°C which is over half the purported global warming of the twentieth century. Taylor cautions that ten years is hardly sufficient to establish a long-term trend and does admit that some warming has happened but not at the alarming level that climate change advocates claim.[24]

Then along comes a counterpoint from *Mother Jones* at the opposite end of the media pole from *Forbes*. The magazine's Chris Mooney points out that one of the principal findings of this AMS survey is that its members who publish less peer-reviewed climate research, or less peer-reviewed research generally, are more likely to be climate skeptics. Mooney also claims that "ideology was a consistently bigger influence on meteorologists, in fact, than their level of scientific expertise."[25] The moral of this story is that even sincere climate experts and media commentators can never completely free themselves from their ideological predispositions. But at least the two sides should be taking each other seriously and trying to find commonalities to better understand why *something* is happening with the climate.

In a comprehensive assessment of the entire climate change clash, Charles Mann observes that the debate itself is hindering practical steps to do something about the problem. Environmental issues became a means for politicians to signal their ideological identity to supporters. As he puts it, "Standing up for your side telegraphed your commitment to take back America—either from tyrannical liberal elitism or right-wing greed and fecklessness."[26]

As a result, very little gets done. Assuming that a massive, worldwide carbon reduction campaign is politically impossible, Mann suggests that retrofitting the world's approximately seven thousand coal burning power plants (responsible for 40 percent of carbon dioxide emissions) would not only be a significant ecological accomplishment, it would prevent sixty-six hundred premature deaths and one hundred fifty thousand childhood asthma attacks each year in America alone. But is even this feasible in the current ideological climate?

Despite the daunting challenges, a worldwide movement is pressing the United Nations, United States, and other countries to take action. On September 21, 2014, the People's Climate March in New York City drew some four hundred thousand demonstrators; and there were smaller marches and rallies around the nation and the world.[27] On September 22, the UN held a high-level discussion of climate change as a run-up to a meeting scheduled in Paris for December 2015 where the aim is to reach a formal agreement among polluting nations.

One would hope that moderate voices on each side might listen seriously to the arguments of their opponents and seek at least some common ground. Conservatives point to the expense of environmental regulations that hinder energy production and the overall health of the world economy. The tactic of raising doubts about the accuracy of global warming to call into question the entire enterprise is now well established. A huge majority of climate scientists, environmental activists, and politicians are warning of the inevitable catastrophic effects of a changing climate. They report that annual global average temperatures have risen 1.8°F (= 1°C) since the late 1800s, and that a rise of one more degree Celsius would be catastrophic for human civilization. These scientists and their political supporters will need to both beat back spurious and questionable arguments from climate deniers and at the same time keep an open mind on the entire topic. Both sides will also need to stop caricaturing and even demonizing their opponents, as nothing will be gained this way. There are an almost infinite number of variables when it comes to the climate of our solar system, and much that even climate scientists don't yet know. Tragically, however, it certainly appears that the Earth is warming, seasonal patterns changing, weather becoming more unpredictable; and we are in for a difficult climate future. It is time for cooler heads (pun intended) to start having serious conversations about this most serious of topics.

SOME GENERAL CONCLUSIONS

Both with respect to the three great debates discussed in this chapter and similar ones (see Chapter 1), true believers need to talk. It might seem quixotic to think that those with opposing positions on immigration, gun rights, and climate change could confer with the express aim of finding consensus. Such conferences might not change the basic stances of the proponents, but—as philosopher Martin Buber wrote in his classic study, *I and Thou*—"All real living is meeting."[28] Unless more of our ideologically committed citizens are willing to listen to one another, they will just keep shouting past one another and playing deaf. But shouting is not real living; it is simply feeling better about one's position and refusing to take the risks involved in genuine dialogue. In the meantime, well-thought-out immigration reform legislation sits in limbo, homicides by gun cause daily tragedies, especially in our inner cities, and little gets done to limit CO_2 above a level generally considered crucial to planetary health, while the debates plod on.

Are we simply engaged, to paraphrase Macbeth, in arguments "full of sound and fury, signifying nothing?" Conservatives have conferences on these issues, so do liberals. But joint conferences by individuals on both sides of these debates with the courage to meet and listen to the other side are a rarity. We are reminded of a sad truth that keeps coming up in our national state of division. Many partisans simply have retreated to the company and familiarity of those who agree with them. There can be no political and ethical center on these issues as long as state and federal legislators and print, Internet, and television professionals and their audiences tack to one side or the other. People find their media ideological comfort zones and seldom leave them. This situation needs to change. We will have more to say about this in subsequent chapters.

NOTES

1. The last time Congress passed immigration legislation was 1986 with the Immigration Reform and Control Act that provided a path to citizenship for about four million undocumented persons, but its provisions for border security and an e-verify system were not implemented.

2. www.people-press.org/2013/06/23/borders-first-a-dividing-line-in -immigration-debate. Retrieved July, 23, 2014.

3. www.numbersusa.com/about. It is the nation's largest grassroots immigration-reduction organization with more than two million members across the country. The organization seeks to persuade elected officials that liberal immigration policies take jobs from American citizens and increase government costs. Retrieved June 10, 2015.

4. November/December, 2013, 15.

5. Quoted in Jim Wallis, *On God's Side: What Religion Forgets and Politics Hasn't Learned about Serving the Common Good.* Grand Rapids, MI: Brazos Press, 2013, p. 84.

6. Southside Presbyterian Church quoted at www.groundswell.mvmt.org /faithshare/sanctuary. Retrieved October 15, 2014.

7. However, in July 2014, a federal judge overturned DC's open and concealed carry ban, and went a step further by determining that nonresidents cannot be barred from carrying handguns there either. Consequently, a resident of Virginia or Maryland could now lock a gun in his trunk, drive into the nation's capital, take it out, and put it in his pocket.

8. www.dailykos.com/story/2014/07/15/1314190/new-study-in-14-states -gun-deaths-exceeded-motor-vehicle-deaths. Retrieved July 25, 2014.

9. www.motherjones.com/politics/2013/01/pro-gun-myths. Retrieved July 25, 2014.

10. www.quinnipiac.edu/news-and-events/quinnipiac-University. Retrieved July 26, 2014.

11. www.factcheck.org/2012/12/gun-rhetoric-vs--gun-facts/. Retrieved July 24, 2014.

12. www.Cato.org/guns-and-self-defense. Retrieved July 25, 2014.

13. http://gunowners.org/fs0404.htm. Retrieved July 29, 2014.

14. Chicago: University of Chicago Press, 1998, p. 19. Available in third paperback ed., 2010.

15. One of the ironies the post–Reconstruction era in the South was that many blacks armed themselves as a protection against the Ku Klux Klan and other white supremacists.

16. In 1994, President George H. W. Bush signed into law the so-called Assault Weapons Ban, outlawing high-capacity magazines. It expired in 2004 and was not renewed by President George W. Bush. Seven states, however, do ban such weapons: California, Connecticut, Hawaii, Maryland, Massachusetts, New Jersey, and New York.

17. www.opensecrets.org/lobby/clientsum.php?id=D00. Retrieved September 7, 2015.

18. Quinnipiac, op cit.

19. George Zornick, "Gun Control after Newtown." *The Nation*, October 6, 2014, p. 25. By the summer of 2015, a total of 21 states had expanded background checks on gun sales and strengthened their gun laws.

20. www.forbes.com/sites/peterferrara/2012/05/31/sorry-global-warming -alarmists-the-earth-is-cooling.

21. http://climateconference.heartland.org. Retrieved July 28, 2014.

22. www.ametsoc.org/policy/2012 climatechange.html. Retrieved August 15, 2014.

23. http://www.forbes.com/sites/jamestaylor/2013/11/20/the-latest-meteorol ogist-survey-destroys-the-global-warming-climate-consensus/. Retrieved August 5, 2014.

24. http://www.forbes.com/sites/jamestaylor/2014/06/25/government-data-shows-u-s-in-decade-long-cooling.

25. www.motherjones.com/blue-marble/2013/12/why-some-meteorologists-still-deny-global-warming.html.

26. *The Atlantic*, September, 2014, p. 90.

27. The guiding force behind the march was Prof. William McKibben of Middlebury College founder of 350.org, an organization fighting global warming, who has won numerous awards for his work. "350" refers to a CO_2 level of 350 ppm that is considered the maximum allowable level for global health but has now been exceeded.

28. English translation by Walter Kaufmann. New York: Scribner's, 1958, p. 62. Kaufmann translates "all real living is meeting" as "all actual life is encounter," but we have used the more popular translation.

Chapter 5

America and the World—Religiosity and the American Character

The United States has tried many approaches to foreign policy over the course of its history, but the ones that are especially resonant in populistic times are neither a Hamiltonian globalism nor a Wilsonian humanitarianism, but a Jeffersonian distrust of the world and a Jacksonian insistence on national honor.[1]

As its title indicates, this chapter's aim is to examine how American religiosity and culture—rooted in the concepts of revivalist Christianity, profound patriotism, and belief in the nation's exceptionalism—have shaped our relations with other nations, especially over the past 70 years since the end of World War II. It is outside the scope and purposes of this book to present a comprehensive analysis of American foreign policy since the country's inception. What we will examine is how differently conservatives and liberals (and libertarians) have understood our place among the nations and our responsibilities to the rest of the human community.

THE EVOLUTION OF AMERICAN RELIGIOSITY

American piety in the colonial period presents a mixed picture. The Puritans came to Massachusetts with the express purpose of living holy lives in the New World, free from the strictures of the Church of England. Their impact on the spiritual and intellectual life of America is unparalleled. Roger Williams, however, dissented from Puritan conformity and moved to Rhode Island, where everyone was free to practice religion in the Puritan manner or in any other way they saw fit. The Calverts (father George and sons Cecil and Leonard) came to Maryland to provide a haven for Roman Catholics, also desiring religious freedom over Anglicanism. William Penn conceived of Pennsylvania as a place where his fellow members of the Society of Friends (Quakers) could practice their faith but without demanding that others embrace it. Delaware became a comfortable place for Lutherans. Dutch Presbyterians landed in New Amsterdam (New York) with mercantile interests in mind but nonetheless brought their Dutch Reformed faith with them. The same kind of motivations prevailed in Virginia, the Carolinas, and Georgia where tobacco and cotton provided the impetus for settlement much more than any desire to propagate Anglicanism. A small colony of Jews arrived in New Amsterdam in 1654 and eventually achieved a foothold there despite Governor Peter Stuyvesant's objections. There were Muslims, too, in the colonial period in the person of the 15 to 20 percent of slaves who brought the faith of Islam with them but had it crushed along with their freedom. (Muslim immigrants would not reappear till the late 1800s.) Of course, the first nations of America, those of the indigenous peoples, had their own religious traditions, centered in the belief that nature is alive and must be respected. Instead, tragically, only the native peoples' often fierce resistance to European colonization was recognized.

This crazy quilt of religiosity, along with memories of religious wars and intolerance in Europe and the Enlightenment philosophy espoused by several of the founding fathers, especially Thomas Jefferson, James Madison, and Thomas Paine, resulted in passage of the First Amendment's mandate that "Congress shall make no law respecting an establishment of religion, or prohibiting the free exercise thereof."

Despite the presence of these many denominations in the colonies, pre–Revolutionary War America was to a considerable extent "unchurched" with insufficient clergy and considerable religious illiteracy. Into this malaise, George Whitefield (also spelled "Whitfield") arrived from England in the mid-1700s as the quintessential revivalist, preaching throughout the colonies in the open air to thousands, including the skeptical Benjamin Franklin who was unmoved by his theology but impressed with his oratory. That oratory sparked the so-called Great Awakening in which many thousands were "born again" and began to take their Christianity seriously. Revivalist fervor cooled during the Revolutionary War and the nation-building that followed, but in the early nineteenth century a second awakening arose with so-called Methodist circuit riders taking the gospel message on horseback to Ohio, Indiana, Illinois, Kentucky, and elsewhere. It, too, grew quiescent as the first debates over slavery and the Civil War itself preoccupied the country. But by the early 1900s, a third revivalist awakening, epitomized by the fervid preaching of Billy Sunday, once again made "born againism" an American hallmark. World War I, the Great Depression, and World War II cooled revivalism once more, but in the late 1940s the nation became aware that "atheistic communism," as it was called, and the Soviet Union posed a menacing threat to its values and maybe even its existence.

Although religiosity, especially the Protestant variety that was so dominant, was always a force in American life, it became even more so in the post–World War II era. And onto the stage strode another revivalist, the Rev. Billy Graham, who would be a friend and confidant to every president from Eisenhower to Obama (though the current president's contact with him has been modest in light of Graham's failing health). In 1952, Graham went to Washington, DC, and, in some respects, made the Capitol his congregation—enlisting members of Congress to serve as ushers at huge revival meetings and staging the first formal religious service held on the Capitol steps. That same year, with Eisenhower's support, Congress established the National Prayer Breakfast. Graham also influenced Congress in 1954 to add the words "under God" to the Pledge of Allegiance and the slogan "in God we trust" on postage stamps that year and on paper money in 1955. The following year it became the nation's official motto. Despite his being very much influenced by Rev. Graham, Eisenhower's revival tent invited in Jews and Catholics along with evangelical Christians.[2] Still, this influx of official religiosity would have shocked Jefferson and Madison.

Although Protestant hegemony would remain until the end of World War II, its informal unity had been cracked by the debate over slavery when northern and southern Baptists and others would part ways over abolition. It was further dismantled by the great debate about the literal interpretation of the Bible that produced two kinds of Protestantism. The first was the conservative-evangelical variety that took its stand on the inerrancy of Scripture, considered factual on all matters—theological, historical, and scientific—and the need to be born again via believer's baptism. By contrast, the liberal or so-called mainline version of Protestantism considered the Bible open to at least some degree of interpretation, for example, concerning the factual nature of the six-day account of creation in Genesis believed to have happened no more than ten thousand years ago, the historicity of the Exodus account of the liberation of Israelite slaves by Moses, or the virgin birth of Jesus.[3] The liberals also enunciated the so-called Social Gospel movement that put less stress on piety and more on social justice and compassion. As discussed in Chapter 4, the battle over biblical interpretation has continued to divide Americans on several issues, including abortion, gay marriage, evolution, school prayer, and, indirectly, climate change and America's role in the world.

Some scholars speculate that a fourth awakening, in some respects anticipated by Rev. Graham, began with the presidency of Ronald Reagan, first elected in 1981, and the rise of the Moral Majority under the Rev. Jerry Falwell and religious broadcaster and one-time presidential candidate Pat Robertson. This contemporary religious awakening coincided with—and was a reaction to—the 1973 *Roe v. Wade* Supreme Court decision that legalized therapeutic abortion in the first and second trimesters of preg-nancy and with two high court decisions a decade earlier that eliminated prayer and Bible reading from public school classrooms (see discussion in Chapter 1). By the 1980s, the gradual evolution of American views on homosexuality that have made gay marriage legal nationwide also contrib-uted to the moral and ethical chasm now existing between conservatives and liberals.

THE TERM "JUDEO-CHRISTIAN" AND ITS RELATIONSHIP TO "CIVIL RELIGION"

Author Ben Hubbard gave a lecture on religion in America to a group of Chinese scholars several years ago and was asked by one of them, hold-ing up a dollar bill, why "in God we trust" was on the currency after he had just spoken about the separation of religion and state as a hallmark of American democracy. He replied that the motto reflected our nation's Judeo-Christian roots and civil religion, and was more ceremonial than lit-eral. However, he was uncomfortable while answering and was not entirely satisfied with his own response. "Judeo-Christian" did not become a famil-iar term until the early 1940s when the National Council of Christians and Jews (now the National Council for Community and Justice) adopted it as a unifying term vis-à-vis anti-Semitism and the rise of Nazism. The term gradually became more identified with conservative religiosity and poli-tics, for example, by President Reagan, evangelical leader James Dobson, and radio commentator and author Dennis Prager. But its use was criti-cized by many leading Jews, including preeminent scholar Jacob Neusner. However, our sense is that the term is now viewed more positively as a symbol of interfaith cooperation, though some religion scholars think the term "Abrahamic religions" might be a better one to describe such coop-eration by including Muslims.

The term "civil religion" was coined by the distinguished sociologist of religion Robert Bellah. He described the concept as "an institutionalized collection of sacred beliefs about the American nation" that are expressed in America's founding documents and presidential inaugural addresses, in our distinctive holidays, of which Thanksgiving is the most unique, and in reverence for the American flag. But even more so, Bellah emphasized belief in the existence of a transcendent being called "God" that required the nation to value liberty, justice, charity, and personal virtue. In short, civil religion is a distinct cultural phenomenon in our society that is more comprehensive than either American politics or denominational religiosity.[4]

AMERICAN EXCEPTIONALISM

In any case, until the end of the nineteenth century, America was very much a Protestant country rooted in the notion that the nation had a kind of providential destiny to be what Puritan leader John Winthrop called "a city on a hill" (cp. Gospel of Matthew 5:14–16) and Ronald Reagan "a *shining* city on a hill." Also in the nineteenth century, the quasi-theological notion of America's having a "manifest destiny" to rule from the Atlantic to the Pacific was popular, though never fully embraced by politicians or the public. However, the concept was used to justify the conquest and sometimes resettlement of Native Americans and the Spanish–American and Mexican–American Wars.

The United States does have exceptional qualities: its courageous break under the fathers of the revolution from an oppressive superpower, an agriculturally bountiful landscape, rich natural resources, oceanic boundaries east and west, peaceful relations with neighboring countries, especially Canada, the reality of a new land where a fresh start on governing could happen, and the genius of the U.S. Constitution. There is also the notion of the "American dream," the idea that America's political freedoms and free enterprise system make anything possible no matter what your background or ethnicity.

Arguments will always persist about whether our form of representative democracy with its three coequal branches of government is superior to other arrangements, in particular, parliamentary systems. But no one disagrees that the Bill of Rights, especially the First Amendment, is an exceptional document. Jefferson and Madison looked around at the great religious diversity in the colonies, reflected on the religious wars and persecution that had plagued Europe off and on since the Protestant Reformation, and concluded that religion had to be unequivocally decoupled from government. So, although the country is predominantly Christian and remains so even today (though not to the same degree),

Christianity has no official standing. Nonetheless, British author G. K. Chesterton could write that America is "a nation with the soul of a church."[5] In stating this, he was reiterating what de Tocqueville had said some 90 years before about an American piety that was thriving without any state sponsorship. One indication of the health of American religiosity is a comparison with Europe. A 2011 Pew survey indicated that half of Americans consider religion very important, compared with 22 percent in Spain, 21 percent in Germany, 17 percent in Britain, and only 13 percent in France. Additionally, Americans are far more likely than Western Europeans to say it's necessary to believe in God to be moral and have good values. More than half (53 percent) feel this way, compared with 33 percent in Germany, 20 percent in Britain, 19 percent in Spain, and 15 percent in France.[6]

Despite our exceptional qualities as a nation and deep religiosity, the history of slavery and the Jim Crow era of lynchings and discrimination that continued for a hundred years after the slaves were freed is a legacy of shame that still haunts us in some respects. Moreover, our treatment of Native Americans was just as shameful, and here, too, a terrible tragedy remains in the continuing plight of so many members of our first nations. The U.S. Senate did finally apologize in June 2009 for the injustice of slavery, and native peoples received a comparable declaration in December 2009 as follows: "The United States apologizes . . . to all Native Peoples for the many instances of violence, maltreatment and neglect inflicted on Native Peoples by citizens of the United States." Included in the nonbinding, bipartisan resolution was an expression of regret for "the forcible removal of native children from their families to faraway boarding schools where their native practices and languages were degraded and forbidden."[7] Between the 1870s and 1930s more than one hundred thousand children were forced from their families into government and religious schools. (In 2005, the Bureau of Indian Affairs had also offered an apology.) It is, of course, true that some one million Americans (mainly young men on both sides) did in some sense atone with their lives for our sins during the Civil War, as did President Abraham Lincoln. Our past mistakes are sensitive matters, especially among more conservative Americans, and there are even debates about the treatment of these matters in high school history textbooks. Yes, we have done some justice to these two groups by way of the civil rights and voting rights legislation of the mid-1960s, but the work is not yet done. The civil disturbances in Ferguson, Missouri, and Baltimore in August 2014 and April 2015, respectively—the most recent of a long string of such riots in our recent history—make this clear. Like individuals, our nation struggles with its past sins. It is in this sense like all the nations.

AMERICAN FOREIGN POLICY SINCE THE END OF WORLD WAR II AND ITS RELIGIOUS DIMENSION

The Formation of the United Nations

The European continent was in shambles at the close of World War II and in desperate need of help. The U.S. Marshall Plan for its recovery was a philanthropic act, a practical necessity, and an indication that the United States would be *the* exceptional nation for the next half-century and to a lesser extent right down to the present. It would be dominant militarily and economically and capable of setting the agenda for the free world on issues of human rights. (More about that below.) However, history might ultimately determine that American exceptionalism began to wane with the 2003 invasion of Iraq. The questionable justification for the war itself, the policy blunders that followed (including those about Iraq's religious makeup discussed in Chapter 1), the disbanding of the Iraqi military's officer cadre, the scandalous treatment of detainees at Abu Ghraib prison, the loss of 4,488 American military, at least 134,000 Iraqi civilians killed directly and another 655,000 who died as a consequence of the war, the immense cost ($1.7 trillion plus $490 billion in war benefits owed to veterans).[8] and the tragic aftermath with the so-called Islamic State now controlling cities and villages in western Iraq—all this has made our nation look less invincible in the eyes of the world. The unprecedented gridlock in the nation's capital with the 16-day shutdown of the government in October 2013 (and the consequent downgrading of our credit by Standard & Poor's) and the perception among our allies that Congress can no longer achieve the people's business have also really hurt our reputation.

Nonetheless, through policies that most would consider positive and through other decisions that liberals would consider unfortunate, the United States has wielded immense influence on international affairs. With decisive American backing, the charter of the United Nations was signed on October 24, 1945, in San Francisco and included 51 nations. Its aims were to "save the succeeding generations from the scourge of war . . . reaffirm faith in fundamental human rights . . . establish conditions under which justice and respect for the obligations arising from treaties and other sources of international law can be maintained, and to promote social progress and better standards of life in larger freedom."[9]

The Universal Declaration of Human Rights

One of the most significant actions taken by the UN General Assembly was promulgation of the Universal Declaration of Human Rights. Among its 30 articles are striking parallels to the U.S. Declaration of Independence and Bill of Rights. Article 1, for example, states that "all human beings are born free and equal in dignity and rights. They are endowed with reason and conscience and should act toward one another in a spirit of brotherhood." Article 2 expands on this concept by stating, "Everyone is entitled to all the rights and freedoms set forth in this declaration, without distinction of any kind, such as race, color, sex, language, religion, political or other opinion, national or social origin, property, birth or other status." Subsequent articles cover freedom from slavery or servitude, torture, or degrading treatment or punishment; freedom of peaceful assembly and association, equality before the law, the presumption of innocence till proven guilty, freedom of movement within a nation's borders; the right to freely marry and found a family, to own property, participate in the government of one's country; the right to special care and assistance for motherhood and childhood, and to a free education (at least in the elementary and fundamental stages). Finally, article 18 deserves full quotation:

Everyone has the right to freedom of thought, conscience and religion; this right includes freedom to change his religion or belief, and freedom either alone or in community with others and in public and private, to manifest his religion or belief in teaching, practice, worship and observance.[10]

It was an extraordinary vision that has borne some fruit, but the subsequent 70 years have seen frequent warfare, genocides, religious persecution, and terrible abuse of women, as is evident in the following discussion.

The Convention on the Prevention and Punishment of the Crime of Genocide

The Convention on the Prevention and Punishment of the Crime of Genocide was adopted by the UN General Assembly December 9, 1948, and became effective on January 12, 1951. Genocide was defined to mean acts committed with the intention to destroy, totally or partially, a national, ethnic, racial, or religious group. These acts included killing (murder), causing serious bodily or mental harm, intentionally inflicting conditions of life meant to cause physical destruction of a group, imposing measures meant to prevent births, and forcibly transferring children of one group to another. Ironically, the U.S. Senate took until 1986 to ratify the Convention and two more years elapsed before the legislation was implemented. Perhaps it was the American psyche's tendency to see itself as exceptional, as not needing to adhere to the same standards as other nations, that allowed almost 40 years to pass before ratification.

There is also an ironic twist here that relates to our nation's long struggle against slavery and the century of Jim Crow laws that followed the Emancipation Proclamation. Under the leadership of black activists Paul Robeson, William Patterson, and W. E. B. Du Bois, the Civil Rights Congress (a radical African American organization begun in 1946 and disbanded in 1956) presented a petition to the UN in December 1951, stating that "the lynching and other forms of assault on the lives and livelihoods of African Americans from 1945 to 1951, especially the frenzied attacks on returning Black American veterans, amounted to genocide." However, Raphael Lemkin, a Polish-born Jewish lawyer and author who coined the term "genocide," and others argued that the situation of American Blacks did not amount to genocide. Although that may be true, our nation has still not completely come to terms with its racist past, as the spate of killings of black men in police custody in recent years—and the demonstrations that followed—make clear.[11]

The Armenian genocide in 1915 of at least 1.2 million persons by the Ottoman Empire during World War I (still not acknowledged as an act of genocide by the Turkish government) and the Holocaust, the destruction of European Jewry by the Nazis during World War II, were the principal inspiration for the Convention. Tragically, this action did not bring an end to genocide in the twentieth century. The murder of about 1.7 million Cambodians by the fanatical Khmer Rouge regime from 1973–79, the 1994 slaughter of eight hundred thousand Tutsis by the Hutus in Rwanda, and the killing of an estimated eighty thousand Bosnian Muslims in Bosnia-Herzegovina along with twenty thousand Catholic Croatians between 1992 and 95 (in particular the slaughter of eight thousand innocent civilians in Srebrenica) bear testimony to this.

In the wake of the disastrous end of the Vietnam War in 1973 and the collapse of the South Vietnamese government in 1975—coupled with Chinese support of the Khmer Rouge—the United States had no stomach for intervention in Cambodia. Rwanda was a different story. There were UN peacekeepers there who requested the United States' assistance as the slaughter began. President Clinton opted against it, though he later expressed regret for this decision. The North Atlantic Treaty Organization (NATO) with U.S. leadership did finally intervene in the genocide against Bosnian Muslims in 1995 with a three-week bombing campaign that forced the Serbs to negotiate. Then in the spring of 1999, another U.S.-led NATO coalition bombed the Federal Republic of Yugoslavia (i.e., Serbia) to stop human rights abuses in neighboring Kosovo and force a Yugoslav/Serb withdrawal of forces.

In the summer of 2004, author Ben Hubbard was attending a conference in New Delhi, India. A reporter for the *Times of India* questioned him about the United States' lack of evenhandedness in the Israeli–Palestinian conflict and its overall failure to protect Muslim human rights. Hubbard responded by reminding the reporter of NATO's and America's rescue of Muslims in Serbia and Kosovo. A satisfying rebuttal perhaps, though the debacle in Iraq would continue to overshadow these rescues in the Balkans.

The International Criminal Court

The International Criminal Court (ICC) is an independent, permanent body, governed by the Rome Statute that tries persons accused of extremely serious crimes of international concern, such as genocide, crimes against humanity, and war crimes. Its creation was spurred by the international criminal tribunals set up to investigate the genocides in Yugoslavia and Rwanda (hence, its discussion at this point, even though it is not actually part of the UN system). The Statute brought about the first-ever, treaty-based international court (located at The Hague, Netherlands) established to help end impunity for those who commit such crimes. The treaty, first ratified by 60 nations in 2002, had 123 signatories as of April 1, 2015. Though independent of any UN member state or the UN itself, the ICC works cooperatively with all of them. As a court of last resort, it will not act if the case is investigated or prosecuted by the judicial system of a member state unless these national proceedings are not genuine, for example, by shielding a person from criminal responsibility. Thus far, 22 cases in 9 situations have been brought before the ICC. In accord with the Rome statute, the prosecutor can begin an investigation on the basis of referral from any state party or from the UN Security Council. Additionally, the prosecutor can initiate investigations on his own based on information about crimes within the jurisdiction of the court received from individuals or organizations. To date, four signatory states have referred situations happening on their territories to the court: Uganda, the Democratic Republic of the Congo, the Central African Republic, and Mali. Additionally, the Security Council has referred to the ICC the situations in Darfur, Sudan and in Libya. Two examples of notorious cases (both from Uganda) are that of the *Prosecutor v. Joseph Coney, Vincent Oti, and Okot Odhiambo*; and the *Prosecutor v. Dominic Ongwen.* The opening of the confirmation of charges hearing for Ongwen is scheduled for January 21, 2016.[12]

Despite the ICC's lofty purpose, the United States has refused to join. The Clinton administration participated actively in the negotiations that led to the ICC's creation, but sought UN Security Council screening of cases (where the United States has veto power). Had this provision been agreed to, the United States would have been able to veto any indictments it opposed. During the same period when the ICC was being formed, the United States had just invaded Afghanistan and the Taliban in response to the terror attack on September 11, 2001. There was concern that American military personnel and politicians might be indicted by the ICC. Our nation has an immense military footprint worldwide and therefore considerable vulnerability to indictments. Once again, the United States, as the indispensable nation, sees itself in some respects as above the fray, capable of great good in the world but also prone to mistakes and miscalculations that might cause problems if it joined the ICC. The George W. Bush administration strongly opposed the ICC, and even began negotiating bilateral agreements with other nations that would ensure immunity of U.S. nationals for prosecution by the Court. As leverage, Washington threatened to end economic aid and withdraw military assistance if such agreements were not made. This was the embodiment of conservative America with the big stick.

By contrast, President Obama's administration is participating with the court's governing bodies and providing support for its ongoing prosecutions. But the current administration, too, fears for the prosecution of U.S. nationals. America is not alone in refusing to join the ICC, as India, Indonesia, China, Sudan, and Israel are also nonmembers. The Palestinian Authority, however, has joined, so there could be indictments of Israelis in connection with the 2014 bombing and subsequent death of civilians in Gaza. (Israel, of course, was responding to missile attacks by Hamas militants.)

Yearly U.S. Reports on Human Rights Practices and Religious Freedom

The United States' record on the prevention of genocide is mixed, as just discussed. Nonetheless, the nation has made signal contributions to the welfare of nations on both human rights practices and religious freedom. The Foreign Assistance Act of 1961 provided that the secretary of state would submit each year to the speaker of the house and the Committee on Foreign Relations of the Senate the Country Report on Human Rights Practices concerning the status of internationally recognized human rights in (a) countries receiving assistance under the act and (b) all other foreign countries that are members of the UN and that are not otherwise covered by the Act. The Country Report utilizes information collected by U.S. embassies and consulates, foreign government officials, nongovernmental and international organizations, and other published material (e.g., media sources and academic research). The Reports are used as a resource for shaping policy, conducting diplomacy, and making assistance, training and other government-related resource allocations (i.e., foreign aid). Three subsidiary reports are linked to the country report: the *International Religious Freedom Report*, the *Trafficking in Persons Report,* and (via the Labor Department) the *Findings on the Worst Forms of Child Labor Report*. Without doubt these reports have raised awareness of abuses around the world and accomplished significant good.

The International Religious Freedom Report for 2013 from the U.S. Department of State (the most recent one available at this writing) is a sad chronicle of religious intolerance worldwide that has persisted and intensified right down to the present. In the city of Homs, Syria, where approximately one hundred sixty thousand Christians lived prior to the outbreak of the Syrian Civil War in 2012, there are now only one thousand. Religious freedom is neither acknowledged nor protected under the law in Saudi Arabia, and public places of worship for non-Muslims don't exist. In the same reporting year, Sunni militants in Pakistan killed more than 400 Shia Muslims in intrareligious attacks as well as more than 80 Christians in one church in Peshawar. In Egypt, organized groups have in several instances attacked Coptic churches and Christian-owned businesses and homes, and then looted and burned the properties. In a three-day period (August 14 to 17, 2012), assailants attacked at least 42 churches throughout the country. Finally, in the Tibetan region of China, police have arrested students, monks, laypersons, and others advocating for liberty, human rights, and respect for freedom of religion—including expressing support for the Dalai Lama. As mentioned in Chapter 8, anti-Semitism is once again on the rise in Europe.

The entire report on worldwide religious bigotry is long and tragic. Yet, the report also describes uplifting acts of communal unity. After the Peshawar church bombing, Muslim community members linked hands around churches during services to show solidarity and resist crazed violence. After an increase in attacks on mosques in the United Kingdom, a neighborhood watch team of Orthodox Jews assisted Muslim leaders to guarantee safe access to mosques and to warn them of possible attacks.

However, the State Department does not simply describe acts of religious intolerance, it actually works through embassies and other governmental agents to help individuals enjoy the benefits of religious freedom. Direct action by U.S. embassy officials in Armenia encouraged the passage of a law to protect conscientious objectors, and brought about the release of 28 Jehovah's Witnesses. Officials from the Departments of Justice and Homeland security are implementing training programs to aid governments in educating local officials about enforcement of nondiscrimination laws. They are also trying to instill cultural awareness of religious minorities. To date, U.S. officials have held successful training sessions in Bosnia-Herzegovina, Hungary, and Indonesia.[13]

The Kyoto Protocol

Under United Nations auspices, the countries of the world came together in 1997 in Kyoto, Japan, to see if they could devise a plan to stem CO_2 emissions and global warming. Unlike some conservative U.S. congress members even to this day, there was a broad consensus that something had to be done. The agreement was straightforward: Industrialized countries would be legally obliged to cut their greenhouse gas emissions 5 percent below 1990 levels during the period from 2008 to 2012. The problem was that developing countries such as China, India, Brazil, and South Africa would not be obliged to make these reductions but instead would be encouraged to adopt greener growth policies. To assist countries in meeting their targets Kyoto offered a range of strategies that could help rich countries offset their emissions by investing in low-carbon projects in less developed parts of the world (so-called cap-and-trade plans). It took eight years for participating countries to ratify the Protocol, but one nation refused—the United States when the Senate voted 95–0 against it. Our senators and President George W. Bush objected to the exemption given to China and India and were responding to the pressure from the oil and gas industries whose powerful lobbies won out. Nonetheless, when Russia in 2004 finally signed on, Kyoto had the necessary 55 signatories to bring the treaty online in 2005. Kyoto has made a difference, as emissions were 22.6 percent below 1990 levels by 2012 among the signatories. Some of the success, though, resulted from independent actions by nations, for example, the United Kingdom's decision to substitute gas for coal. Still, the cap-and-trade concept and the significant consciousness-raising aspect of Kyoto have been valuable.

There is no doubt that Kyoto was a flawed protocol, especially the exemptions given to China and India, which are now much more like developed countries than developing. But if the United States had ratified Kyoto, perhaps with qualifications, the world might be in a very different place environmentally than it is. Data from the Dutch Capital PBL Environment Agency released in late 2014 indicates that CO_2 emissions reached a new record of 35.3 million gigatons that year, 0.7 million higher than in 2013.[14] We are an exceptional nation, but we sometimes make exceptions to what would promote the greater good of the world. As discussed in the section on climate change in Chapter 4, conservatives in Congress and in the country still dispute the reality of global warming. Their views need to be taken seriously, because environmental science is immensely complex. We wish, however, they would take much more seriously the global consensus that we are on a collision course to a considerably warmer climate whose effects are already being felt through increased droughts, the intensity of storms, and rising sea levels—especially on South Pacific islands such as Kiribati (elevation 2 meters above sea level) where levels are rising at twice the global average (2.9 mm. versus 1.2 mm.)—and even in South Florida.

America and Israel

On November 29, 1947, the newly formed United Nations voted 33–13 with 10 abstentions to approve the division of Mandate Palestine into two nations, Israel and Palestine, with Jerusalem as an international city under UN auspices. Israeli leader David Ben-Gurion announced that Israel would declare its independence on May 14, 1948. In the brief period just prior to the declaration, an epic struggle took place in the Oval Office between President Harry Truman and the legendary General of the Army and Secretary of State George C. Marshall over recognition of the new nation. The State Department had a strong Arab bias based both on some anti-Semitism in its ranks and the nation's growing need for Mideast oil that Saudi Arabia, Iraq, and the Gulf states possessed. Truman, by contrast, was motivated by the need for a democratic state in the midst of Arab dicta-torships, the Holocaust, the desperate need for the Jews to have their own state, and a profound sense that doing so was just and righteous. Truman also had a close Jewish friend and former business partner, Edward Jacob-son, who on several occasions in 1947 and 1948, corresponded or met with Truman to urge recognition of the fledgling state. Ironically, the Reform Jewish community in America largely opposed Zionism at the time (as did ultra-Orthodox Jews), and so it appears Truman's decision was not based on wanting to secure the Jewish vote in his reelection. Through the remarkable skill of presidential advisor Clark Clifford, Secretary Marshall remained neutral on the decision, and a few minutes after Israel's declaration of its independence, the president signed the letter of recognition.[15]

The War of Independence followed, during which five Arab armies attacked the newly born state in hopes of driving it into the sea and ending the Zionist project. Though Israel prevailed, the struggle for its existence resulted in several more wars with growing American military assistance. The defining war for Israel, a war that has complicated its existence right down to the present, was the Six-Day War of June 1967. Arab armies were massed for an attack on Israel, but in a preemptive strike that wiped out Arab airpower, Israel took control of Egypt's Sinai Desert, the West Bank, including East Jerusalem and the Temple Mount, the Gaza Strip and the Syrian Golan Heights. It was a dizzying triumph for the Israelis and a second catastrophe for the Palestinians (the first being Israel's creation itself). But it would further complicate America's relationship with the Arab world and with Israel, which would gradually begin to extend its borders by building settlements in the West Bank and Gaza (those in Gaza were vacated in 2005). Time and again, the United States would criticize Israel for the extension of these settlements (where some three hundred fifty thousand Israelis now live, mostly in border towns along the 1967 armistice line, but eighty thousand in isolated settlements that could not remain in a final, two-state peace agreement).

Through all these difficulties, the United States would remain steadfastly committed to Israel's existence within secure borders through economic and military assistance exceeding $3 billion per year. Israel was an anchor of democracy and security in a troubled and dictatorial region, a source of military intelligence, and a provider of scientific and medical breakthroughs that have benefited the rest of the world. In short, the United States and Israel had shared values and a special relationship. But the state of the Jewish people was also a problem child, as it pursued its expansionist program in the West Bank to the frustration of every presidential administration from Lyndon Johnson to Barack Obama. Israel had always argued that the settlements—which had become in many cases thriving suburbs—were justified for security purposes in light of the various wars and the history of terrorism on the part of Palestinians. Among both Israel's secular right-wing and its religiously Orthodox community, there was the conviction that the West Bank was part of "greater Israel." Religious conservatives (both in Israel and the United States) argued further that the entire region belonged to it by biblical mandate. After Israel's War of Independence, American Jews of all branches gradually closed ranks behind Israel, so that today almost all support its continued existence. However, a significant minority in such largely Jewish organizations as Americans for Peace Now and J Street are very critical of its settlement policy.

In Chapter 6, we will discuss further the unwavering support of Israel by evangelical Christians who find scriptural backing for such support along with the conviction that the birth of a Jewish nation and its capture of the Temple Mount in 1967 are harbingers of the end times. A Pew Research study of American Jews in 2013 found that 40 percent of this community believes the land that is now Israel was given to the Jewish people by God. But, as a stunning sign of evangelical Christian support for the Jewish state, 55 percent of American Christians accept this belief, including 64 percent of (mainly conservative) Protestants.

One of many reasons why conservatives are critical of the United Nations, even to the point of wanting to cut off funding, has been that body's obsessive focus on the perceived sins of the State of Israel. The most extreme example was UN General Assembly Resolution 3379 in November 1975 that "determined that Zionism is a form of racism and racial discrimination." It passed by a margin of 72 to 35 with 32 abstentions. The U.S. ambassador to the UN, Daniel Patrick Moynihan responded with an impassioned speech warning that "the UN is about to make anti-Semitism international law." (The Zionism-as-racism resolution was finally rescinded by the General Assembly in 1991 by Resolution 46/86.) Moynihan's stance typified the way the United States defended Israel at the UN year after year. Beginning in 1972 with President Nixon, America has vetoed in the Security Council 42 resolutions of the General Assembly critical of Israel.

Whether America's steadfast defense of Israel will continue is an open question, as pressure mounts in the UN to finally get a peace agreement between Israel and Palestine. The West Bank settlements are an open sore for American foreign policy in the Middle East. The 1.8 million inhabitants of Gaza live in a region that *New York Times* columnist Roger Cohen has described as "little better than an open air prison."[16] This is a principal reason for the so-called Boycott-Divestment-Sanctions (BDS) movement on many college campuses that seeks to characterize Israel as an apartheid state resembling South Africa before it dismantled its discriminatory policies in 1994. Nonetheless, Israel faces the constant threat of Palestinian acts of terror, the implacable hatred of Hamas that controls Gaza and seeks Israel's destruction, and Hezbollah, de facto ruler of South Lebanon, that has the same aim. Making concessions for peace in this neighborhood is not easy. In the end, the U.S. commitment to Israel will probably continue no matter who the next president is, but America and the world are growing impatient.

President Obama's Outreach to the Muslim World

On June 4, 2009, President Obama—fewer than six months into his presidency—made an historic speech to the Muslim world at Al-Azhar University in Cairo. The president came, he said,

to seek a new beginning between the United States and Muslims around the world, one based on mutual interest and mutual respect . . . upon the truth that America and Islam are not exclusive and need not be in competition. Instead, they overlap, and share common principles—principles of justice and progress; tolerance and the dignity of all human beings.[17]

He stressed the need to overcome crude stereotypes that exist in both the Muslim world and America about each other, and the way American Muslims were flourishing. He emphasized our nation's "unbreakable" commitment to Israel, but also noted that the situation of the Palestinian people was "intolerable." He noted how he had told the leaders of Iran that America was very prepared to move forward diplomatically, especially in convincing that nation to give up its nuclear weapons ambitions. (The president had earlier sent a personal message to Iran's leader Ayatollah Ali Khamenei in hopes of thawing relations between the two countries. Though that hasn't happened, an historic agreement limiting Iran's nuclear program was signed in Vienna on July 14, 2015, between that nation and the United States and five other world powers.) It is difficult to know how much impact the speech has had on subsequent relations with the Muslim world. As discussed in Chapter 1, radical Islam in groups such as ISIS and Al Qaeda despise America, while we have maintained good relations with Egypt, Jordan, Saudi Arabia, and many other Muslim-majority states. But the tragic legacy of Iraq, the long complex war in Afghanistan, drone strikes in Pakistan and Yemen—these have meant that relations between the two civilizations remain tense and complex. One ironic twist resulting from Obama's Cairo speech was his receiving the Nobel Peace Prize in October of the same year, "for his extraordinary efforts to strengthen international diplomacy and cooperation between peoples." It was the promise of better relations between the two civilizations that seems to have inspired the choice of the young president. He himself was embarrassed by his selection and even his supporters and admirers were flummoxed. In his acceptance speech on December 10, 2009, he interpreted the award as a "call to action, a call for all nations to confront the common challenges of the twenty-first century."[18]

American Philanthropy as Part of the American Character

For the sake of national security, business promotion, and humanitarian concerns (e.g., health promotion and education), our government in 2013 provided $37.7 billion in foreign aid (over $23 billion for humanitarian assistance and international development, and more than $14 billion in foreign military assistance), amounting to only 1 percent of our national budget yet still more than any other country. Since the end of World War II, the United States has disbursed more foreign aid than any other country in almost every year. No surprise—we are the world's richest country and have global interests unlike any other nation. The largest current recipient of U.S. aid is Afghanistan, though for many years Israel was number one. While our governmental largess is to a considerable degree tied to enlightened self-interest, that is not true of private philanthropy. In some years, America has ranked first in per capita world philanthropy, though in 2013 we were in thirteenth place (behind the UK, Canada, and others).[19] Still, we donate over $200 billion per year of which about $71 billion goes overseas. About 65 percent of U.S. households make charitable donations and we volunteer about 200 billion hours annually to charitable activities (six times more frequently, for example, than Germans). A countervailing tendency overall in U.S. generosity is American resistance to the welfare state as compared to Europe. Yes, there is plenty of welfare (aid to families with dependent children, food stamps/WIC, etc.), but there is still a strong sense that people need to fend for themselves, pull themselves up by those old bootstraps.

CONCLUSION

We are a highly religious people compared to our European counterparts. This has shaped our character as a nation with respect to our overall foreign policy, human rights, and foreign aid. We are a generous people, though the problems of the urban poor in our own country continue to bedevil us. We have exceptional strengths and resources, and a philanthropic spirit that has benefited the world immensely since the end of World War II. But whether we are a chosen nation à la Puritan theology and are distinctively exceptional among the nations is open to debate. This is because civil religion and the American character will always be very much tied to nationalism and America's bottom line. This is particularly true on the issue of climate change where business interests, especially those linked to the oil and gas industries, have kept us from being the world's environmental leader, as we should be. We have to wonder whether a more cooperative and functioning Congress would not have made a huge difference in solving the environmental challenge, and other international problems. In a word, would a less contentious and more effective national government have made us even more exceptional?

NOTES

1. Alan Wolfe, *Does American Democracy Still Work?* New Haven: 2006, p. 156.
2. See Kevin M. Kruse, *One Nation under God—How Corporate America Invented Christian America*. New York: Basic Books, 2015.
3. We discussed in Chapter 1 the debate between evolution and creationism/intelligent design that began with the Scopes trial in 1925 and is ongoing.
4. http://hirr.edu/ency/civilrel.htm. Retrieved May 3, 2015.
5. www.chesterton.org/america/. Retrieved April 18, 2015. The quotation is from the first chapter of Chesterton's 1922 book *What I Saw in America*.
6. www.pewglobal.org/2011/11/17/the-american-western-european-values-gap/.
7. www.tolerance.org/blog/American-apology-long-overdue. Retrieved April 30, 2015.
8. www.businessinsider.com/the-Iraq-war-bi-numbers-2014-6.

9. www.history.com/this-day-in-history/the-United-nations-is-born. Retrieved April 20, 2015.

10. Universal Declaration of Human Rights. www.un.org/en/documents/udhr. Retrieved April 20, 2015.

11. www.wikipedia.org/wiki/Genocide_Convention#United_States. Retrieved April 23, 2015.

12. www.icc-cpi.int/en_menus/icc/about%20the%20court/Pages/about%20 the%20court.aspx. Retrieved April 26, 2015.

13. www.state.gov/j/drl/ris/irf/religiousfreedom/index.htm#wrapper. Retrieved April 23, 2015.

14. www.rtcc.org/2015/02/16/Kyoto-protocol-10-years-of-the-worlds-first-climate-change-treaty/.

15. Richard Holbrook, "Washington's Battle over Israel's Birth." *Washington Post.* www.washingtonpost.com/wp-dyn/content/article/2008/05/06/AR 2008050602447.html.

16. www.nytimes.com/2014/12/21/opinion/sunday/roger-cohen-what-will-israel-become.html.

17. www.Whitehouse.gov/the_press_office/Remarks-by-the-President-at-Cairo -University-6-04-09.

18. www.en.wikipedia.org/wiki/2009_Nobel_peace_prize/. Retrieved May 7, 2015.

19. https://philanthropy.com/article/Americans-rank-13th-in/153965. Retrieved May 3, 2015.

Chapter 6

What Matters to the Right

We mentioned previously the 2014 survey of ten thousand adults by the Pew Research Center that illustrated how dramatically polarized the nation has become in the past 20 years. As we move to Chapters 6 and 7 to discuss what matters to the right and the left, respectively, we begin by highlighting the main findings from the survey.

1994–2014: DRAMATIC INCREASE IN POLARIZATION

The percentage of Americans who express consistently conservative or liberal opinions doubled between 1994 and 2014 from 10 percent to 21 percent. Moreover, ideological thinking is more closely connected to partisanship than in the past. Consequently, ideological overlap and a commonality between the Democrats and Republicans has diminished. At the time the survey was conducted (January–March 2014), 92 percent of Republicans were to the right of the median Democrat and 94 percent of Democrats were to the left of the median Republican. Moreover, 27 percent of Democrats in 2014 viewed the Republican Party as a "threat to the nation's well-being" compared to 16 percent in 1994. Conversely, 36 percent of Republicans in 2014 considered the Democratic Party a threat compared to 17 percent in 1994.[1] However, these opinions are not shared by the majority of Americans, who do not have consistently conservative or liberal viewpoints and do not see either party as a threat to the nation. Most survey respondents think their representatives in Congress need to meet halfway to settle contentious disputes rather than holding out for all or most of what they want. But here's the rub: Many people in the ideological center remain on the edges of the political playing field, relatively disengaged, while the true believers on each side make their opinions known through greater activism at every stage of the electoral process—voting, writing letters to elected officials, volunteering, or donating to a campaign.

Another measure of the great divide is the growth in *very* unfavorable impressions Republicans and Democrats have of each other: 43 percent of Republicans (versus 17 percent in 1994) view the other party in strongly negative terms, while 38 percent of Democrats (versus 16 percent in 1994) feel this way. Even geography enters into the political split: 50 percent of consistently conservative individuals say it's important to live in a place where most people share their political views, and the same is true of 35 percent of the consistently liberal. In a parallel way, 63 percent of the consistently conservative report that most friends share their politics, while 49 percent of ideological Democrats feel this way. There is even a mixed marriage dynamic to all of this: 30 percent of consistent conservatives would be unhappy if an immediate family member married a Democrat, while the same is true of 23 percent of consistent liberals. Finally, and not surprisingly, "Consistent liberals and conservatives define political compromise is one in which their side gets more of what it wants."[2]

SMALLER GOVERNMENT, LOWER TAXES

Reducing the size of government, especially at the federal level, and lowering taxes are at the heart of the conservative creed. President Ronald Reagan (1981–89), became the patron saint of those on the right because his massive tax cuts and reduction in federal spending gave a tremendous boost to the nation's faltering economy. Inflation and unemployment were cut dramatically, the gross national product rose by 26 percent, and 20 million jobs were created. Reagan's successor, President George H. W. Bush, tried to maintain the Reagan revolution, but the national debt was growing alarmingly and he was forced to recant his pledge: "Read my lips, no new taxes." It may have cost him reelection.

Today's antitax champion is Grover Norquist who does not hold political office but heads a powerful organization, Americans for Tax Reform (ATR), which he founded in 1985 at President Reagan's request. ATR works to limit the size and cost of government by opposing higher taxes at the federal, state, and local levels, while supporting tax reform that would result in taxing consumed income once at one rate. ATR's principal tool for accomplishing this is the Taxpayer Protection Pledge that asks all candidates at the federal and the state levels to commit in writing that they will oppose all tax increases. In the 113th Congress, 219 house members and 41 senators took the pledge; at the state level, 14 governors and 1,035 state legislators have done the same. Norquist chairs the Washington, DC–based "Wednesday Meeting," a weekly confab of 150 elected officials, political activists, and movement leaders that began in 1993. There are now 60 comparable meetings in 48 states.[3] As the 2016 presidential election looms on the horizon, every serious Republican candidate will probably take the Norquist pledge.

DEFICIT REDUCTION

Most politicians on both the right and the left are deeply concerned about the national debt, which, on February 12, 2015, was $18,123,477,036.05 and has grown at an average rate of $2,380,000,000 *per day* since September 30, 2012. With an estimated U.S. population of 320 million, that works out to about $56,600 of indebtedness per person. However, Republicans are much more willing to cut domestic spending—particularly on Medicare, Medicaid, and Social Security—to shrink the yearly deficit. Spending on this social safety net is growing rapidly as baby boomers reach retirement age and the cost may eventually become unsustainable. Conversely, military spending remains largely untouchable for conservatives. America's role in the world as the "indispensable nation" cannot continue, they maintain, without a strong military posture. Overall, they maintain that the deficit results from overspending not undertaxing.

OVERTURNING *ROE V. WADE*

We discussed the long-standing and intensely emotional debate about the morality and legality of abortion in Chapter 1 in some detail. To conservatives, in almost all instances abortion amounts to murder and is a kind of silent genocide of the unborn. Consequently, liberal support for abortion symbolizes to conservatives that there is something fundamentally wrong with the liberal worldview. This, in turn, affects the entire posture of those on the right toward those on the left. If liberals condone the murder of the unborn, their whole political agenda is called into question and seen as suspect. The same is true to a lesser extent of liberal support of LGBT rights. Homosexual acts are considered unnatural, perverted, and unbiblical by most conservatives. Consequently, liberal support for gay rights is viewed as weakening the moral fabric of the nation and in some sense threatening heterosexual marriage. As the nation has moved closer and closer to universal acceptance of gay marriage and attitudes have changed, the moral force of the anti-LGBT argument has lessened somewhat. Moreover, allowing gay people to marry and have sexual relations may be objectionable to social and religious conservatives, but it does not involve the taking of what they consider to be a human life in the womb. In our opinion, the conservative–liberal divide that is now so stark will not be bridged as long as the abortion issue continues to fester without some compromise or resolution.

REPEALING THE AFFORDABLE CARE ACT/OBAMACARE

The House of Representatives voted to repeal the ACA for the fifty-sixth time on February 3, 2015. This will put all new House members on record as opposing the act, even though President Obama would veto the repeal if it were passed by the Senate. To conservatives, Obamacare is big government at its worst. They think it will increase the national debt; that it puts undue financial strain on businesses, especially smaller ones, and is a form of socialized medicine running contrary to free enterprise. Spending on Medicaid, the federal health care program for the poor that is now connected to the ACA, is up a massive 23 percent since October 2014 (the start of the 2015 fiscal year). Stephen Moore, columnist for the *Orange County Register*, writes that "in an era of almost no inflation, Obamacare has turned out to be, just as feared, the largest expansion of government since the Great Society programs of the 1960s."[4] Moore explains that an increasing number of people are now on Medicaid, because so many are unemployed and do not get health insurance through their nonexistent employer. Moreover some employers are dropping their health coverage and dumping employees on Medicaid and the Obamacare exchanges. In Chapter 7, under the "Social Safety Net" subhead, we discuss the unsuccessful challenge to the ACA that the Supreme Court ruled on in June 2015 (*King v. Burwell*) and that was the Republicans' last hope for crippling the ACA.

PUBLIC SCHOOL ISSUES: PRAYER, EQUAL TIME FOR INTELLIGENT DESIGN, AND VOUCHERS

We analyzed both the Supreme Court's decisions outlawing prayer in public schools and decisions by the high court and a federal district court in Pennsylvania banning the teaching of intelligent design in science classes in Chapter 1. Many conservatives would like to somehow reverse these decisions, but this appears highly unlikely. In 1982, President Ronald

Reagan proposed an amendment to the Constitution that read as follows: "Nothing in the Constitution shall be construed to prohibit individual or group prayer in public schools or other public institutions. No person shall be required by the United States or by any state to participate in prayer."[5] There was widespread support in Congress and with the public for the amendment, but Congress could not muster the needed two-thirds majority in each house to put it before the states for ratification. Reluctance by some in Congress to tamper with the Establishment Clause of the First Amendment probably led to the amendment's defeat.

The Catholic Church has been advocating for public support of its school system since the nineteenth century. In 1884, the U.S. Catholic bishops issued a pastoral letter to Catholic clergy spelling out the necessity for a parochial school system. Archbishop John Hughes of New York was in the forefront of the battle, but he and his fellow bishops did not prevail. As with school prayer, the Establishment Clause has always kept parochial schools from getting anything like full funding. However, there has been a campaign for school vouchers going back to President Reagan's administration, also advocated by President George W. Bush. These vouchers, also referred to as "opportunity scholarships," are state-funded subsidies that pay—usually only partially—for students to attend private schools rather than public ones. These private institutions must meet minimum academic standards set by state legislatures and contain specific eligibility requirements. These voucher programs usually pertain to students from poor families, students with disabilities, and students attending chronically underperforming schools. These criteria came into play dramatically in 1989 when the Wisconsin legislature passed the country's first modern school voucher program targeting students from low-income households in Milwaukee. In 2001, Florida enacted the John M. McKay Scholarship Program for Students with Disabilities, thereby becoming the first state to offer private school vouchers to kids with disabilities. Then in 2002 in *Zelman v. Simmons-Harris*, the Supreme Court ruled 5–4 in favor of an Ohio voucher plan that set aside $5 million for a pilot project in Cleveland. The Ohio plan provided vouchers worth up to $2,250 to parents who can then decide where to use them. Private schools benefiting from the vouchers must agree not to discriminate in their admissions on the basis of race, religion, or ethnic background. In 2004, Congress enacted the first federally funded and administered voucher program for Washington, DC, and offered private-school vouchers to low-income students with priority given to those attending low-performing public schools. In 2011, Indiana established the country's first statewide voucher program for low-income students. However, in Utah in 2007, a statewide voucher program available to any student and with no limitations on eligibility was defeated in a ballot measure. And California has twice defeated voucher proposals: Proposition 174 in 1993 and Proposition 38 in 2006. In sum, the voucher debate is far from over and conservatives will undoubtedly press to extend its reach in the years ahead.

LESS ENVIRONMENTAL REGULATION

The current stance of conservatives on protection of the environment goes hand-in-hand with their skepticism about climate change and global warming. The Republican-dominated 114th Congress would like to rein in environmental regulations, for example, by changing the makeup of the Environmental Protection Agency's Science Advisory Board. In fact, the House, on a mostly party-line vote on November 18, 2014, passed legislation that would, among other things, allow industry experts to be members of the panel as long as their potential conflicts of interest were disclosed. Even if the legislation were reintroduced in the current Congress and passed by both houses a presidential veto would be likely. Conservatives have consistently argued that the EPA overregulates and thereby threatens the coal, oil, and natural gas industries. Environmentalists have been particularly concerned about hydraulic fracturing or fracking, which has succeeded in retrieving tremendous amounts of oil and natural gas from shale but has polluted groundwater and caused other environmental damage. However, conservatives with the backing of the energy industry strongly support fracking.

Ironically, it was Republican President Richard M. Nixon who established the EPA in 1970. And Republican President Theodore Roosevelt, a prominent conservationist, promoted policies that eventually led to the creation of the National Park Service. Yet, President George W. Bush opposed, and the Senate failed to ratify, the Kyoto Protocols that set international standards for regulating greenhouse gas emissions. The protocols were adopted in 1997 by 192 nations and entered into force in 2005,[6] but without U.S. ratification they cannot realize their full potential.

OPPOSITION TO IMMIGRATION REFORM

The debate over immigration was analyzed in depth in Chapter 4, where we discussed the profound objections to liberalizing immigration law by the very conservative Tea Party wing of the Republican Party. Because those objections were keeping any kind of immigration reform in limbo, President Obama, shortly after the November 2014 elections, issued an executive order, the Deferred Action for Parents of Americans program, and an expansion of the Deferred Action for Childhood Arrivals program, that will permit as many as five million illegal aliens to apply for a work permit and be protected from deportation for a period of three years. Those affected are either parents of U.S. citizens or long-term permanent residents who have lived in the country for at least five years. The Republican response, spearheaded by House Speaker John Boehner, was a full-throated "no" to the order. He feels the president has overstepped his authority and that his action is illegal. The executive order was set to go into effect on February 16, 2015, but U.S. district judge Andrew S. Hanen of Brownsville, Texas, issued an injunction temporarily halting it. Texas and 25 other states had sued to stop Obama from proceeding with the order. The administration appealed the judge's decision on February 23, 2015, asking Judge Hanen to lift his injunction while it appealed his ruling to the Fifth U.S. Circuit Court of Appeals. However, on May 26, 2015, the Obama administration's appeal was disallowed and the judge's injunction was left in place while the appeal worked its way through the court system.

Ironically, Tamar Jacoby, president of Immigration Works USA, a national federation of small-business owners favoring immigration reform, contends that most GOP Congress members support relief at least for the so-called dreamers (children brought here illegally by their parents who have lived here most of their lives), and that many support legal status for unauthorized immigrants. But once again polarization is the problem: Congressional Republicans feel the need to strike back at President Obama for his presumed illegal action in issuing the executive order, and they are therefore unlikely to do anything about immigration. Jacoby believes the president did overreach, "but being right isn't always enough in politics—you also have to win the war of perceptions. And right now, the GOP is losing that war . . . Americans aren't hearing the message about the president's abuse of authority. They're hearing the GOP says it hates immigrants."[7] The immigration battle will have profound effects on who Republicans nominate for president in 2016 while the fate of 11–12 million undocumented human beings continues to be uncertain.

THE ATTACK ON CONSERVATIVE RELIGIOUS VALUES

It has happened every Christmas in recent years: Conservative talk radio and Fox Cable News claim that the religious core of the holiday gets hollowed out—"Merry Christmas" becomes "Happy Holidays," the Nativity scene or crèche is barred from public property, and what remains is a mix of Santa Claus, reindeers, and beautifully decorated (Christmas) trees. Conservatives seem to forget that the First Amendment maintains a wall of separation between religion and the state, and in doing so has guaranteed religious freedom for all Americans and kept religious groups alive and well. However, liberals sometimes ignore that the nation has a Judeo-Christian matrix and is still about 78 percent Christian. This, in turn, might help explain why the U.S. Congress has a chaplain, our coinage contains the words "in God we trust," the Pledge of Allegiance contains the phrase "one nation under God," and December 25 is a national holiday because it celebrates the birthday of Jesus Christ.

Conservative Christians feel under siege from liberals who sometimes describe them as narrow-minded fundamentalists or "Bible thumpers." Their more conservative lifestyle, their protests against sexually explicit material on TV and in films, and their vehement objections to abortion and gay marriage are often ridiculed, especially by the secular left. Donald Wildmon, a United Methodist pastor in Mississippi, founded the American Family Association (AFA) in 1977 to fight back against the deluge of sexually explicit material on television and in film, and to promote traditional family values. It has some two million supporters and its journal goes out to one hundred eighty thousand subscribers. AFA started American Family Radio in 1991, which now has 160 stations in 40 states and is available on the Web. Earlier in its history, the AFA launched boycotts against companies that sponsor indecent sexual content, in particular, the Disney Company because of the content of some films of its subsidiary companies. The boycott was lifted in 2005 after Michael Eisner's resignation as chair of the company and its divestiture of Miramax Films. Today, the AFA has become more focused on its antigay agenda, which led the respected civil rights organization the Southern Poverty Law Center (SPLC) to describe the AFA as a hate group because of what the SPLC considered its blatant misrepresentations of the LGBT community.[8]

Nationally syndicated talk-radio host and public intellectual Dennis Prager identifies another aspect to the attack on conservative values: the crushing of dissent. He provides several examples, one being that the *Los Angeles Times* has announced it will not even publish letters to the editor that question the man-made global warming theory. On the issue of opposition to same-sex marriage, the CEO of Mozilla/Firefox, Brendan Eich, was forced to resign in 2014 because it was discovered he had given $1,000 to the successful Proposition 8 campaign that amended the California Constitution so that marriage was defined as the union of one man and one woman (it was overturned by the Supreme Court in 2014). When Eich refused to recant, he was forced to resign despite the fact that gays who work at Mozilla all acknowledged how equitably they were treated both as individuals and couples under his watch. And there was the case of black African, feminist, atheist Ayaan Hirsi Ali who is a critic of Islam for its treatment of women. She was scheduled to receive an honorary doctorate from Brandeis University in May 2014. But, after some Brandeis students and the Council on American Islamic Relations objected, the invitation was withdrawn. Yet, playwright Tony Kushner, himself Jewish but extremely anti-Zionist, was allowed to receive an honorary doctorate from Brandeis despite protests from pro-Israel alumni and pro-Israel students there. The left, according to Prager, "destroys its opponents personally and professionally . . . It is, therefore, a different America, as neither liberals nor conservatives engaged in this practice in the past."[9]

Ironically and sadly, liberals often echo the same complaint about squelching dissent. Comedian Bill Maher is an unabashed lefty and is quite critical of radical Islam and religion generally. After he was asked to address the December 2014 commencement ceremony at UC Berkeley, Muslim students and others protested. The student speaker selection committee then voted to disinvite him and a petition on Change.org netted more than six thousand signatures. Fortunately for the cause of free speech, the university's president overruled the students and Maher delivered his address to applause and only a few protesters. The moral of the story is that political correctness, the theory that no one need be offended in the public square, is the enemy of the kind of vigorous debate about politics and culture that enables a society to thrive.

UNEQUIVOCAL SUPPORT FOR THE STATE OF ISRAEL

Since Israel's establishment in 1948, the United States has been its strongest, most reliable supporter and friend among the nations. A February 2015 Gallup poll reports that 70 percent of Americans view that country favorably, and 62 percent say they sympathize more with the Israelis than the Palestinians in their century-long conflict. By contrast, 17 percent view the Palestinian Authority favorably, and 16 percent sympathize more with the Palestinians than Israel. These numbers are quite consistent with prior Gallup surveys over the past 25 years. However, a key reason that America's sympathy for Israel has remained so solid is that Republicans' support for the state of the Jewish people has risen from 53 percent in 2000 to more than 80 percent today, with just 7 percent choosing the Palestinian Authority. Support for Israel among Democrats has also risen since 2000 but not as sharply as with Republicans.[10] Both political liberals and liberal Protestant churches, such as the Presbyterian Church USA, have criticized certain Israeli policies, especially Jewish settlements in the West Bank. In 2004, the General Assembly of the Presbyterian Church USA passed a phased divestment policy from certain companies, such as Caterpillar,

that do business in Israel. However, in 2006—after American Jewish organizations protested the policy—the Assembly modified the resolution to
focus on negotiation rather than divestment, and also expressed regret for
past anti-Semitism.

By contrast, the conservative and evangelical Christian community
has almost universally defended Israel and made their opinions known
in elections. They take seriously God's words to Abraham in Genesis 12,
where God makes a far-reaching commitment to the patriarch and his
descendants:

I will make of you a great nation, and I will bless you, and make your name great,
so that you will be a blessing. I will bless those who bless you, and the one who
curses you I will curse; and in you all the families of the earth shall be blessed.
(Genesis 12:2–3)

Because the Bible is seen as absolutely without error by evangelicals,
these verses have become their motto and made support for Israel a non-
negotiable element of their faith. Perhaps the most ardent of the conservative Christian supporters of Israel is the Rev. John Hagee (mentioned in
Chapter 1) who made a controversial statement about how the Holocaust
was a blessing for making possible the founding of Israel. Rev. Hagee had
been a very public supporter of 2008 presidential candidate John McCain
who then distanced himself from the preacher. Hagee was apparently
trying to show how Israel's founding was providential, but his statement
backfired and he later apologized. Nonetheless, the preacher, his twenty
thousand–member Cornerstone Church in San Antonio, Texas, and the
organization he founded, the 1.3 million–strong Christians United for
Israel, has raised $80 million toward humanitarian causes in Israel and
promoted tourism to the Holy Land. Every year CUFI sponsors a summit in Washington, DC, where delegates meet members of Congress and
speak on behalf of Israel.[11]

OPPOSITION TO LABOR UNIONS

Since the 1920s, Republicans have strongly opposed labor unions. For
them, free enterprise runs contrary to the control a union can exercise
over a corporation. The poster child for conservative opposition to unions
might be the International Longshore and Warehouse Union that wields
tremendous power over the nation's ability to import and export goods.
In fall 2014, the west coast branch of the union began a significant work
slowdown that jammed up ports from Los Angeles to Seattle and had a
major impact on the economy. President Obama finally called in Secretary

of Labor Thomas Perez to mediate the labor action and an agreement was reached in late February 2015. What particularly annoys conservatives is that full-time ILWU employees may make as much is $147,000 per year plus good benefits, though the average wage is probably nearer $100,000—but not bad compared to what most other unionized workers earn.

By far the most significant legislation affecting labor unions was the 1947 Labor-Management Relations Act (usually referred to as the Taft-Hartley Act after its Congressional authors) that amended the Labor Relations (Wagner) Act of 1935. It gave state legislatures the power to weaken unions by making the so-called closed shop illegal. The new union-shop policy meant that workers could not be forced to join a union even though they might benefit from union agreements that raised wages. These non-union employees still had to pay union dues or at least that portion of dues used to pay for union negotiations with management. However, Taft-Hartley made possible another option: the right-to-work law. It permitted state legislatures to pass such a law under which an employee cannot be forced to join a union or pay union dues. In March 2015, Wisconsin—under Governor and former presidential candidate Scott Walker—became the twenty-fifth right-to-work state. In these states, most of which are in the South and West, though also including Indiana and Michigan more recently, union membership has plummeted. Almost one-third of workers belonged to unions in the 1950s, while today the number is about one-tenth. Right-to-work states have attracted new businesses, such as the auto industry, because of the lower wages workers are paid in most of these states. And union power to affect elections is weaker because its bank accounts are smaller.

CONCLUSION

As we have tried to show, conservatives are interested in preserving core values in American society and keeping the nation true to its original principles: small government, Judeo-Christian morality, secure borders, a strong national defense posture, support for free enterprise (without interference from unions), greatly reducing our huge yearly budget deficits and the gigantic national debt, and keeping God and religious values in public schools. As we turn to Chapter 7 on what matters to the left, the contrasts will become very evident. Hopefully, the comparison of these two value systems will make citizens more aware and appreciative of the closely held views of those in the other camp. This, in turn, might help move everyone closer to the "endangered center" so that the business of governing and promotion of the common good is enhanced.

NOTES

1. www.people-press.org/2014/06/12/political-polarization-in-the -American-public/.

2. Ibid.

3. www.atr.org/about-Grover. Retrieved February 12, 2015.

4. *Orange County Register*, Opinion section, February 15, 2015.

5. Quoted in Edwin S. Gaustad, *Proclaim Liberty throughout the Land: A History of Church and State in America.* New York: Oxford University Press, 2003, p. 92.

6. www.unfccc.int/Kyoto_protocol/items/2830.php. Retrieved February 20, 2015.

7. "The GOP, Trapped," *Los Angeles Times*, February 19, 2015.

8. www.splc.org/get-informed/intelligence-report/browse-all-issues/2010 /winter/the-hard-liners

9. "Crushing Dissent in America," *Los Angeles Jewish Journal*, May 2–8, 2014, p. 34.

10. www.Gallup.com/poll/181652/seven-in-10-Americans-continue-to-view -Israel-favorably.

11. www.jhm.org/home/about/pastorJohnHagee. Retrieved February 23, 2015.

Chapter 7

What Matters to the Left

As we move from Chapter 6, discussing what matters to the right, to Chapter 7 to discuss the core values of the left, let's reflect on what matters to all of us. What are the commonalities that almost everyone in the republic considers of personal concern? The list is not meant to be exhaustive, but suggestive of why we are still one people whose aims are, among others, to, "establish Justice [and] . . . promote the general Welfare" (preamble to the U.S. Constitution). Of course, the Declaration of Independence and the Constitution matter greatly to those on the left and right and everyone in between. Interpretations will differ but, as with the Bible, the documents remain sacred—a core part of our civil religion.

- Balancing the federal budget on a fixed timetable.
- Creating more jobs and lowering the unemployment rate.
- Making America energy-secure within the next 20 years.
- Reforming the rules currently governing Congress (e.g., the Senate filibuster) so that government works more efficiently to get the people's business done.
- Reforming Medicare and Social Security so that they remain secure for another 75 years. There are, of course, conservatives who would like to abolish or radically alter both programs; but each of them has such overwhelming support that "reform" is the only realistic approach to the problems with each.[1]
- Unemployment and underemployment and the economic and psychological effects this has on families.

- Improving our educational system from prekindergarten to graduate school. The public school system, in particular, is underfunded, underappreciated, and overwhelmed by family and societal problems.
- The severe problems of homelessness and poverty, especially as they affect children (one of every 45 children is homeless in a given year).
- All forms of religious persecution, especially anti-Semitism and the repression of Christians in the Middle East.
- Combating the growing problem of bullying in our schools and on the Internet.
- Reforming our prison system so that more people who are mentally ill or drug addicted get treatment rather than incarceration.
- Combating the plague of drug and alcohol addiction by providing better educational opportunities, counseling services, and community policing.
- Doing more to prevent suicides, especially in the military and among veterans.
- Weakening the attraction and power of street gangs.
- Combating sex slavery, not only abroad but on the streets of our major cities.
- Support for Israel as the one state of the Jewish people.
- Responding to the threat of terrorism in this country and overseas, and the growth of Islamic radicalism as manifested in groups such as the so-called Islamic State/ISIS, Al Qaeda, etc.

Granted, conservatives and liberals have differing solutions to these challenges, but a broad consensus exists that we must address them and there is some common ground in which to do so. We will analyze most of these common problems in detail in the next chapter.

The following discussion of what matters to the left is meant to be descriptive and does not aim to provide solutions to these complex problems. Instead, it will be suggestive of the need for conservatives, liberals, and libertarians to seek comprehensive solutions by tacking to the center and finding compromises. On these monumental issues, no constituency will get everything it wants; but we believe there can be modest improvements for everyone. Once a platform of mutually acceptable solutions is adopted, greater trust and even more progress will result.

"MONEY MAKES THE WORLD GO 'ROUND"

The line from the musical "Cabaret" points to the age-old problem of the distribution of wealth: why some people have so much of it and why an immense majority do not. It is not our task in this book to evaluate the relative merits of economic theories, such as those of John Maynard Keynes or Milton Friedman. However, the evidence is indisputable that the income gap between the richest and poorest Americans is greater than it has been in almost a century. There is something amiss, for example, when one family, the Waltons, has amassed a fortune comprising 40 percent of total U.S. private wealth!

To liberals like Senators Bernie Sanders (I-VT), Elizabeth Warren (D-MA), and UC Berkeley professor (and former secretary of commerce) Robert Reich, this income gap is a fundamental injustice that needs to be corrected. Reich reports on research indicating that the richest one-tenth of one percent of Americans now possess over 11 percent of the nation's total wealth. This translates to sixteen thousand people each worth at least $110 million. By way of comparison, in 1978 the average wealth holder in the top .01 percent was 220 times richer than the average American. By 2012 that individual was 1,120 times richer. In the mid-1980s, the bottom 90 percent of Americans held 36 percent of the country's wealth but today hold less than 23 percent.

Moreover, the wealth of the superrich is changing the political game. In the 2012 election cycle (the last for which good data is available) contributions from the top .01 percent accounted for over 40 percent of all campaign donations (versus 10 percent of total contributed by the very wealthiest in 1980). These investments have paid off handsomely. As the top .01 began investing seriously in politics, corporate profits in the stock market have risen substantially, enlarging the wealth of this class by an average of 7.8 percent a year since the mid-1980s.[2] Senator Sanders notes that Americans today are working longer hours for lower wages. "Since 1999, the median middle-class family has seen its income go down by almost $5,000 after adjusting for inflation, now earning less than it did 25 years ago."[3]

Warren, in her 2014 autobiography, *A Fighting Chance*, discusses how big corporations can hire armies of lobbyists to get million-dollar loopholes into the tax system and then persuade their congressional friends to support laws that keep the field of play tilted in their favor. She also writes that the federal government has permitted an unregulated financial industry to prey on the middle class.[4] In short, progressives believe the chasm between the rich, the middle class, and especially the poor is unacceptable and needs to be rectified.

Another worrisome development, in the opinion of progressives, is that the middle class is shrinking. The percentage of people in the population earning between $35,000 and $100,000 a year decreased (in today's dollars) from 53 percent in 1967 to 43 percent in 2013. Moreover the fastest-growing segment of the middle class are people 65 and older with good retirement benefits, 19 percent of whom are still working part-time. In stark contrast, married couples with children, who once comprised 60 percent of the middle class, today make up 25 percent.[5] The decline in well-paying blue-collar jobs is one reason for this situation; another is the number of good jobs lost during the Great Recession. And many progressives maintain that millions of people are simply not being paid a decent wage. A good illustration of this comes from the CBS-TV program *Undercover Boss* where the disguised chief executive, seeking to better understand how his company works on the ground, invariably makes numerous mistakes on an assembly line, in a restaurant kitchen, and so on. It takes a dedicated team to run a business, but in the opinion of many on the left it seems those at the top are being disproportionately rewarded.

The precursor to the critiques of income and wealth disparity by Sanders, Warren, Reich, and others was the Occupy Wall Street (OWS) movement. It began September 17, 2011, in Zuccotti Park near New York City's Wall Street financial district. Essentially a consciousness-raising movement, the OWS protesters' main complaints were social and economic inequality, greed, corruption, and the sense that corporations were having disproportionate influence on government. The OWS slogan was "we are the 99 percent," referring to income inequality and distribution of wealth between the richest 1 percent and the remainder of Americans. The protesters were forced out of the park on November 15, 2011, after which they made several unsuccessful attempts to reoccupy that location and then turned their focus to the occupation of banks, corporate headquarters, board meetings, and college and university campuses. Although the movement eventually ran out of steam, it did spark a conversation about income inequality that remains alive.

Raising the minimum wage is another important goal of people on the left. As 2015 began, 3.1 million low-paid workers in 20 states received raises that are higher than the federal minimum of $7.25. These increases are expected to generate $826.8 in new economic growth as these workers began spending their higher salaries. Over the next two years, via ballot initiatives or legislative campaigns, a number of additional states will probably see minimum wage increases, as will many cities. Finally, there is the scandal in the eyes of liberals that 43 million private-sector workers have no paid sick leave (only California, New Jersey, and Rhode Island mandate that benefit). The Obama administration is urging the other states to require seven leave days. The United States is also the only country in the developed world that does not provide paid maternity leave. In short, the grievances of working people are many and serious.

There are other economic complaints by the 99 percent, for example, the tax exemption provided to the National Football League, farm subsidies provided to huge agribusinesses, the dodging of taxes by large corporations when they move their headquarters offshore, and the dropping of some safeguards in the Dodd-Frank Banking Act. This makes it easier for major financial institutions to undertake riskier investments that could fail and end up in the lap of taxpayers. This is what contributed to the Great Recession in 2008 when big banks and mortgage companies took huge pools of mortgage funds and used them to make speculative investments. As so often in the past, some progressive legislators, for example, Representative Christopher Van Hollen (D-MI) proposed in early 2015 a tax break for those earning less than $200,000 per year. It would be offset by a financial transaction tax that would apply to every transaction, for example, the sale or purchase of stocks or bonds, and would be aimed at high-frequency traders. Their behavior, Van Hollen argues, makes markets more volatile.

CLIMATE CHANGE AND GUN CONTROL

Both these issues were discussed at length in Chapter 4. The major point here is that powerful interests have largely kept the problems associated with a warming climate and an alarming handgun death rate from getting the kind of attention that a wide segment of the public believes is desperately needed. Liberals, in particular, are frustrated when a respected conservative commentator such as Dennis Prager or a veteran lawmaker like Orange County's Dana Rohrabacher (R-CA)—as well as Senator James Inhofe (R-OK), new chair of Senate Committee on Environment and Public Works—consider climate change to be nonsense. The National Oceanic and Atmospheric Administration and the NASA reported that 2014 was the warmest year since record-keeping started 135 years ago. (The oceans, too, are warmer: 60.9 degrees Fahrenheit versus the twentieth-century average of 59.6). Regarding gun control, while 70 percent of the public favor universal background checks, the NRA and similar groups resist the idea vehemently. And, as noted in Chapter 4, there is almost no conversation going on between opponents on these issues. The field is ruled by polluters like the coal industry and handgun manufacturers like Colt and Remington.

ANIMAL RIGHTS

Like defending motherhood, everyone across the political spectrum opposes cruelty to animals and their unnecessary exploitation in the production of food for humans. However, those on the left have displayed a much more intense commitment to the rights of animals. While almost everyone applauds the work of the Humane Society and the American Society for the Prevention of Cruelty to Animals, the work of two groups, Greenpeace and PETA (People for the Ethical Treatment of Animals), is viewed differently by conservatives. That's because both groups have really pushed hard for changes in the human–animal relationship. PETA is the nation's largest animal rights group with 300 employees and three million members. It works for the humane treatment of animals in four areas: factory farms, the clothing trade, research laboratories, and the entertainment industry.[6] It does so through education, investigations of animal cruelty, research, animal rescues, legislation, and protest campaigns—and it pushes hard. For example, it has infiltrated numerous fashion shows in the United States, Europe, and elsewhere and scattered blood on the runways to protest the use of fur.

Although the mission of Greenpeace is to protect the environment, and in particular the world's oceans, its efforts to protect whales have garnered the most attention. In 1986 its efforts brought about a worldwide ban on commercial whaling and helped bring some whale species back from the brink of extinction. However, Japan, Norway, and Iceland continue to do some whaling. In response, Greenpeace's vessels have repeatedly attempted and often succeeded in foiling whale hunts—and they have done so at considerable personal risk to the ships' crews.

THE SOCIAL SAFETY NET

As noted earlier, the ultraconservative wing of the Republican Party would not shed a tear if the entire safety net were massively cut back. Since this is simply not going to happen, Republicans and their supporters will seek to reduce Social Security payouts, for example, by using a more conservative consumer price index formula to determine increases in SSI payments. They would also like to put stricter criteria on eligibility for Social Security disability payments and to shrink the food stamp/Women, Infants and Children program (WIC). Of course, their greatest grievance is against "Obamacare," the Patient Protection and Affordable Care Act. In the 114th Congress, now controlled by Republicans in both houses, and with the largest majority in the house since 1932, legislation to repeal or dramatically cut back on the ACA has been repeatedly introduced but remains theoretical because of the president's veto threat. The conservatives' best hope, as mentioned in Chapter 6, was to challenge the act based on a loophole that can be interpreted to mean only states with their own health care exchanges—and there are just 14 of these plus Washington, DC—can provide federal ACA benefits to those states. However, by a 6–3 decision in

King v. Burwell the Supreme Court dashed that hope. Liberals, of course, argue that the safety net is already unraveling—that many elderly retired folks are barely getting by on Social Security and that, despite Obamacare, millions still do not have adequate health care, let alone dental or vision coverage. They also point out that one in 45 children (1.6 million) experience homelessness each year in this country. Such children are sick four times more often than other children, go hungry at twice the rate of other kids, and are twice as likely to have learning disabilities.[7]

REDUCING THE COST OF HIGHER EDUCATION

Something really appears skewed in our economic priorities, say liberals, when aggregate student debt exceeds total credit card debt. Only mortgage indebtedness is higher. Average student debt is now about $28,000, a number that has doubled in about ten years and that makes qualifying for a mortgage difficult. Senator Warren attempted in 2014 to get the interest rate lowered to 3.86 percent (the current rate) for loans issued before 2010 but without success.

Along with the problem of indebtedness, there is the looming issue of the country's ability to turn out enough college graduates to sustain the workforce. Demographer William Frey has calculated that, if we don't improve the college completion rate, the share of Americans with at least a four-year degree will begin declining as soon as 2020 and not return to its 2015 level until at least 2050. In California alone, economists predict that by 2020 the state will have a shortage of highly skilled workers. A principal reason for this grim scenario is that the percentage of Latinos and African Americans in the population is rising quickly, such that in the 2014–15 school year a majority of all K-12 public school students were nonwhite. Moreover, completion rates for these students are considerably lower than those for whites.

At the start of 2015, as the new Congress convened, President Obama rolled out "Americans College Promise," a program that would make community colleges tuition free. He is proposing to Congress that $60 billion be allocated over the next ten years to help cover tuition for full- and half-time students who maintain a 2.5 GPA and make good progress toward completion of their degrees. The administration estimates the program could save a full-time student $3,800 per year. Although community college tuition averages about $3,330 a year and is further offset by Pell grants for poor and working-class students, tuition accounts for only about 20 percent of the total cost of attendance at these colleges. A program like the one posed by the president was started in 2007 in the City University of New York and has dramatically increased student success. Whether he will have any luck with this proposal remains in doubt, especially because of the massive federal deficit and Republicans' distaste for such attempts at what they see as social engineering. However, a community-college associate's degree is now the equivalent of a high school degree a century ago. So unless we train students for technical or vocational programs, or for entry into four-year universities, the country could be in a desperate situation by 2030 when the number of working age whites will have fallen by 15 million. Education has always been the engine of American greatness, without which we are likely to become a second-rate nation.

OVERTURNING THE *CITIZENS UNITED* AND *MCCUTCHEON* SUPREME COURT DECISIONS

The Supreme Court's 5–4 decision in *Citizens United v. Federal Elections Committee* (2010) was arguably the most momentous and controversial decision ever in the area of campaign fund-raising. Prior to this, corporations or unions could not make direct contributions to candidates. If they wished to fund advertising for or against a candidate, they could do so only through individual contributions from their employees, or their members, to Political Action Committees. Because of restrictions on how much an individual might contribute to a PAC, there were absolute limits on how much it could raise and how much it could contribute to a particular candidate. Because the contributions and expenditures of PACs were subject to disclosure requirements, the public could see who was making the contributions.

After *Citizens United*, these limitations and disclosure requirements no longer controlled electioneering advertising and independent expenditures, and an avalanche of dollars broke loose to create essentially unrestricted campaign activity. Hence, billionaires such as the Koch brothers, Sheldon Adelson, Tom Steyer, and George Soros have become paymasters who can massively influence election results all over the country. *Citizens United* came ten years after the Bipartisan Campaign Reform Act cosponsored by Senator John McCain (R-AZ) and former Senator Russ Feingold (D-WI) had required candidates to disclose their major funders and to utilize only voluntary individual donations through PACs rather than corporate or union treasury money. It's a new ballgame now.

To add to the campaign finance problems created by *Citizens United*, the Supreme Court in 2014 in *McCutcheon v. Federal Election Commission* overturned, by another 5–4 decision, a section of the Federal Election Campaign Act. It had imposed a two-year combined limit on contributions by individuals and national party federal candidate committees. While the decision kept in place the $2,600 limit on how much an individual could give to any one candidate in an election cycle, it meant that this amount could be contributed to virtually an unlimited number of candidates. The floodgates of political giving were now almost completely open. Politicians and those seeking office are now engaged in a race to raise money that became even more desperate during the midterm congressional election in the fall of 2014. Many Americans on the right and the left could barely keep up with the daily volume of e-mails and letters begging us to give, give, really give.

But there is a postscript: Tacked onto the bill passed in late December 2014 to raise the debt limit was an amendment raising the limit on how much an individual may contribute to a political party from $129,600 to $777,600. As Philip Bump wrote in the *Washington Post*, "If money is speech, political parties are about to get a lot louder."[8] As a preview of what's coming in the 2016 presidential contest, Freedom Partners, a network of conservatives led by the Koch brothers, plans to spend $887 million to elect a Republican. On the 2012 race, the Republican National Committee spent less than half of that—$404 million. The only sure winners in the next election cycle will be television stations raking in millions for running political ads.

A movement is under way in Congress to repeal *Citizens United* through a constitutional amendment, but the current makeup of Congress makes the amendment seem like a long shot. Nonetheless, the "Democracy for All Amendment" (Senate Joint Resolution 19) would restore democracy by reestablishing the authority of Congress and the states to regulate and limit campaign spending. In September 2014 the resolution was actually passed by the Senate 54–42, but a two-thirds majority for the vote was needed to send it to the House for a comparable vote and then to the states, three-quarters of whom would have to ratify it. The proposed (Twenty-Eighth) amendment would enable Congress and the states to pass legislation ending corporate spending on elections, eliminating dark or anonymous money in elections, imposing limits on total election spending, and allowing for the implementation of active systems of small-donor and public financing. In summer 2014, the progressive advocacy group Public Citizen commissioned a poll conducted jointly by Democratic and Republican polling firms among 800 likely voters. It indicated that voters opposed *Citizens United* by almost 3 to 1, with Republicans opposing it by 2 to 1. Moreover, by a 6-to-1 margin, survey respondents held an unfavorable view of spending in elections by special interests and lobbyists. Thus far, 16 states and some 550 cities and towns along with more than 160 former and current members of Congress have endorsed the amendment, as has President Obama.

SHUTTING DOWN "GITMO"

President Obama had hoped to shut down the Guantánamo Bay military prison in Cuba (Gitmo) during his first year in office, but was blocked by Congress and by the legal complexity of the situation. Nonetheless, he advocated closing the prison again in his 2015 State of the Union address. The number of prisoners there was reduced from 780 in 2003 to 122 by early 2015. The Obama administration is seeking countries willing to take 54 prisoners cleared for release by security officials and is evaluating how many of the remaining prisoners could be safely freed. In December 2014, Pope Francis appealed to diplomats at the Vatican to open the doors of their nations to take prisoners marooned because of turmoil in the prisoners' home countries. Of the 88 released since Obama took office, only 6 are known to have become reinvolved in terrorism or insurgency groups. In 2010, Congress passed legislation banning transfer of detainees to the maximum-security prison in Thomson, Illinois. So it would be difficult for the president to override this law by an executive order.

But sentiments in Congress might change if the number of detainees got to be less than 40 or 50. It costs more than $3 million per year to house a prisoner at Guantánamo versus $78,000 at a supermax prison on U.S. soil. In November 2013, Senator John McCain (R-AZ)[9] read a letter on the floor of the Senate from 38 retired generals and admirals that supported shutting the facility. It said in part, "Guantánamo is a betrayal of American values. The prison is a symbol of torture and justice delayed. More than a decade after it opened, Guantánamo remains a recruiting poster for terrorists, which makes us all less safe."[10] Nonetheless, a 2014 Gallup Poll indicated that 66 percent of respondents oppose closure of the facility (versus 53 percent in 2007) and 29 percent favor doing so (versus 33 percent in 2007). The frequency of terror attacks by Muslim extremists is probably influencing public opinion. Still, the existence of a prison on what is technically foreign soil (Cuba) where alleged acts of torture and humiliation occurred, and where detainees languish, is fodder for extremist anti-American propaganda and makes winning the war on terror more difficult.

A final irony in the Gitmo mess was the release in January 2015 of *Guantánamo Diary* by Mohammedou Ould Slahi, a prisoner there for the past 12 years. His account of sleep deprivation, being shackled for days in a freezing cell, being doused with ice water, beatings, and threats has been substantiated by multiple government investigations. Yet, Slahi, like so many other Guantánamo detainees, has never been formally charged. Federal judge James Robertson reviewed Slahi's habeas corpus[11] petition in 2010 and concluded that the government's evidence was "so attenuated, or so tainted by coercion and mistreatment, or so classified that it cannot support a criminal prosecution."[12] The judge ordered his release, but the Obama administration appealed the decision and it was overturned. Perhaps publicity about the book will further weaken the case for keeping the prison open.

PROTECTING VOTING RIGHTS

The arc of voting rights has certainly bent toward justice since the Constitution originally enfranchised only white, property-owning males. The Fifteenth Amendment gave African Americans the right to vote, the Nineteenth provided women that right, the Twenty-Fourth abolished the poll tax, and the Twenty-Sixth enfranchised 18-year-olds. The 1965 Voting Rights Act (VRA) included provisions to guarantee that blacks and other minorities were able to vote, thus making the theoretical guarantees of the Fifteenth Amendment a reality. Congress extended the VRA several times and then in 2006 extended it for an additional 25 years. In 2013, however, the Supreme Court in *Shelby v. Holder* overturned, 5–4, the provision in the VRA that required certain states with a history of voting restrictions to get preclearance from the attorney general or the DC federal district court for any changes in voting eligibility. The high court's majority noted that voting discrimination still exists but that the current variable treatment by the states imposes current burdens that must be justified by current needs.

So the VRA needed to be amended but the proposal to do so got stuck in the legislative thicket. Since then, 15 states have enacted various restrictions on voting eligibility, most controversially in Texas (seven other states had passed restrictions since 2010). The Lone Star State passed a voter identification law requiring registered voters to present a certain kind of photo ID card and making it difficult for those without the card to get one. The law was challenged and ultimately ended up in the Supreme Court, which in November 2014 allowed it to stand. Consequently, at the time of the 2014 election, more than six hundred thousand registered voters in Texas did not have the required ID.[13]

This is admittedly a complex issue made more so because each state under the Constitution determines its own voting rules. Thus, on the bright side, online voter registration is now available in 20 states. However, the disturbing trend is that being able to vote has become more difficult in too many parts of the country, while the evidence that voter fraud has influenced the outcome of any election is quite thin.

PROTECTING REPRODUCTIVE RIGHTS

The abortion rights controversy was discussed at length in Chapter 1. Suffice it to say that the struggle continues between the pro-choice and pro-life camps with no end in sight. This could change if a Republican were elected president in 2016 and an opening emerged on the Supreme Court, thus giving the new president the opportunity of appointing a more conservative jurist. In this circumstance, overturning *Roe v. Wade,* or placing even more restrictions on it, might very well happen. At the beginning of the 114th Congress in early 2015, Republicans in the House had initially hoped to bring forth legislation forbidding abortions after 20 weeks of a pregnancy. However, more centrist Republicans, especially women, strongly objected and the idea was shelved. President Obama would veto such legislation if it were approved by Congress, so the matter is only a theoretical possibility for the moment. The real action, as already noted, is in conservative states where the antiabortion vice continues to tighten.

DEFENDING LGBT RIGHTS

We analyzed religion's gay-rights dilemma in Chapter 1, and will make only a few additional points here. As discussed, the Supreme Court decided in June 2015 that homosexual unions are legal in all 50 states. As David Von Drehle stated in *Time* magazine before the court's decision:

It defies belief to think that the same justices who joined [Supreme Court Justice Anthony] Kennedy's 2013 opinion, with its emphasis on the equal dignity of same-sex couples, would allow gay marriages to spread from coast-to-coast, then turn around and enforce state bans. Such a ruling would potentially invalidate thousands of unions.[14]

That, of course, is precisely what happened; yet, struggles continue as when Rowan County, Kentucky, clerk Kim Davis refused on religious grounds to issue a marriage license to a gay couple. U.S. District Court Judge David Bunning jailed Davis for contempt, but released her after five days. He warned, however, that he might re-arrest her if she did not permit her deputy clerks to issue licenses to gay and lesbian couples. Presidential candidate Mike Huckabee accompanied Davis from jail. This religiously fueled controversy may be with us right through presidential primary season.

The rights of transgender individuals may be the final battleground in this complex struggle. Such individuals still face significant discrimination in many parts of the country. In January 2015, three transgender women of color were murdered in Virginia, Kentucky, and Texas, respectively. In 32 states there is no protection for "trans" people from being fired. However, in the same month the Department of Justice (DOJ) explicitly clarified that discrimination claims are covered under Title VII of the Civil Rights Act. Diane Schroer, after a 25-year career in the Army, had applied for a position as a terrorism analyst at the Library of Congress. She was offered the position under the assumption that she was a man, but she thought she should tell her prospective employer of her plans to transition to a woman. Once she did so, the offer was rescinded. In 2005, the ACLU filed a lawsuit on her behalf and, although the DOJ vigorously fought the lawsuit, the court ruled in Schroer's favor. The 2015 clarification further vindicates her case and parallels a 2012 decision by the Equal Employment Opportunity Commission that found that transgender individuals are protected under laws banning sex discrimination.

Another development that will give increased visibility to the issue of transgender rights is the transition of 1976 Olympic decathlon champion and reality TV star Bruce Jenner to a woman, Caitlyn. A new reality show on the E! network, *I Am Cait*, focusing on Jenner's transition, ran from July 26 to September 13 in eight weekly episodes.

THE MILITARY-INDUSTRIAL COMPLEX LIVES BUT SHOULDN'T

It is a source of amazement and frustration, at least to liberals, that the U.S. defense budget is larger than that of the next eight countries combined (China, Russia, Saudi Arabia, France, United Kingdom, Germany, Japan, and India).[15] That budget totaled $613.6 million in 2014 with a Department of Defense request for $636.6 million in 2015. These are perilous and complicated times, and even those on the far left acknowledge the need to confront the so-called Islamic State or ISIS and other threats. However, it is the waste, duplication, and political meddling that bothers liberals. Author Ben Hubbard, while on active military duty, was sitting in his office in the old Presidio Army headquarters in San Francisco when he saw a new desk coming in the door to replace his current, perfectly usable desk. His commanding officer later explained that the headquarters needed to use up its entire budget for that year or there would be fewer dollars in the next. This is a game long played by many public agencies and is symptomatic of financial abuse in the Pentagon.

A much more serious example of waste involved the Pentagon's purchase of huge C-127 cargo planes at $50 million apiece that went directly from the factory into mothballs because they were not needed. What makes this more unbelievable is that the planes were purchased from Italy and then shipped to an Air Force facility in Arizona nicknamed "the boneyard." These aerial corpses had joined thousands of other aircraft and 13 aerospace vehicles at the boneyard at a cost of $35 billion by the end of 2013.[16] The explanation often given in these and other cases by politicians on Capitol Hill is job creation, especially, of course, when the planes or armaments are made in the United States. Why not take the money and hire people to upgrade America's ailing roads and bridges?

A final sad example of wasteful military spending is the hulking Abrams tank. In 2013, Army Chief of Staff Ray Odierno stated that the military did not want to spend $436 million on additional tanks (it has 2,400 already, two-thirds of which are an improved version of the Abrams), but would prefer to use the funds in other ways. However, the nation's only tank plant is located in Lima, Ohio, and that state's congressional delegation, especially Republican Representative Jim Jordan and Senator Rob Portman, and Democratic Senator Sherrod Brown, have used the old "national security" rationale to keep the spending in place. Then in December 2014, Congress allocated $120 million for Abrams upgrades despite Army objections. The dance goes on as our infrastructure creaks and our social safety net frays—at least that's how progressives see the matter.

CONCLUSION

Progressives believe strongly that addressing the issues described in this chapter would make for a more just society and would "promote the general welfare." Regarding the health of the planet, fighting climate change might be the most serious challenge, while overturning the *Citizens United* and *McCutcheon* high-court decisions might be most important to the health of our democracy. But all of the issues really matter to those on the left and they will fight to support their causes. Of course, these folks realize that, given the makeup of the 114th Congress and the mood of the country, painful compromise is inevitable. Politics, as German Chancellor Otto von Bismarck said in 1884, is "the art of the possible."[17] Liberals will need to be artful if they want to see what they hold dear become reality in even a modified form. As we saw in Chapter 6, "What Matters to the Right," it is also evident that compromise by conservatives on many issues is the only road to improved health for the nation. Their issues, too, involve serious matters that they feel the nation must address for the greater good. So the hope is that the analysis of key issues in these two chapters might provide perspective for citizens—for voters—as the 2016 election draws nearer.

NOTES

1. These first five commonalities were drawn from the "National Strategic Agenda" proposed by the organization No Labels, cofounded in 2011 by a bipartisan group of experienced politicians and now led by former Utah Governor Jon Huntsman. See full discussion in Chapter 11.

2. www.robertreich.org/post/102926070780.

3. www.huffingtonpost.com/rep-Bernie-Sanders/an-economic-agenda -for-America-12-steps-forward.

4. Jill Lepore, "The Warren brief," *The New Yorker*, April 21, 2014.

5. www.nytimes.com/2015/01/26/business/economy/middle-class-shrinks -further-as-more-fall-out-instead-of-climbing-up.html.

6. www.peta.org/about-peta/. Retrieved February16, 2015.

7. www.family homelessness.org/children.php?p=ts.

8. www.WashingtonPost.com/blogs/the-fix/WP/2014/12/10/campaign -contributions-are-about-to-go-way-up-heres-what-that-looks-like-in-one-massive -graph.

9. Since then, McCain has changed his position and opposes closing the facility.

10. Quotation from www.nytimes.com/2015/01/18/opinion/sunday/perpetuating -Guantanamos-travesty.

11. A legal document requiring that a person be brought before a judge or court, especially to determine if the person has been detained or imprisoned legally. *Random House Webster's Collegiate Dictionary*. New York: Random House, 2001, p. 589.

12. www.nytimes.com/2015/01/26/arts/Guantanamo-diary-by-mohamedou -ould-slahi.

13. January 2015 letter from Brennan Center for Law and Justice. www.brennan center.org

14. *Time*, February 2, 2015, p. 18.

15. www.pgpf.org/chart/archive/0053/_defense-comparison. Retrieved January 3, 2015.

16. http://Jonathanturley.org/2013/10/08/military-buying-Italian-planes-at -50-million-a-piece-and-sending-them-to-boneyard/

17. www.thisdayinquotes.com/2009/12/politics-is-not-exact-science-said. html. In 1863, while still a Prussian statesman, Bismarck made a similar comment to members of his parliament: "Politics is not an exact science, but is it an art?"

Chapter 8

What Matters to the Center and Why It's Endangered

We examined what matters to the right in Chapter 6 and the left in Chapter 7 to help the reader gain an appreciation for some of the deeply held views of each side. In Chapter 8 we examine those issues that, in one way or another, matter to almost everyone across the political and cultural spectrum. The aim is to make clear that common goals for the nation still exist and can be implemented. Next we assess the work of the bipartisan movement "No Labels," some of whose goals we have incorporated among the issues that matter to those in the middle and are indispensable to more effective government. Then, we look at the increase in independent voters, aligned with neither political party and frustrated by polarization, who tend to cede more power to those on the hard right and hard left. Finally, we provide some reflections on American pragmatism and how it might show a way forward out of our political and cultural impasse.

ISSUES THAT MATTER TO ALL OF US

Balancing the Federal Budget on a Fixed Timetable

As discussed in Chapter 6, when a nation goes $2.4 billion further in debt every day, there's a problem. Currently, interest rates are low, but that will inevitably change at some point and the cost of borrowing will rise. According to the nonpartisan Congressional Budget Office the total amount of federal debt held by the public is now equivalent to about 74 percent of the economy's annual output or gross domestic product (GDP). This is a higher percentage than at any time in U.S. history except a brief period around World War II and is almost twice the percentage at the end of 2008. By 2039, federal debt in the public's hands would be on an upward path that could not be indefinitely sustained. The economy has recovered since the Great Recession, which should keep deficits between 2.5 percent and 3 percent of GDP through 2018. After that, however, pressure stemming from an aging population, rising health care costs, and expansion of federal subsidies for health insurance will cause deficits to balloon once again.[1] This is a grim picture, and 2039 is not that far off for the millennials who are reading this book. The bipartisan Concord Coalition has been working for many years on deficit reduction and is currently proposing an idea to presidential candidates, "First Budget." It asks candidates to acknowledge the severity of the long-term debt, to make it a top policy priority in their campaign, to put forward a plan for fixing it, and to engage and educate the public about the tough choices needed to solve the problem. It also urges the newly elected president in 2016 to outline in his *first budget* concrete steps to reduce our chronic debt: slowing the cost of health care spending, making social security sustainable and secure for future generations, simplifying the tax code, and protecting critical investments to promote economic growth and opportunity.[2]

Creating More Jobs and Lowering the Unemployment Rate

Although the rate has dropped since the end of the Great Recession, it is still far from ideal. Many people have simply given up the search for a job, many others are employed only part-time when they need full-time work, and a troubling share of college graduates are working in low-paying jobs below their educational levels. A February 2015 Pew Research Center survey that 60 percent of respondents felt that the job situation had only partially recovered, 7 percent fully, and 32 percent "hardly at all."[3] The wage situation is also troubling: The real value of the minimum wage has fallen by nearly one-third since 1968.

Making America Energy-Secure within 20 Years

The United States has been kowtowing to oil-rich Middle East nations, especially Saudi Arabia, Libya, and the Gulf states, since the end of World War II. Our thirst for oil from Saudi Arabia, in particular, has led us to tolerate abuses of human rights, especially women's rights. This, in turn, has enabled the Saudis to propagate their extremely conservative view of Islam by bankrolling mosques and educational centers in North America, Europe, and elsewhere. The situation has changed dramatically in the past decade with the discovery of shale oil that can be extracted by using hydraulic fracturing or "fracking." The problem, however, as mentioned in Chapter 7, is that this procedure has caused environmental damage, especially to groundwater. It may be some time before the extent of the damage is understood and addressed, but it is real and long lasting. On a much more positive note, the advent of the Toyota Prius and other hybrid and completely electric vehicles, the significant growth in solar and wind energy, and other new technologies are beginning to make a real difference in the extent of our energy independence. Iowa and South Dakota are each generating at least 26 percent of electricity needs from wind farms, and Texas 10 percent. In Denmark the figure is 34 percent and in Portugal and Spain about 20 percent. China now gets more electricity from wind farms than from nuclear power plants.[4] So, along with general agreement on the need for energy independence, there is growing optimism for the future. As astrophysicist Stephen Hawking has said, "Where there is life, there is hope."

Reforming the Rules Governing Congress to Make It Run More Efficiently. Case in Point: The Filibuster

Article 1, section 5 of the Constitution permits each house of Congress to "determine the rules of its proceedings." In the past almost 230 years since Congress first convened, rules aplenty have been adopted, some of which have ceased to work well. The most problematic of these is the filibuster (from a Dutch word meaning "pirate"), a stalling tactic used in the Senate when controversial legislation is being considered. A senator can talk a bill to death by speaking incessantly. Though the procedure was adopted in 1806, it was not employed until 1837 and was rare for the next century. In 1917, the Senate adopted a cloture rule that made it possible to end a filibuster with a two-thirds vote (later reduced to 60 percent). But in 1975, a "virtual filibuster" was put in place enabling other Senate business to continue even while the filibuster remained in place. By 1990 there had been a grand total of 413 filibusters, but since the beginning of the twenty-first century the tactic has been used over 600 times. Virtual filibusters on motions to proceed with Senate business can gum up the institution and keep important legislation from even being considered. In September 2013, Senator Ted Cruz of Texas employed an actual filibuster as he stood and talked for more than 21 hours to prevent a vote on raising the national debt ceiling that delayed passage of the funding bill, contributed to a three-week shutdown of the entire government, and cost the federal government $2 billion in lost productivity and the economy $4 billion in lost activity.

One of the most damaging results of the filibuster is its use to prevent a vote on nominees to the federal judiciary. There are now at least 85 vacancies in the federal court system that have slowed its work and placed a heavier burden on sitting judges. It is true that a new rule adopted by the then–Democratic-controlled Senate in 2013 made confirmation of federal judges possible by a simple majority vote, but that was not the end of the matter. The Senate also has a so-called blue slip custom whereby a senator can block the nomination of a federal judge to be appointed within his or her state. A 2011 survey by Public Policy Polling in a cross-section of 10 states found that 81 percent of respondents felt the Senate "does not deal with important issues facing the country in a timely manner," and by a 62 percent to 20 percent margin that there should be only one opportunity to filibuster a bill instead of four, as current Senate rules allow. Regarding the judiciary, the poll found that, by a 75 percent to 17 percent margin, "people who have been nominated to serve as judges have an up or down vote on their nomination in a more timely manner."[5]

Reforming Medicare and Social Security to Keep Them Solvent in the Current Century

We discussed protecting the social safety net in Chapter 7 and noted that those on the far right would to be happy to completely revamp the system, for example, by replacing Social Security with a 401(k) retirement plan or something similar. That might not be the case with Medicare, but conservatives might well reduce its benefits and make all retirees foot more of the bill. Because of the spiraling costs of these programs, especially as the population ages and more and more baby boomers participate in them, some difficult but realistic changes seem unavoidable. Perhaps no issue among those being considered in this chapter is more complex, emotional, and seemingly insoluble. But the current generation of senior Americans and the Congress owe it to the millennial generation to make painful decisions to rescue and reform these two immensely beneficial programs. One among many suggestions is to increase the top salary from which SSI deductions are made. It is currently $118,500, but more and more upper middle-class individuals are making well above that amount and need to pay their fair share. Also, the wealthy should be expected to pay a larger share of their medical expenses within the Medicare program. This issue is, of course, tied to the challenge of balancing the federal budget, discussed above.

"London Bridge Is Falling Down"—Repairing Our Crumbling Infrastructure

This issue might not seem of concern to everyone, because conservatives are reluctant to raise the taxes needed (e.g., by raising the gasoline tax) to repair the nation's infrastructure. They would like to see other expenditures (Social Security, Medicare, food stamps, etc.) reduced before spending more on bridges and roads, and such spending has been reduced significantly in recent years. In fact, however, the entire nation is in serious danger from collapsing bridges, unrepaired highways, inefficient electrical grids, and aging water mains. An estimated sixty thousand bridges (more than 10 percent of the total) are in serious need of repair. On August 2, 2007, a major bridge in Minneapolis on Interstate 35W collapsed over the Mississippi River killing seven people and injuring at least 60 more. A significant water main bursts on average every two minutes somewhere in the United States, resulting in 6 billion gallons of water wasted per day.[6] At this writing, the National Highway Traffic Safety Administration was nearly out of money. As usual, there will be a temporary fix, but this is no way to run a railroad or a government.

Improving Our Educational System from Pre-K through Graduate School

The American educational system was once the envy of the world, which is still the case in our colleges and universities. However, the pre-K through high school picture is far less stellar. Some rankings may help illustrate this:

- The United States ranks fourteenth in cognitive skills and educational attainment out of 40 ranked countries.
- In overall educational performance, we rank seventeenth.
- The average reading literacy score for U.S. 15-year-old students is 498 out of 1,000, putting us in twenty-fourth place.
- And we are in eleventh place in fourth-grade math proficiency.

A principal reason for these discouraging numbers is the socioeconomic disparity in American society. In affluent parts of the country—which really means rich neighborhoods from city to city and state to state—schools are well equipped, teachers are happy to teach there, and fringe benefits abound. And students from these school districts are college-bound more often than in poorer districts. But America is still a very segregated society, so school districts with high rates of unemployment, poverty, and homelessness feel the effects in behavior problems, truancy, fewer pre-K programs, poor diets, and the presence of gangs, among other issues. Though considerable effort by federal and state agencies has gone into remedying these disparities, they remain to some extent intractable. Still, a strong consensus exists that we must do better as a nation.

In a new book, *Our Kids: The American Dream in Crisis*,[7] the distinguished sociologist Robert Putnam paints a grim picture of how serious this issue is. Basing his conclusions on a wide-ranging sociological survey, Putnam reports that poor children are missing more than just tangible goods. They have few mentors and are half as likely as rich kids to trust their neighbors; and their schools offer fewer competitive sports, so they are less likely to take part in after-school programs. The study also reports that more than 60 percent of children whose mother's education ended after high school will now spend at least some of their life by age seven in a one-parent household. In the 1970s, Putnam notes, there was very little difference in how much time educated and less-educated parents spent on activities such as reading to infants and toddlers that matters so much to intellectual development. Today, however, affluent children receive 45 minutes more per day than poor ones on reading and other parent–child activities. Putnam is hoping to make unequal opportunity for children the central issue in the 2016 presidential election. A quixotic goal perhaps, but when one looks around at this educational disparity, especially in black and Latino neighborhoods, one realizes how much America's future will depend on closing this awful gap.

When it comes to college, cost is perhaps the biggest problem across the country, and it has risen dramatically in the past 20 years. In 2013–14, the median published tuition and fee price at public and private four-year institutions was $11,093.[8] Room and board adds several thousand dollars more. Of course, tuition at elite universities and in graduate and professional schools is considerably higher. All of this has created a student loan crisis burdening more than 41 million Americans and adding up to $1.3 trillion in total indebtedness that puts many young people in a kind of servitude. Former Florida governor and presidential candidate Jeb Bush paid just $100 a year in tuition at the University of Texas in the early 1970s. Today an in-state undergraduate pays over $18,000 at the same school,[9] and the average debt of a graduating student is $33,000. A young health professional and friend of co-author Ben Hubbard reports that she may never get out of debt and never own her own home. This, after eight years of higher education. President Obama has proposed a Student Aid Bill of Rights that would add transparency to the loan process, but whether the current Republican Congress will give the proposal serious consideration is uncertain.

Preventing Bullying and Cyberbullying

Bullying appears to be a part of our human communal nature that will never be completely eliminated but can be reduced and blunted. It typically involves intense or continuous aggression, direct or indirect, that may be physical, verbal, or nonverbal, especially by way of gestures. The aim is always negative and malicious, and frequently involves a power imbalance between the parties involved. The result of such bullying can be serious and cause long-term emotional, physical, and academic consequences. As many as 30 percent of schoolchildren are either bullies or victims of bullying, and one hundred sixty thousand kids stay home daily because of fear of being bullied. One of the missions of the Southern Poverty Law Center, among other religious and communal organizations, is to prevent bullying, especially against LGBT youth and racial minorities. Their *Teaching Tolerance Magazine* is distributed twice yearly to four hundred fifty thousand schools in all 50 states and Canada. (However, even as widely respected an organization as the SPLC has its conservative critics, for example, the Family Research Council. According to the FRC, "Teaching Tolerance program materials, sample curricula, and resources focus disproportionately on conveying acceptance of the Lesbian, Gay, Bi-sexual and Transgender [LGBT] community."[10] Once again, the religious and ethical debate over the acceptability of the LGBT lifestyle becomes a factor even in a discussion of a problem that matters to most everyone in the nation.)

A new and ominous aspect of bullying, cyberbullying, has evolved over the past 20 years as a tragic by-product of the creation of the World Wide Web. According to the National Crime Prevention Council, 43 percent of teens report having been victims of cyberbullying in the past year. Like real-world bullying, the Internet variety may include sending hurtful, hateful, derogatory, harassing, or threatening messages to others; spreading rumors about them; and/or sending personal or embarrassing information about, or pictures of, other individuals with the intent of intimidating, frightening, ridiculing, or harming them.[11] About 70 percent of students report seeing frequent bullying on the Web, and 81 percent think online bullying is easier to get away with than the in-person variety. Children who were bullied in the real or virtual worlds suffer as a result in ways that can interfere with their social and emotional development, along with their school performance. And bullying victims are two to nine times more likely to consider committing suicide.

Remedying the Severe Problems of Poverty and Homelessness, Especially Affecting Children

A November 2014 report by the National Center on Family Homelessness provides a really shocking statistic: One child in 30 (or nearly 2.5 million) was homeless—that is, either on the street or without permanent housing—at some point in 2013. In fact, homelessness increased by

8 percent between 2012 and 2013. This will inevitably produce devastating effects on children's educational, emotional, physical, and social development, as well is on their parents' health, employment prospects, and parenting abilities.[12] That, in turn, will have long-term consequences on society, especially regarding school drop-out rates, teen pregnancy, crime, and poverty.

A single mother in her late 20s with two children is the most common family type experiencing homelessness. A January 2013 census of the homeless in Los Angeles, found that 39,463 people were sleeping on the street or in shelters, and another 18,000 were "precariously housed," that is, in grave danger of ending up on the street. Author Ben Hubbard will never forget taking a group of Japanese exchange students to Little Tokyo in Los Angeles several years ago and seeing the shock on the students' faces as we passed through skid row. We are shocked as a nation and must do better. Everyone agrees, but solutions are elusive, though a realistic living wage and more public housing would help considerably.

Combating the Plague of Alcohol and Drug Addiction

We tried prohibition in the 1920s, but the Eighteenth Amendment banning alcohol was repealed by the Twenty-First in 1933; yet, alcoholism remains a huge problem. Author Ben Hubbard attended the funeral of a friend and recovering alcoholic in October 2014. The event was a de facto Alcoholics Anonymous (AA) meeting in which several recovering alcoholics paid tribute to their deceased friend and indicated how many years they'd been sober. The group included a Hollywood producer, a member of a famous musical group, and ordinary citizens. Although alcohol had been a problem for some of his own family members and friends, this was the first time Hubbard had experienced AA up close and realized both the depth of the problem and the hope for recovery that AA and other therapies provide. Alcohol continues to be the leading cause of motor vehicle deaths and injuries, and contributes to criminal activity, date rape, family violence, divorce, and other problems. We stress its seriousness here because it is so widespread yet, in one sense, so taken for granted. The tragedy is that so few young people—in families that consider moderate drinking acceptable—are taught at home how to drink responsibly. No American celebrates alcoholism and problem drinking, yet the problem cries out for expanded treatment programs and better education about its potential dangers.

The war on drugs that began in the 1970s under President Nixon has, on the one hand, partly contributed to a one-third drop in the illegal drug use since then. On the other, it has cost over $1 trillion, filled our prisons with marijuana smokers and cocaine addicts, and given America the highest per capita incarceration rate in the world. The country is finally beginning to come to its senses about the futility of locking up so many individuals, most of whom needed treatment not prison. Once again, however, as with the educational disparity discussed above, poverty is a breeding ground for drug use. Nonetheless, drugs are everywhere—in our high schools, colleges, at rock concerts, and in affluent suburbs. Ten percent of eighth graders report they have used drugs in the past month. One in eight weekend drivers will test positive for an illicit drug when stopped by law enforcement. The estimated business cost *per second* in lost business productivity, health care expenses, and so on, from drug abuse is $6,120. The legalization of recreational marijuana in Washington State, Oregon, Colorado, and Alaska, and of medical marijuana in 19 other states, may prove to be a step in the right direction. But almost any adolescent in the country can get the weed easily; and long-term use can result in abnormal changes in brain structure that damages one's memory.[13]

As if the epidemic of illegal drugs were not enough, the abuse of prescription drugs, for example, OxyContin, has reached crisis levels. Every day, 50 people die from overdosing on a prescription drug and six million suffer from abuse of these drugs. In March 2015, Senators Rob Portman (R-OH) and Sheldon Whitehouse (D-RI) began a campaign for passage of the Comprehensive Addiction and Recovery Act (CARA). The act would expand prevention and educational efforts—particularly aimed at teens, parents, and aging populations—to prevent the abuse of opioids and heroine and to promote treatment and recovery. It would also expand the availability of naloxone to law enforcement agencies and other first responders to assist in the reversal of overdoses to save lives.[14]

People use drugs and alcohol for many reasons—pleasure, thrills, escapism, self-medicating to blunt emotional problems, or to mask the lack of meaning in their lives. And the solutions, none perfect, include supportive families, teachers, mentors, and clergy; counselors and therapists; and a more level economic playing field. Unless the American left, right, and center commit to addressing, even in small ways, this plague of addiction, we are in for more national heartache.

Weakening the Grip of Gangs on Our Inner Cities

This common concern flows out of the last, the addiction plague, because gangs thrive on drug trafficking and attract young people who can find no other meaning in their lives. The National Youth Gang Survey's most recent analysis estimates that there are 850,000 gang members, two-thirds of whom live in larger cities and suburban counties. The total number of gang-connected homicides averaged nearly 2,000 from 2007 to 2012. Since on average there are about 15,500 homicides yearly in the United States, gang-related murders, accounted for about 13 percent of the total. However, in Chicago and Los Angeles, half of the homicides involved gangs.[15] And so in these cities and other large metropolitan areas, there are no-go areas where, especially at night, you enter at your own risk. This is a dirty little secret that we don't want to talk about but that spawns a kind of inner-city terrorism among the innocent heart, hard-working people who live there.

Blunting the Appeal and Violence of Hate Groups

The Southern Poverty Law Center reported the existence of 784 hate groups in 2014, down from the previous few years but significantly higher since Barack Obama became president. All of these groups espouse beliefs or practices that attack or malign an entire group of people, usually for their immutable racial characteristics.[16] Most despise African Americans and other racial minorities, Jews, and the LGBT community. One organization, the Institute for Historical Review, is dedicated to questioning the existence of the Holocaust (or at least its severity). Although in a given year these groups do not carry out a large number of violent acts, they do so occasionally in vicious ways. In 1998, James Byrd Jr., a black man, was beaten, chained behind a pickup truck, and dragged 1.5 miles by two known white supremacists and a third man and died when his head hit an object in the road and was severed. That same year, Matthew Shepard, a gay 21-year-old student at the University of Wyoming, was beaten and tortured, strapped to a fence and left to die. His assailants had expressed antigay sentiments. These two heinous murders led to the passage in 2009 of federal legislation, the Matthew Shepard and James Byrd Jr. Hate Crime Prevention Act. According to the Bureau of Justice Statistics, there were about two hundred sixty thousand reported and unreported hate crimes in 2012.[17] The climate of fear and animosity perpetrated by hate groups creates a toxic atmosphere in society and makes racial, ethnic, and religious minorities feel like they don't belong here.

Combating Human Trafficking Both Abroad and on Our Nation's Streets

The trafficking or enslavement of human beings is a worldwide problem and has, of course, a tragic history in the United States. An estimated seventeen thousand persons are trafficked to or within our nation yearly, most of whom are women and children to be used for sexual purposes, though forced labor is another aspect of the problem. The causes are closely related to our earlier discussion of poverty, homelessness, and lack of economic opportunity. Desperate and vulnerable individuals are tricked by the promise of a legitimate job and are ensnared before they know it. As many as three hundred thousand American youth are at risk of becoming victims of this practice. Sex trafficking, the core of the problem, is the fastest growing business of organized crime and the third largest criminal enterprise in the world according to the FBI.[18] In January 2006, the Trafficking Victims Protection Reauthorization Act became federal law and has had some impact on the problem. In March 2015, the Senate, with bipartisan support, was about to pass the Justice for Victims of Trafficking Act (approved earlier by the House). The act was intended to change the federal criminal code by making the soliciting of sex from a trafficking victim a crime equivalent to sex trafficking itself, even when a defendant doesn't know the individual was forced to do so. It also authorizes and funds a variety of community, state, and federal initiatives aimed at prosecuting human trafficking, along with efforts to fight other illicit sexual conduct, illicit e-commerce, and cybercrime. Although some critics think the act spread too wide and complex a net, the legislation had a motherhood-apple pie quality that should have made passage relatively easy. However, buried in the recesses of the lengthy bill was a provision prohibiting any funding for abortion if, for example, a trafficking victim becomes pregnant. Democrats, who were not at first aware of that clause, said they will not vote for the act unless it was removed. Majority leader Mitch McConnell responded by saying he would not bring up for a vote the confirmation of Atty. Gen.–designate Loretta Lynch until the bill in its present form passed. Eventually a compromise was reached, Obama signed it on May 29, 2015, and Lynch was confirmed on April 27 after waiting more than five months . Even though this story finally had a happy ending, the old Washington tit-for-tat game was again on full display .

Addressing All Forms of Religious Persecution, Especially Widespread Anti-Semitism and Anti-Christian Persecution in the Middle East

Anti-Semitism has been called "the longest hate," and its history is persistent and tragic, stretching from the persecutions and expulsions of the Middle Ages to the Holocaust. After World War II, Germany and the rest of the Western world began examining its corporate conscience about the extent to which denigration and hatred of Jews over many centuries—often inspired by the false notion of Jews as "Christ killers"—had provided the ground for the Nazis' final solution to the Jewish problem. In the postwar era, beginning especially in the 1960s and 1970s, there was tremendous growth in Christian–Jewish understanding and dialogue, and more accurate Christian scholarship about the role of Jews in Jesus's crucifixion and the deep Jewish roots of Christianity. A document of the Second Vatican Council, "In Our Era" (*Nostra Aetate,* 1965), made clear the predominant role of the Romans in the death of Jesus and the need for Catholic–Jewish dialogue and cooperation.

In the past 15 years, however, hatred of Jews has returned to Europe with vandalism and physical attacks perpetrated, in particular, by extremist elements of Europe's growing Muslim community. In summer 2014, demonstrators in the German cities of Dortmund and Frankfurt chanted, "Hamas, Hamas; Jews to the gas." On the eve of Bastille Day that year, a group of Parisian Jews were trapped in a synagogue by a pro-Palestinian mob and had to be rescued by police. In March 2012, four people were murdered in a Jewish day school in Toulouse, France, and the Jewish community center there was firebombed in July 2014. Then there was the killing of four Jews in a Parisian kosher market on January 7, 2015, the same day seven others (one of whom was Jewish) were slaughtered at the offices of satirical journal *Charlie Hebdo.* As distinguished Holocaust scholar Deborah Lipstadt wrote in the *New York Times,* "70 years after the Holocaust, many Jews in Europe no longer feel safe. Hiring an armed guard to protect people coming for weekly prayer is not the action of a secure people."[19] In a powerful essay in *The Atlantic,* Jeffrey Goldberg surveys the alarming extent of reborn anti-Semitism on the continent and asks in the title, "Is it time for the Jews to leave Europe?" Goldberg concludes the piece this way:

I am predisposed to believe that there is no great future for the Jews in Europe, because evidence to support this belief is accumulating so quickly. But I am also predisposed to think this because I am an American Jew—which is to say, a person who exists because his ancestors made a run for it when they could.[20]

In the contemporary Muslim world, Christians have also felt the wrath of extremist Islam. Nine of the ten countries with the worst records for persecution of Christians include populations that are at least 50 percent Muslim, according to an assessment by Open Door USA's World Watch List 2015 and information published by the State Department and the Central Intelligence Agency. (North Korea placed first on the list.) An estimated 100 million Christians are persecuted worldwide and as many as one hundred thousand are killed yearly, making them the most vilified religious group in the world. Since the U.S. invasion of Iraq in 2013, over 70 percent of Christians have fled the country, and seven hundred thousand Syrian

Christians have left there since the Civil War began in 2011. According to Open Doors, this persecution included beatings, physical torture, confinement, isolation, rape, severe punishment, imprisonment, slavery, discrimination in education and employment, and even death.

After finishing medical school in Egypt, author Ben Hubbard's former ophthalmologist, a Coptic Christian, was accepted into a residency program for eye doctors. But he was told by the program's Muslim director that he could expect no help or encouragement in finishing his training. He left for England and ultimately ended up finishing his ophthalmology studies in America. So it is no surprise that a century ago the Christian population of the Middle East was 20 percent while today it is 5 percent. Undoubtedly, the legacy of Western colonialism in the Mideast, the invasion of Iraq and the plague of dictatorships in so many of these countries has contributed to the persecution of Christians. Moreover, as we will discuss shortly, many thousands of Muslims, too, have felt the wrath of radical Islam. Tragically, Islam, with a rich history of tolerance and scientific achievement in the Middle Ages, is now in the grip of fanatical forces such as Al Qaeda, the so-called Islamic State, Hamas, Hezbollah, Boko Haram, and similar groups that hate the United States, Israel, and Western culture and have come to see Christianity as the enemy of Islam.

Ironically, Muslims in Europe have also felt the sting of persecution and discrimination from right-wing groups. Most of them immigrated there for economic reasons and have often been marginalized, especially in France with its large population of Muslims originating from North Africa. In some instances, European Jewish and Muslims organizations have cooperated in maintaining kosher and halal animal slaughtering customs, as well as circumcision. Jewish and Muslim social-media groups known as Salaam-Shalom have begun in several countries. But this is a still small voice.

The Islamic state, though Sunni Muslim in orientation, persecutes any Muslim in Iraq and Syria who does not conform to its fanatical and fundamentalist interpretation of the religion. In March 2015, two mosques in Yemen were bombed in the midst of Friday prayer, killing 135 of the faithful and wounding hundreds more. When religion becomes cancerous, it can generate a particularly vile kind of hatred.

Confronting Terrorism in All Its Forms

During his military service in the early 1960s, author Ben Hubbard was able while in uniform to carry an unloaded .45 caliber pistol onto a commercial airliner. Oh, how the world has changed since then. Every time someone passes through security at an airport, they are aware that we live in a world always somewhat on edge—and in some parts of the world very much so. Suicide terror seemed almost unimaginable back in the 1960s, even though most of us had heard of Japan's kamikaze pilots and their willingness to die for the Japanese Emperor during World War II. Today, terror attacks and attempted attacks worldwide are very imaginable. The murder of nearly three thousand people on September 11, 2001, has shaped the American psyche like no event since the attack on Pearl Harbor on December 7, 1941. The other major terrors on U.S. soil—the bombing of the Alfred P. Murrah Federal Building in Oklahoma City in 1995, the first World Trade Center attack in 1993, and the Boston Marathon bombing in 2013—have all been horrific, but 9/11 is in a unique category.[21] Estimates of foiled plots vary, but there had been at least 60 through 2013. Among these, the so-called shoe bomber, underwear bomber, and SUV plotter in New York's Times Square stand out. Israel has felt the wrath of terror attacks over the past quarter century, as have Iraq, Pakistan, and so many other countries. It is an unimaginable kind of evil that everyone in the civilized world decries and that is abhorred by people of all political, religious, and ideological persuasions with the exception of a tiny group of fanatics poisoned by hate.

Although Islamist extremism has been the source of almost all these attacks and foiled attacks, antigovernment extremist Timothy McVeigh bombed the Murrah Building, killing 168 people, including 19 children, and injuring 450 others. There was a rush to judgment that the act must have been committed by Islamic extremists, but in this case the hate-group ideology discussed above triggered a terrible massacre.

Other issues that matter to the left, right, and center might have been analyzed here: reform of our prison system, greatly expanded facilities for the seriously mentally ill, the high rate of suicides, the ongoing slaughter of elephants and rhinoceroses in Africa that feeds the commercial ivory trade, and the hookup culture that exacerbates sexually transmitted diseases (STDs). Hopefully, however, the point of the preceding exercise is clear.

Reflections on the Issues That Matter

We would not reach utopia if these common problems were significantly alleviated, but our nation and the world would be immensely healthier and safer. Almost everyone—left, right, and center—cares about the issues described here. Their solutions would differ to some extent; but the overlap is immense and, we hope, demonstrates that making common cause to alleviate them might bring liberals and conservatives closer together. This, in turn, could help them think more empathetically and seriously about why particular issues are of great concern to the other side, and not scoff at and dismiss what matters to the political and cultural "other." We live in an age of widespread political cynicism and distrust. President Reagan ironically quoted a Russian proverb while commenting on negotiations with the former Soviet Union: "Trust, but verify." Both trust and verification are indispensable in the political arena, yet we have had far too little of either.

THE POTENTIAL OF THE "NO LABELS" MOVEMENT

The nonpartisan, nonprofit organization No Labels, though not without its detractors, has real potential to bring conservatives, liberals, and independents together with a philosophy emphasizing cooperation, efficient government, and civility. Founded in 2010 by Nancy Jacobson, a Democratic fund-raiser, Mark McKinnon, a Republican political strategist, and former U.S. Comptroller David Walker, its goal is to move from the old politics of point scoring toward a new one of problem solving. It hopes to do this by getting politicians from across the political spectrum to work together to solve common problems (for example, the gargantuan national debt).

On December 13, 2011, No Labels issued an action plan, "Make Congress Work," that included four major goals:

1. Create 25 million new jobs over the next ten years.
2. Balance the federal budget by 2030.
3. Secure Medicare and Social Security for the next 75 years.
4. Make the United States energy-secure by 2024.[22]

It hopes to get the House of Representatives to pass a resolution "expressing the sense of the House . . . regarding establishing a National Strategic Agenda" (anchored in the four goals above). A petition to that effect is circulating online.

It includes such items as automatic pay-docking for Congress if the federal budget is not passed on time, an up-or-down vote on all presidential appointments within 90 days of their nomination, five-day work weeks for Congress, and a bipartisan leadership council similar to one proposed by former Senator Olympia Snowe of Maine. The following year, No Labels offered suggestions for making the presidency work better, for example, by instituting a question time between Congress and the president similar to what happens in parliamentary systems. On its website, the organization lists nine proposals for increased efficiency and cost saving in government, for example, "don't duplicate, consolidate," that would eliminate duplicate federal agencies and programs identified in 2013 by the Government Accountability Office.

The organization is now cochaired by former Utah governor and 2012 Republican presidential candidate Jon Huntsman and Senator Joe Manchin (D-WV). It published an e-book in 2014, *No Labels: A Shared Vision for a Stronger America*.[23] The book restates the movement's goals, especially the need for problem solvers to change U.S. politics by finding shared goals before the policy-making process begins. No Labels also has a weekly online radio program hosted by Huntsman. The group, which boasts five hundred thousand members and 87-plus members of Congress, can claim one legislative victory: "No Budget, No Pay" became law in February 2013. It directed both the House and the Senate to adopt a budget for fiscal 2014 but did not require a budget conference. If not accomplished, members' pay will be held in escrow, though not docked permanently, as No Labels had proposed. Moreover, a growing number of moderate Blue Dog Democrats and the Tuesday Group of moderate Republicans now hold meetings once a month.

Nonetheless, according to Senator Susan Collins (R-ME) and media observers, of the group's $4.5 million budget for 2014, only 4 percent was slated for "Congressional relations."[24] The rest went for administrative expenses, travel, and fund-raising. As an example of its missteps, the organization gave its "Problem Solver Seal" in April 2014 to Republican Senator Cory Gardner of Colorado, who was then challenging Democratic incumbent Mark Udall. Gardner then boasted of the seal as an election endorsement from No Labels, which incensed the Senate Democratic caucus. Needless to say, No Labels was forced to clarify the matter. So this new, idealistic organization is experiencing real growing pains. And it remains to be seen whether or not it can help spur a return to civility and cooperation in Washington any time soon. It is one thing for individual members of Congress to reach across the aisle in the name of bipartisanship, but it is another when the congressional leadership of one's party begins leaning on the member not to get out front of the party caucus. In fact, that's precisely what happened during the government shutdown in fall 2013 when No Labels congressional members were told to back off from their efforts to end the shameful gridlock. Civility in theory is attractive, but on the ground, in the halls of Congress, it is immensely challenging. Nonetheless, efforts at consensus—such as that being attempted by No Labels—must be made by legislators and citizens, because not doing so is an abdication of responsibility with dire consequences.

THE RISE IN THE PERCENTAGE OF "INDEPENDENT" VOTERS

Chapter 6 began with a discussion of the dramatic increase in polarization among the electorate, with 21 percent expressing either consistently conservative or liberal opinions in 2014, compared to 10 percent in 1994 according to a Pew survey. A corollary of this phenomenon is the increase in the number of voters who identify as independents. In a 2013 Gallup poll, 42 percent of about eighteen thousand respondents identified as political independents, the highest percentage since the organization began conducting interviews by telephone 25 years ago. At 31 percent, democratic identification has remained fairly stable over many years, though it peaked at 36 percent in 2008, the year President Obama was first elected. The Republican tally fell to 25 percent, the lowest in 25 years and nine points below its high of 34 percent at the start of George W. Bush's second term in 2004. When Gallup then asked about how these independents were "leaning," Democrats had a 47 percent to 41 percent advantage.[25] One conclusion is that party affiliation simply does not mean as much as it did in the past, because the two major parties have lost much of their credibility. There is, of course, nothing wrong with being an independent, but such folks usually don't go to political meetings and rallies or donate to candidates. In fact, one prominent political theory known as "dealignment," argues that political parties play a crucial supportive role in democracies by regulating the type and number of people seeking election, mobilizing voter turnout, and providing the kind of coalition-building that enables officeholders to govern parties. They also serve as reference points for voters by framing issues and supplying and filtering information. Without parties, candidates rely more heavily on mass media (with its simplistic sound bites) for communication, and political action committees (PACs) for funds (as noted elsewhere in this study). Ticket-splitting becomes more common, resulting in divided government and making the implementation of policies even more difficult.[26]

THE LOSS OF PRAGMATISM IN AMERICAN POLITICS

Pragmatism was a philosophical tradition popular in the late nineteenth and early twentieth centuries, especially as articulated by Charles S. Peirce, William James, and John Dewey. It emphasized what James called "the cash value of an idea." It was a practical philosophy that mirrored the down-to-earth, roll-up-your-sleeves temperament of the American people. It helped the nation recover from the Great Depression in the 1930s through the Work Projects Administration (WPA) and the establishment of the Social Security system. It inspired America to enact the Marshall Plan that did so much to rescue Europe from the ravages of World War II, and the G.I. Bill that made a university education possible for a huge segment of the public that once considered it unattainable. Pragmatism was also the impetus for the Peace Corps that sent young idealistic Americans to impoverished regions of the world and burnished our nation's image. There was also the pragmatism of President (and former five-star general) Dwight D. Eisenhower who cautioned the nation about the growing power of the "military-industrial complex." Despite his tragic flaws, President Richard M. Nixon inaugurated the Environmental Protection Agency in 1970 and initiated the historic opening to China.

President Ronald Reagan and House Speaker Tip O'Neill were also superb pragmatists who, despite huge ideological differences and some personal animus, got things done in Washington during their joint tenure, 1980–86. They worked their way to agreements that reformed the tax code, saved Social Security, and helped achieve their common cause of bringing peace to Northern Ireland. O'Neill's behind-the scene support helped Reagan engineer his historic Cold War–ending bond with Soviet leader Mikhail Gorbachev.[27] Finally, President Bill Clinton and House Speaker Newt Gingrich, though sometimes battling bitterly in public, managed to cooperate on historic welfare reform legislation and on balancing the federal budget, a feat never again achieved.

Where is the pragmatism today? President Obama and Speaker John Boehner might play a round of golf once in a while, but they're not getting very much of the people's business done. Liberals will point to the obstructionism in Congress that faced Obama from the moment he became president; conservatives will note Obama's penchant for going it alone on health care, immigration, and other issues. Neither has shown sufficient skill in the art of compromise, the art of the possible.

NOTES

1. www.cbo.gov/publication/45471. In 2025, federal spending on major health and retirement programs and interest on the debt will account for 67 percent of total federal spending. See www.fixthedebt.org/blog/warnings-on-the-debt -grow_#1.VPjhieGz_g2.

2. www.concordecoalition.org/. Retrieved June 9, 2015. Compare this organization's goals on deficit reduction to those of the group No Labels, as discussed in Chapter 12.

3. www.people-press.org/2015/03/04/most-say-government-policies-since -recession-have-done-little-to-help-middle-class-poor/modest-change-in-views -of-recession-personal-impact/.

4. Lester R. Brown, *The Great Transition—Shifting from Fossil Fuels to Solar and Wind Energy*. Washington, DC: Earth Policy Institute, 2015. Also see www .earth-policy.org.

5. www.fixtheSenatenow.org/news/entry/American-public-strongly-backs -us-senate-rules-reform#.VP4YT_nF9wU.

6. www.bafuture.org/facts-quotes/all?page=3.

7. New York: Simon and Schuster, 2015.

8. www.trends.collegeboard.org/sites/default/files/college-pricing-2013-full-report.pdf.

9. www.finaid.txstate.edu/undergraduate/cost.html.

10. www.frc.org/issuebriefs/southern-poverty-law-centers-teaching-tolerance-project. Retrieved April 14, 2015.

11. www.mass.gov/ago/about-the-attorney-generals-office/community-programs/bullying-and-cyber bullying/cyber bullying.html. Retrieved April 14, 2015.

12. www.huffingtonpost.com/2014/11/17/children-homelessness-us_n_6169994.html

13. www.psychologytoday.com/blog/the-athletes-way/201403/heavy-marijuana-use-alters-teenage-brain-structure.

14. www.portman.senate.gov/public/index.cfm/2015/2/portman-and-white house-renew-push-to-combat-drug-addiction-and-support-Americans-in-recovery.

15. www.nationalgangcenter.gov/survey-analysis/measuring-the-extent-of-gang-problems. Retrieved March 16, 2015.

16. www.splc.org/hate-maps.

17. Intelligence Report (published by the Southern Poverty Law Center), spring, 2015, p. 68. The magazine (pp. 43–53) provides a breakdown of the 784 hate groups: Ku Klux Klan (72), Neo-Nazi (142), White Nationalist (115), Racist Skinhead (119), Black Separatist (13), Neo-Confederate (37), Christian Identity (21), and general hate (165).

18. www.huffingtonpost.com/rachna-choudry/slavery-and-human-trafficking-promotion_b_654-3924.html. Posted January 27, 2015.

19. www.nytimes.com/2014/08/21/opinion/deborah-e-lipstadt-on-the-rising-anti-semitism-in-europe.html.

20. *The Atlantic*, April, 2015, p. 75.

21. Army Maj. Nidal Hasan, MD, murdered 13 people and wounded 24 others at Fort Hood, Texas, on November 5, 2009. Hasan seems to have been motivated by the killings of Muslims in the Middle East and a desire to strike back rather than by terrorism in the usual sense.

22. www.nolabels.org/goals-no-labels-national-strategic-agenda/. Retrieved March 23, 2015.

23. Edited by Governor Huntsman. New York: Diversion Books, 2014. Now available in paperback.

24. "Bipartisan Group Finds Bridges Hard to Build" by Tracy Jan. www.bostonglobe.com/news/nation/2013/12/01/bringing-partisan-Warriors-together

25. www.gallup.com/poll/166763/record-high-americans-identify-independents.aspx.

26. http.en.wikipedia.org/wiki/independent_(voter)#Realigning_elections.

27. See Chris Matthews, *Tip and the Gipper: When Politics Worked*. New York: Simon and Schuster, 2013.

Chapter 9

The New Centrists—Can They Rescue Our Struggling Democracy?

In fact, it may be that this religious and political center is one tonic to sustain the entire American experiment, to keep it afloat and somehow renewable in the face of hostile ideologies and depressing news about the environment and the economic system . . . Motivated by faith, but instructed by an inner compass of civic values and experience living in a modern democracy, the moral and religious centrists follow their heads and hearts at the same time. They match up priorities to reach personal decisions that may not always be in lockstep or predictable. Add to this the agnostics and humanists who also are guided by moral considerations, but who may be put off by aspects of organized religion or the posturing of TV evangelists. Regardless of these people's views on the existence of God, they constitute values-based constituencies across a wide spectrum of the population.[1]

In American politics, it has always been the center that holds, that keeps the ship of state afloat, and that resists extremism from either the right or the left. Steve Burgard's (Ben Hubbard writing) eloquent wisdom in the quotation above provides a kind of text for which this chapter is the interpretation. Time and time again, surveys have shown that America is a centrist nation, sometimes tacking to the left, sometimes to the right, but always correcting itself in the long run. However, as the title of this book indicates, the center is currently "endangered" and conflicted as ideologues on both the left and the right in Congress, statehouses, and city councils push agendas based on absolutist views of what is best in government and society.

Washington Post columnist and political philosopher E. J. Dionne describes the period since Teddy Roosevelt assumed the presidency in 1901 the era of the "Long Consensus" that created the American Century. Government grew in this era, but so did individual liberty. The state assumed new roles, but opportunities for individuals grew. "New regulations protected the air and water, the integrity of food and drugs, the safety of workplaces and consumer products—and American capitalism flourished."[2] Moreover, labor unions enhanced a more social form of capitalism producing widespread property ownership and upward mobility. Dionne believes the Long Consensus is under assault from the "individualistic right" that has always been part of American politics but is gaining power in response to the failures of the Bush administration and the liberal policies of Obama's presidency, especially Obamacare.[3]

This assault, in the person of the Tea Party Republican block in Congress, abetted by some progressives lacking the art of the deal—the ability to compromise—has caused that body to be constipated, unable to reach compromises on important issues such as confronting the Islamic State/ISIL by constitutionally approving the president's right to wage war against it or by fixing our broken immigration system; and it often ends up playing chicken with important matters of state, only voting at the last minute on important legislation. At the end of May 2015, for example, the Senate stalled so long that revisions to the 2001 Patriot Act rules about domestic surveillance contained in the new USA Freedom Act expired. The Upper Chamber finally did ratify the House version a few days later, but the entire mechanism for monitoring suspect phone conversations shut down and then had to be restarted. No way to run a railroad, in our view, but certainly the way many in Washington play hardball.

As we discuss in some detail in an excursus to Chapter 10, absolutist religious views have had a significant impact on American politics in the past quarter century. Religion has always influenced politics in this country from the abolitionists to the Christian temperance movement to the civil rights and voting rights struggles to the morality of war and abortion, and to what constitutes a just and compassionate society. In Chapters 1 and 4, we examined some of the controversies and debates that have divided voters. Then in Chapters 6, 7, and 8, we examined what matters most to the right, the left, and "the many," respectively. Although the differences described in Chapters 6 and 7 over abortion, health care, immigration, climate change, and so on, are substantive and not fully reconcilable, the extent of the mutual concerns of the left, the right, and to most of us, discussed in Chapter 8, gives cause for hope. For the fact is, a huge cadre of moderate citizens wants to balance the federal budget in a reasonable time frame, reduce unemployment, make the nation's energy supply largely independent of foreign sources and reliable, keep Medicare and Social Security fiscally secure (even if painful adjustments are necessary), improve our struggling educational system, reduce poverty and homelessness, combat alcohol and drug addiction, eradicate gangs and hate groups, combat human trafficking, end religious persecution worldwide, and eradicate terrorism. As we mentioned in Chapter 8, and will elaborate upon further in Chapter 12, the nonpartisan No Labels movement represents centrist thinking on several of these issues.[4]

PEW SURVEY OF POLARIZATION IN AMERICAN POLITICS

The Pew Research Center's survey of ten thousand adults between January and March 2014 indicated that polarization in the electorate has increased from 39 percent to 49 percent between 1994 and 2014. (The motivation for writing this book stems in part from that dramatic change.) Here are the principal findings of the survey:

1. The portion of Americans who express consistently conservative or consistently liberal opinions has doubled in the past two decades from 10 percent to 21 percent, and the extent of ideological overlap between two parties has shrunk.
2. The share of Republicans expressing very negative opinions of the Democratic Party jumped from 17 percent to 43 percent in the 20-year period, and the share of Democrats with a very unfavorable take on the Republican Party rose 22 points to 38 percent.
3. A favorability index or "ideological silo" has also increased so that 63 percent of consistent conservatives and 49 percent of consistent liberals responded in the survey that most of their close friends share their political views (see further discussion of this phenomenon in Chapter 12).
4. Similarly, three-quarters of consistent conservatives state they would prefer to live in a community where, "the houses are larger and further apart, but [even though] schools, stores and restaurants are several miles away." By a nearly identical margin (77 percent) consistent liberals prefer smaller homes closer to stores, parks, and so on. Nearly four times as many liberals as conservatives say it is important their community has racial and ethnic diversity, while three times as many conservatives as liberals say it is important that a majority in the community share their religious faith.
5. The political center has diminished—39 percent of Americans currently take about an equal number of liberal and conservative positions, down from 49 percent in surveys conducted in 1994 and 2014. However, despite the mixed ideological views of those in the center,

they tend to express very passionate views on such issues as immigration, gun control, and health care policy.

6. The most ideologically oriented Americans carry through their opinions by means of greater participation in every stage of the political process. Voting rates are higher among those on the right than the left on the basis of self-reports, but higher among those on the left than people in the middle. And these highly committed conservative and liberal individuals donate to political campaigns at about twice the national average.

7. Not surprisingly, "compromise" for each side means it gets more of what it wants in the political arena, with 62 percent of liberals saying the ideal compromises between President Obama and the GOP should be closer to what the president wants, and 57 percent of conservatives saying the best deals should be more on GOP terms.[5]

Despite this shrinkage in the political middle, it remains a significant factor and still determines elections. Although 43 percent of registered voters belong to strongly ideological voting blocs (27 percent on the conservative side, 17 percent liberal) neither party has a large enough base to win national elections without extending its appeal to the 57 percent of voters who are less partisan and less predictable. The Pew researchers put it as follows: "The political landscape includes a center that is large and diverse, unified by frustration with politics and little else. As a result, both parties face formidable challenges in reaching beyond their bases to appeal to the middle of the electorate and build sustainable coalitions."[6] For example, the cohort known to political scientists as "young outsiders," who constitute 15 percent of registered voters, lean moderately GOP but diverge from the party on such issues as environmental regulation and gay rights. On the other hand, the so-called hard-pressed skeptics (13 percent of registered voters) are battered by the economy and resentful of government; yet they back more government generosity for the needy. Then comes the "next generation left" (13 percent of voters) who are young and relatively affluent but have reservations about the cost of social programs. Finally, the very religious and racially diverse "faith and family left" (16 percent of voters) are not comfortable with the slow pace of social change. Andrew Kohut, founding director of the Pew Research Center, and his research team conclude that, although Republicans and Democrats have come increasingly to hold different values, enough variability exists in the middle of the electorate to ensure political change. So it is more a matter of the each of the *two political parties* having become more homogeneous in their values and basic beliefs than it is of the *nation overall* being fundamentally divided. In support of his conclusion, Kohut notes that between 2000 and 2012, a period of rapid growth in political polarization, the middle gave four victories to the GOP and three to the Democrats in nationwide elections.[7]

INDEPENDENT VOTERS: CENTRISTS OR MAVERICKS?

A new record was set in 2014 when 43 percent of respondents identified as independents in a Gallup poll of 16,479 adults. That was significantly higher than the number of self-identified Democrats (30 percent) or Republicans (26 percent). Since 2008, the percentage of political independents has steadily increased from 35 percent to the current 43 percent, and both parties have suffered as a result. The decrease in identification with both over recent years is correlated with dissatisfaction with government, according to the poll, and is now seen as one of the most important problems facing the nation. Additionally, trust in government to handle nationwide problems overall is the lowest that Gallup has ever measured, with Americans' favorable ratings of both parties at or near historic lows. *Notice the correlation between increased polarization and growth in the number of independents—the people in the center don't like what they see.*

When the Gallup pollsters asked the respondents how they were leaning politically, 45 percent identified as Democrats and 42 percent Republicans. (The remaining 13 percent were apparently core curmudgeons.) This outcome was among the Democrats' smallest advantage over the past quarter century. (These results seem to indicate that the 2016 presidential election will probably be close and that the state of the economy will be a deciding factor. One is reminded of President Bill Clinton's campaign slogan, "It's the economy, stupid!" Jeffrey M. Jones, author of this Gallup poll, opines that, with Republicans controlling Congress and Democrats the White House, Americans' frustration with the political process is ongoing. He thinks this could mean that the number of independents will continue to increase.[8] The sharp divisions in Congress have also exacerbated another problem—the growth of the "Imperial Presidency," the situation in which a president, Republican or Democrat, frustrated over Congress's inability to pass legislation, takes matters into his own hands and rules by executive order. This was the case with President Obama when in 2012 he initiated the Deferred Action for Childhood Arrivals (DACA). It permitted several million young, undocumented individuals who arrived here before 2007 the right to obtain work permits. In 2014, just after the elections, he attempted a similar maneuver with undocumented adults, Deferred Action for Parents of Americans and Lawful Permanent Residents (DAPA). However, 26 states sued to block this executive order, and a federal district court judge in Texas agreed, as did the U.S. Court of Appeals for the Fifth Circuit. As discussed in Chapter 6, DAPA is on hold and effectively blocked unless the Supreme Court eventually takes it up.

Whether divided government will persist after the 2016 elections remains to be seen, but it very well might. Hence, the themes of this book: Better communication between the parties, greater willingness to make painful compromises, and more commitment to the "general Welfare" must develop if effective government is to endure.

In an informal 2012 CNN poll of one hundred independents, they listed the following as reasons for their political stance: not wanting to be labeled, which can lead people to make assumptions about one's opinion on various issues; voting for the lesser of two evils, indicating dissatisfaction with both major parties; not wanting to be restricted by either parties' platform; feeling lost politically and disillusioned with both parties; and the need to remain a free thinker politically.[9] Here again, a sense of frustration with politics as currently practiced is evident.

So, how do we answer our own question? Are independents capable of forming a moral middle of pragmatic voters, frustrated with the machinations and indecisive stalling of both parties, but potentially able to force them to tack more to the center and care more about the greater good than the party's good? We think so, but the billion-dollar avalanche of campaign spending that lies ahead in the 2016 election, the "gotcha" politics of Fox News Channel and to some extent MSNBC, right-wing radio commentators such as Rush Limbaugh, and the ongoing values debates still percolating are daunting challenges. Nor are those on the left without sin, such as comedian Bill Maher whose sweeping denunciation of much of the Muslim world goes too far. The 24-hour news cycle, the deluge of often-nasty political commentary on the Internet, blogs, Twitter, and Facebook, all make it difficult for centrists to arrive at fair and accurate conclusions about public affairs.

VOTER TURNOUT AS A SYMPTOM OF FRUSTRATION WITH POLITICS

Voter turnout of 36.4 percent in the 2014 midterm elections was the lowest since 1942 (as World War II raged) at 33.9 and has been dropping ever since the high of 49 percent in 1964. Turnout is higher during presidential election years: 59 percent[10] in 2012 versus 63 percent in 2008, 61 percent in 2004, but only 55 percent in 2000. Among the affluent nations in the Organization for Economic Development and Cooperation, the U.S. ranked thirty-first of 34 nations, although six of these have compulsory voting. Political observers offer the following reasons for low voter turnout:

1. Disillusionment and frustration with the entire political process (including its polarization), along with the perception that the "ruling class" determines elections. For example, it costs between $1.6 and $2 million to mount a campaign for the House and approximately $10.4 million for a Senate run. And, as noted earlier, Congress members spend a disproportionate amount of their time raising money for their reelections.

2. The perception that corruption and influence peddling is rampant in Washington and that campaign promises are often not fulfilled.

3. The current single-party dominance in 38 of the 50 states where the governorship and the legislature belong to the same party. Why vote if you're in the minority in such a state?

4. The fact that voter registration is a two-step process in every state except Minnesota—where a person can register to vote while getting a driver's license, and can even register on election day—and Oregon, which permits online registration. In most of the rest of the democratic world the government knows the names, ages, and addresses of its citizens and registers them automatically. Not so in the United States where no such records exist.

5. Holding elections on Tuesdays. In 1845, Congress established the first Tuesday after the first Monday in November as the nationwide date for federal elections. Back then, most Americans lived on farms, and it could take all day to get to the county seat to vote. Moreover, many Americans observed the Sabbath ban on travel, so Tuesday provided the white male farmers, who alone had suffrage, the most realistic voting day. Today, consequently, unless a working person votes absentee, they must get to the polls either before work or afterward (though some companies do allow time off to vote during working hours).

6. The disenfranchisement of felons. Among 31 developed democracies, ours is the only one barring felons for life from voting in at least some states. Eleven of those 31 countries, including Canada and the states of Maine and Vermont, allow felons to vote from prison. Most states let felons vote after being released from prison, but in four states ex-felons are barred for life from voting. More than 3 million convicts and ex-cons who had not regained their right to vote came from six neighboring southern states—Alabama, Florida, Kentucky, Mississippi, Tennessee, and Virginia. As a result of this felon disenfranchisement, 23 percent of blacks in Florida, 22 percent in Kentucky, and 20 percent in Virginia were barred from voting, a rate four times higher than for the non–African American population.[11] This smacks of Jim Crow racism.

Absentee balloting has been a significant boost to voter participation, but one has to wonder why the technology to permit secure online voting has not been developed. We pay bills with online banking and use credit cards to make Internet purchases. Though computer hacking poses challenges to online voting, the digital gurus in Silicon Valley and Seattle ought to be challenged to come up with a solution.

IS THERE A CORRELATION BETWEEN POLITICAL "NONES" AND RELIGIOUS "NONES"?

A Pew Research Center report, "America's Changing Religious Landscape,"[12] reflects a sharp drop in the number of Americans affiliated with a religion. The Christian share of the U.S. population is declining while the number of adults not identifying with any organized religion is growing. Further, these changes are taking place across the whole religious landscape and are affecting all parts of the country and many demographic groups. The drop in Christian affiliation is particularly pronounced among younger adults but is happening among Americans of all ages and ethnicities, both college graduates and those with only a high school education, and among women as well as men. Between 2007 and 2014, the Christian portion of the population dropped from 78.4 percent to 70.6 percent, mainly through declines among mainline (liberal) Protestants and Catholics.[13] Correspondingly, the number of unaffiliated adults or "nones" grew from 16.1 percent to 22.8 percent. These "unchurched" Americans now number approximately 56 million and are more numerous than either Catholics or mainline Protestants; and about 35 percent of them are millennials (those born after 1980). Among the unaffiliated, about 31 percent are atheist or agnostic (versus 7 percent in the population as a whole) while the remainder believe in God or a higher power of some kind. Among the "nones," ironically, 40 percent state that religion is important or somewhat important in their lives. On the other hand, among the 70.6 percent of affiliated Christians, many are CEOs (Christmas and Easter Only adherents!). Non-Christian religions (Judaism, Islam, Hinduism, Buddhism, Sikhism, etc.) were the only ones seeing an increase in numbers: from 4.7 percent in 2007 to 5.9 percent in 2014.

What to make of these statistics? Although the United States remains much more religious than its European counterparts, it is becoming more secular and will probably continue in this direction. There is still a strong well of spirituality in the country, but it is often not finding a home in organized religion. Several factors may account for this: the child abuse scandals in the Catholic Church; past and present scandals among TV evangelists; the culture wars over abortion, gay rights, the ordination of women, the teaching of evolution, and so on, that tend to produce cynicism about religion, especially among younger adults; the sense that organized religion is about raising money and building churches, synagogues, and so on; the sheer size of many evangelical megachurches that may tend to turn people off; and a general sense of disillusionment in a world where the 1 percent control so much of the nation's wealth and where religion, rightly or wrongly, is seen as part of the Establishment.

There is clearly a significant overlap between religiously unaffiliated Americans and politically independent ones. Both are turned off by political and religio-cultural wars, and by the polarization that affects both the body politic and the body religious. As we discuss further in the following chapter, evangelical Christians comprise 51 percent of all Christians or about 87 million adults. Yet, they are engaged in almost no interfaith dialogue and cooperation with Catholics, mainline Protestants, Jews, Muslims, and others, even though these nonevangelicals wish it were otherwise. People, in other words, tend to sort themselves out both religiously and politically. And those who are not on the conservative or liberal political wings of society remain in the center, sometimes without a political or religious allegiance. Of course this is not always true, because many mainline Protestants, Catholics, and Jews are centrists. But there is a big gap, and it affects how we feel about politics and religion.

Before we turn to a focus on the new centrists or moral middle, it needs to be stated that evangelical Christians and Orthodox Jews[14]—though they seldom dialogue or cooperate with their liberal counterparts—are certainly compassionate and philanthropic toward "the least of these"[15] in our society, and espouse the same high ethical standards as more liberal religionists. The work of Pastor Rick Warren's Saddleback Church to alleviate AIDS in Africa and to increase awareness of mental illness is just one example of such loving kindness. But we wish conservative Christian leaders would seek more common ground and more cooperation on those issues that matter to most everyone discussed in Chapter 8, for example, reducing poverty and homelessness, combating drug and alcohol abuse and human trafficking, and so on.

THE CENTER IS MORAL, MODERATE, AND DESPERATE FOR PROGRESS

There *is* a political and moral middle in America, the 57 percent of citizens discussed above who do not hold strong ideological positions on abortion, gun control, climate change, and so on. Many of them care deeply about the welfare of the nation and the chronic problems besetting it. A cynic, however, might say they are the "muddled" moral middle—either unsure of what positions to take on complex issues, overwhelmed by the realities of holding down a job and raising a family, or simply unconcerned about matters they feel they have no control over. That would be an unfair assessment, though clearly the issues are immensely complicated and just "taking care of business" on a daily basis can be daunting for most of us. Nevertheless, events such as Occupy Wall Street in 2011, the 2013 March on Washington for gun control, the 2014 People's Climate March in New York City, and the 2015 Million Mom March on Washington against police mistreatment of suspects all demonstrate that many people care about justice and will march if they think they can make a difference.

As the following examples attempt to illustrate, the center resists absolute standpoints on the big values issues:

Gun Control. We analyzed the "great debate" about gun control in Chapter 4. But on the specific issue of requiring background checks for the purchase of weapons, 91 percent of all Americans in a 2013 *Washington Post*–ABC poll were in favor, including 74 percent of NRA members.[16] A comparable 2014 poll by the University of Massachusetts at Lowell Center for Public Opinion found that 78 percent of respondents favor more thorough background checks for gun purchasers and 80 percent favor closing the gun show loophole.[17] In short, Americans want their handguns and rifles, but a huge majority favor the middle position—guns but reasonable restraints on them.

Abortion. As with gun control, we previously discussed (in the Chapter 1) this emotional issue. Here, too, the moral middle wants the option of abortion to be available at least in some cases. A 2012 National Opinion Research Center (NORC) survey has found consistently over many years that 87 percent of the American public approves abortion when a woman's health is seriously endangered, 78.3 percent when pregnancy results from rape, and 77.1 percent when a serious defect in the fetus exists.[18] A 2014 Gallup Poll found that 28 percent of respondents thought that abortion should be legal under any circumstances, 50 percent under only certain circumstances, and 21 percent illegal in all circumstances. That means that 78 percent of respondents considered abortion legal at least in some circumstances, but this is 9 points lower than in the NORC survey. There is no question that support for abortion has softened in recent years, but a significant majority still believes the option of abortion must be available at least in difficult situations.

Climate Change. In April 2015 researchers at Yale and Utah State Universities unveiled a new statistical technique allowing a national county-by-county analysis of American's attitudes toward global warming. It found that, of 3,143 total counties, a majority in 99 percent of them believe in global warming. These data align broadly with a recent 98–1 Senate vote that climate change is real and "not a hoax." However, a majority of U.S. counties (80 percent) remain unconvinced that the change is caused "mostly by human activities."[19] This corresponds roughly with a 2014 Pew Political Typology survey that found 60 percent of respondents agree temperatures are rising but only 40 percent of those concur that the cause is human activity. The debate over climate change is probably the most polarizing issue in American politics today. This might help explain the disconnect between what the public feels about climate change and the huge consensus among scientists that it is "extremely likely" humanity is the main cause of warming. So the best we can say is that those in the center recognize the reality of climate change but are conflicted about its causes.

Gay Marriage. As we discussed in Chapter 1, the morality of gay and lesbian marriage is still a point of profound contention between conservative and liberal politicians and people of faith. However, there has been a dramatic turnabout in how the nation overall, including the Supreme Court, feels about the need for justice for the LGBT community. We think it reflects the wisdom of the center and that the nation is better for its acceptance of this community. A Social Issues survey by Gallup in May 2015 reports that 63 percent of the public finds gay or lesbian relations morally acceptable (versus 40 percent in 2001).[20]

CONCLUSION

The center still holds in American political and cultural life, but it is a somewhat shaky hold. Still, although we may be a country of passionate opinions, we are also a country that eschews extremism on the left or right and seeks a balance on the many truly complicated issues facing the nation—from national security and religious tolerance to gun control, abortion, and climate change. But the center is deeply frustrated by the inability of Congress to strike reasonable compromises on these issues and several others, such as immigration and health care, and sometimes expresses its discontent by retreating from the political process, especially by not voting. The "new centrists" can play a role in rescuing us from our polarization and discontents. People across the political spectrum care deeply about a range of issues that affect the nation's well-being—as we discussed in Chapter 8 on what matters to all of us—but our political leaders will need to show more courage through the art of compromise, the art of the possible, despite the tremendous pressures they are under to get reelected. To foster that courage, the center will need to increase its political pressure on them. Are centrists really "fed up" and not willing to take it anymore (to paraphrase the movie *Network*)? Time and the 2016 election will tell.

NOTES

1. Stephen Burgard, "Memo on the Religious and Moral Center," Chapter 9 in S. Burgard (ed.), *Faith, Politics and Media in Our Perilous Times,* 2nd ed. Dubuque, IA: Kendall Hunt Publishing Co., 2010, pp. 123–24.

2. E. J. Dionne, *Our Divided Political Heart: The Battle for the American Idea in Age of Discontent.* New York: Bloomsbury, 2012, p. 7.

3. Ibid., p. 8.

4. www.nolabels.org/.

5. www.pewresearch.org/fact-tank/2014/06/12/7-things-to-know-about -olarization-in-America.

6. www.pewresearch.org/fact-tank/2014/08/01/the-political-middle-still -matters.

7. Ibid.

8. www.gallup.com/poll/180440/new-record-political-independents.aspx.

9. www.cnn.com/2012/11/02/politics/irpt-independent-voters/.

10. The Pew Research Center reports a somewhat lower figure of 53.6 percent. www.pewresearch.org/fact-tank/2015/05/06/u-s-voter-turnout-trails-most -developed-countries/. The numbers used here are from www.fairvote.org/research -and-analysis/voter-turnout/.

11. www.minnpost.com/eric-black-ink/2014/why-turnout-so-low-US-elec tions-we-make-it-more-difficult-vote-other-democracies.

12. www.pewforum.org/2015/05/12/America's-changing-religious-land scape/. The survey of more than thirty-five thousand Americans was conducted between June 4 and September 30, 2014.

13. The Evangelical Protestant share of the population fell only slightly from 26.3 percent to 25.4 percent.

14. Though both members of the Church of Jesus Christ of Latter-day Saints/ Mormons and most U.S. Muslims are religiously quite conservative, they do participate in interfaith work.

15. Gospel of Matthew 25:40.

16. www.washingtonpost.com/blogs/the-fix/WP/2013/04/03/90-percent-of -Americans-want-expanded-background-checks-on-guns-why-isnt-this-a-slam -dunk/.

17. www.uml.edu/News/press-releases/2014/gun-control-full-2014.aspx.

18. www.norc.org/pdfs/gss%20reports/trends%20in%20attitudes%20 about%20abortion_final.pdf.

19. www.slate.com/bloggs/the_slatest/2015/04/06/new-climate_change_poll _shows_Americans_believe_in_global_warming.html.

20. www.Gallup.com/poll/183413/Americans-continue-shift-left-key-moral -issues.

Chapter 10

"A Battlefield of Values"—Politics, Culture, and Religion in Orange County, California

THE POLITICAL EVOLUTION OF ORANGE COUNTY

Orange County, California, represents a tale of two worlds—the conservative bulwark that birthed the John Birch Society and helped elect several Republican presidents,[1] and the culturally diverse county that has grown steadily more centrist, even though conservatives are still politically dominant.

One illustration of the political divide in Orange County mirrors the national chasms we've been discussing in this book. In July 1990 the Nixon Presidential Library and Museum in Yorba Linda was dedicated. It was run by the nongovernmental Nixon Foundation, a group of Nixon friends, family, and supporters. All of the other 12 presidential libraries have been operated in connection with the National Archives, but this did not happen with the Nixon library until 17 years later. In July 2007, the National Archives brought millions of pages of documents to the library and appointed historian Timothy Naphtali as its director. However, the foundation that raises funds for the library and museum remained a separate entity. Naphtali and the foundation eventually clashed over his makeover of the museum's Watergate exhibit. It was much more critical of Nixon's role in the Watergate break-in, the subsequent cover-up, and his ignominious resignation. And while the Nixon Foundation tended to invite conservative speakers such as Dick Cheney, Newt Gingrich, and Ann Coulter, Naphtali invited many scholars with a broader point of view. Eventually these differences led to his resignation, in November 2011, and the absence of a director until January 2015, when Michael Ellzey, a nonexpert in the museum world and former director of the Great Park in Irvine, was selected. In fairness, both the Bill Clinton and George W. Bush libraries have been criticized for downplaying controversial aspects of their presidencies.

Orange County is a kind of mirror opposite to Los Angeles with its liberal politics supported by legions of movie stars. The county was for many years considered LA's bedroom community. It is still dominated by LA media where all the major television and radio stations are located,[2] by the Hollywood entertainment industry, and by the dominant culture of Los Angeles with the Hollywood Bowl, Getty Center, Disney Concert Hall, and art museums.

But starting in 1955 with the opening of Disneyland in Anaheim and Segerstrom Center for the Arts (formerly known as the OC Performing Arts Center) in Costa Mesa in 1986—as well as the development in 1967 of South Coast Plaza, the largest shopping mall on the West Coast—the county has come into its own. It has a population of 3.2 million, greater than that of 21 states, and in many ways resembles one single metropolis—the OC. In fact, when visiting other parts of the country, people tend to say they are from "Orange County" rather than a particular city (of which there are 34). There are two professional sports teams: baseball's Los Angeles Angels of Anaheim (moved from LA in 1966) and hockey's Mighty Ducks of Anaheim (1993). Two major universities also emerged in the same postwar era, California State University, Fullerton (1959), and the University of California, Irvine (UCI; 1965). They joined a distinguished private university, Chapman in the City of Orange (1954, though founded in 1861 as Hesperian College in Woodland Hills, California). In some respects the universities, with their strong liberal tendencies, have tempered the county's conservatism. On the other hand, the conservatively oriented military was for many years a power in South County when both the El Toro Marine Air Station and Marine Corps Base Camp Pendleton were in operation. El Toro was a major presence from 1943 until its closing in 1999. Camp Pendleton opened in 1942 and remains the Marines' West Coast base of training and operations. Former Marine Corps brigadier general Thomas F. Riley ended his military career at Camp Pendleton and later served for 20 years on the OC Board of Supervisors. In a similar vein, it is not surprising that Orange County's airport is named after legendary movie star and longtime resident John Wayne whose huge statue adorns the airport entrance.

A significant influence on Orange County's conservatism has been its longtime newspaper, the *Orange County* (formerly *Santa Ana*) *Register*, founded in 1905. However, it took on its unique personality when Raymond C. Hoiles purchased the paper in 1935. Two years later, he began writing a bylined column called "Common Ground" in which he articulated his libertarian philosophy of limited government, free markets, property rights, and individual liberty—along with opposition to public schools, collective bargaining, social welfare laws, and taxes.[3] The paper continued to mirror the county's conservatism long after Hoile's death in 1970 and right down to the beginning of the new century. By this point, newspapers were really beginning to struggle in the new digital world and the county's demographics were changing. Gradually, under current publisher Aaron Kushner, the paper's opinion pages have become a bit more centrist, though far from liberal.

Like the rest of the country, Orange County has pockets of significant affluence and others of considerable poverty. Newport Beach, Irvine, Laguna Beach, Mission Viejo, Rancho Santa Margarita, Aliso Viejo, Villa Park, and Tustin are at the high end (and that's where reality TV's *The Real Housewives of Orange County* reside); while there is considerable poverty in Anaheim, Santa Ana, and elsewhere. Compare this to the situation in Chicagoland, the boroughs of New York City, and many other large cities, and you get a similar picture—a lot of affluent citizens, many poor, and a shrinking middle class.

A UNIQUE ETHNIC MIX

The county's demographics mirror the growing ethnic diversity in the country as a whole but with one big exception: far fewer African Americans and far more Asians. Whites still hold a slim majority at about 44 percent, followed by Hispanics/Latinos (34 percent, well above the national average), and Asians (19 percent). But the African American population is 1.7 percent, far below the national average. A century ago the Ku Klux Klan was strong in Anaheim. That, along with the historic conservatism of the county, continuing pockets of racism, and the high cost of living in many areas may account for the very low numbers. Most Latinos are of Mexican origin, and their numbers have grown significantly in the past quarter century. The most surprising demographic change, however, is the growth in Asian Americans who now number almost six hundred thousand, a 41 percent increase between 2000 and 2010, and the third-largest such population in the country. The affluent, planned community of Irvine is 43 percent Asian and its university, UCI, has an enrollment that is about 58 percent Asian versus 28 percent white!

Although there are a significant number of Americans of Chinese, Korean, and even Japanese ethnicity, it is Vietnamese Americans who have left the most significant mark on the county. They have developed a whole sub-culture surrounding Little Saigon in Garden Grove. It has been historically conservative, reflecting the anti-Communism of that immigrant commu-nity whose members either fled Vietnam when Saigon (now Ho Chi Minh City) fell in 1975 or came later, some as part of the so-called boat people who fled in subsequent years. And they are making their mark in politics. Van Tran, who escaped from Saigon at age ten, a week before it fell, represented the county as a Republican in the California Assembly from 2004–10. (He then unsuccessfully challenged Congresswoman Loretta Sanchez.) In 2014, Bao Nguyen was elected (by 15 votes) mayor of Garden Grove as a *Democrat* and became the first Vietnamese American mayor of a city of over one hun-dred thousand people. The 34-year-old Buddhist was born in a Thai refugee camp—a classic example of the American dream. The same year, former county supervisor Janet Nguyen (no relation) decisively defeated former state assemblyman José Solario for the 34th District seat in the state Senate. The County Board of Supervisors has one member of Vietnamese ethnicity, Andrew Do, who was chief of staff to former supervisor Janet Nguyen. He very narrowly defeated former state assemblyman and Senator Lou Correa in a special election in 2015. Ironically, though the Latino population of the county is much larger than the Vietnamese, the latter vote in significantly larger numbers, helping explain the defeat of Solario and Correa.

Bob Dornan was a longtime congressman from both LA and Orange Counties who, as a fervently conservative supporter of strong national defense spending, got the nickname "B-1 Bob." Redistricting finally put Dornan in a heavily Latino congressional district in central Orange County and he was defeated in 1996 by Loretta Sanchez who continues to represent the district. But it was a sign that the OC's conservatism was beginning to weaken. In fact, between 1994 and 2014 the share of registered Republicans in the county shrank from 50 to 41 percent while Democrats went down only modestly from 35 to 31.7 percent, and the number of independents grew from 10 to 22.7 percent. Latinos are over twice as likely to register as Democrats than Republicans, and their share of the county's electorate is growing. They are now 18 percent of registered voters but 34 percent of the population; and, as more of them become citizens and reach voting age, their electoral impact will increase.[4] This Orange County trend of Latinos favoring Democrats is happening throughout most parts of the country and poses a tremendous electoral challenge for Republicans in the 2016 elec-tion. Unless they can devise a way to attract more Latino voters, especially by proposing an immigration plan acceptable to conservatives, electing a Republican president will be difficult. Florida Senator Marco Rubio, son of Cuban immigrants, and former Florida governor Jeb Bush, who is married to a Mexican American, might give them the best shot at increasing their share of the Latino vote.

POLARIZATION IN MINIATURE: THE BATTLE FOR COSTA MESA

Costa Mesa, home to author Ben Hubbard, is a medium-sized city of one hundred thirteen thousand in the center of the county where the OC Fairgrounds are located and, as noted, Segerstrom Center for the Arts and South Coast Plaza. It lacks the affluence of its posh neighbor Newport Beach and has a significant lower-income Latino population on its Westside. Its politics were quite conventional for most of its history since incorporation in 1954, but the 2008 election brought to the five-member City Council[5] strongly conservative Jim Righeimer along with fellow conservative, and current mayor, Steve Mensinger. They joined Councilman Gary Monahan to comprise a council majority. Faced with the kind of ballooning pension obligations affecting other cities in California and throughout the country, the Council, in March 2011, sent layoff notices to nearly half of its employees with the aim of outsourcing many positions and avoiding further pension costs. The six-month termination notices affected 213 of the city's 472 full-time employees and cut across several departments: firefighters, maintenance workers, jail staff. The workers and their union were stunned, and they attacked the decision vehemently; one city worker jumped to his death from Costa Mesa City Hall, apparently over the prospect of getting a slip. Union members, especially the police union, fought back and eventually almost all of the layoff notices were rescinded.

Nonetheless, a climate of alienation and suspicion resulted with bizarre consequences. In the run-up to the 2012 Council elections, Righeimer was tailed from Councilman Monahan's Goat Hill Tavern by a private investigator, Chris Lanzillo. He alerted police that Righeimer might be driving under the influence, and the councilman and then-mayor was forced to take a sobriety test in his front yard. Result: stone sober, and Righeimer even produced a receipt from the tavern for two diet cokes. Mensinger has charged that Lanzillo placed a GPS tracking device on the undercarriage of his truck—and checked it covertly at night—apparently to see if his opponents could discredit him in some way. In November 2012, the two councilmen filed a lawsuit in Superior Court against the police department's union, the union's former law firm, Lackie, Dammeier, McGill, and Ethir, that had hired Lanzillo, and the private investigator himself. It was pending at the time of this writing. (Lanzillo and a second investigator were charged in December 2014 with four felonies resulting from their dirty tricks against Righeimer and Mensinger. Lanzillo testified at a preliminary hearing on August 26, 2015, that will determine whether there is enough evidence to bring him to trial.) Alienation between the current city council majority and the police department's union, which fired Dammeier's now-defunct law firm after the incident with Lanzillo, is still apparent. In fact, the department continued to be understaffed in 2015 with only 108 sworn officers in contrast to the 136 that would put it at full strength, although it hoped to be fully staffed by July 2016. Rob Dimel, president of the Costa Mesa Police Association, has stated that the inability to keep the department at full strength—with officers either retiring or taking other jobs—is a result the hostile work environment created by Righeimer.

In the 2014 election, a former councilwoman Katrina Foley was elected with a significant majority, but Righeimer squeaked by his opponent, former councilman Jay Humphrey, by only 47 votes. In an interview with *Daily Pilot* newspaper, Righeimer said, "The message is that the community is 50–50 on important issues. As an elected official, you have to look at that. They didn't go out there and give you a mandate to do whatever you're doing and continue to do."[6] What that will mean for the future of the city's operations remains to be seen, but the city remains very divided.

One has to seriously question whether the abortive firing of those city employees in the interest of balancing Costa Mesa's books was a prudent fiscal and political decision. Other cities have dealt with comparable pension problems by offering less generous retirement plans for new hires and requiring current employees to contribute more of their salaries toward retirement. There is no question that this is a huge national problem, as became clear in March 2015 when Wisconsin Governor Scott Walker succeeded in breaking the power of that state's powerful public unions by making it a right-to-work state. But the "nuclear options" taken by the Costa Mesa Council and Governor Walker—as opposed to tough negotiations and painful concessions from both sides—has made toxic the political and civil climate in Costa Mesa, California, the state of Wisconsin, and other feuding constituencies. This is not "the art of the possible" but the art of the confrontational. So Costa Mesa has become a microcosm of the sort of pugilistic politics afflicting cities, states, and our national government. And it is not working.

RELIGION IN THE OC: THRIVING BUT DIVIDED

When co-author Ben Hubbard moved to Orange County 30 years ago, he quickly became aware that it was not only the home of Disneyland but also a kind of religion land—with the imposing Crystal Cathedral spires not that far from the famed amusement park—as well as a robust Evangelical Christian community that he had not experienced in other parts of the country. The fish logo (a coded reference to Christianity) on automobile bumpers was one of many indicators that this was different religious territory. He knew of the late Rev. Robert Schuller's *Hour of Power* television program and that the John Birch Society, with its conservative and evangelical roots, had been very active in Orange County. Co-author Steve Burgard lived in the county for 12 years and continued to visit yearly on academic research breaks for the succeeding 13 years until his untimely death in 2014. What both of us have found remarkable is the religious vibrancy of the area, the pioneering interfaith work that has gone on, and the amazing growth in Latino Catholicism paralleling the significant influx of Hispanic immigrants from Mexico and other parts of Central America. At the same time, however, conservative churches in the county have little interaction with their liberal counterparts and exist in a kind of parallel, yet very vibrant, religious universe.

THE NONDENOMINATIONAL MEGACHURCHES

In contrast to some other megachurches in Orange County, the Crystal Cathedral in Garden Grove (a city in the central part of county), was a member of an established denomination, the Reformed Church in America. And Schuller's theology was closer to mainline Protestant thought than to the biblical conservatism or even literalism that governed evangelical theology. It was Norman Vincent Peale's power of positive thinking rather than Billy Graham's born againism that inspired Schuller to begin his ministry in 1955 in a rented drive-in movie theater and eventually raise the funds for the majestic glass cathedral (the largest all-glass structure in the world). Schuller also started his highly successful television ministry, the *Hour of Power,* which at its height was watched by 1.3 million viewers in 156 countries.

Ironically, it was his amazing success that led to his ministry's downfall, as he over extended himself with lavish Christmas and Easter pageants and unrealistic salaries for family members, and as he failed to recognize demographic changes occurring in his part of the county. The Crystal Cathedral filed for bankruptcy in 2010 and was purchased by the Roman Catholic Diocese of Orange two years later and renamed Christ Cathedral. The former Crystal Cathedral ministry moved into St. Callistus Catholic Church in July 2013 and renamed itself Shepherd's Grove. In turn, the church and its parochial school moved onto the cathedral campus. The cathedral is being refurbished to accommodate celebration of the mass by 2017 (masses are now celebrated in the arboretum on the campus).

Along with Schuller's hubris and mismanagement, the Crystal Cathedral's downfall was the result of the movement of his kind of white, conservative congregants to the southern part of the county, the huge influx of Latinos to central Orange County, and the preference of white suburbanites for a more conservative Bible-based theology.

Another evangelical ministry founded virtually from scratch was the Rev. Chuck Smith's Calvary Chapel. The church began in 1965 in Costa Mesa with 25 congregants and a biblically fundamentalist approach. In 1968, Smith and his team reached out to the hippies and surfers who inhabited Orange County beaches with the right message at the right time, and the "Jesus movement" was under way. Today there are more than fifteen hundred Calvary Chapels worldwide, and the mother church includes a variety of ministries and a K-12 parochial school. Ben Hubbard attended the eighth-grade graduation ceremony of a friend's child several years back at Calvary. The school's principal, in his message to graduates, told them how important it was that they had accepted creationism and rejected evolution. It is one thing to know this in theory, but quite another to realize the impact such teaching has on a significant number of young people in the country. Smith died in 2013, but his ultraconservative movement is alive and thriving.

A kind of offshoot of Calvary Chapel, the Association of Vineyard Churches was actually rooted in a Bible studies movement in the LA music community. It came into its own under John Wimber's leadership. A talented pastor and musician, Wimber in 1977 had founded a Calvary Chapel in Yorba Linda, but his stress on healing and the other gifts of the Holy Spirit led to a split with Smith. For the next 20 years until his death, he spread his charismatic movement resulting in more than fifteen hundred churches worldwide and now headquartered in Sugar Land, Texas.

Then there was the Melodyland Christian Center founded in 1969 by Pastor Ralph Wilkerson. Like the Vineyard, it had a charismatic orientation and at one time included a school of theology and a junior college, Anaheim Christian. As with the Vineyard's Wimber, when Wilkerson retired in 1998 the center lost some of its luster, Disneyland absorbed the site, and the ministry relocated to the more affluent city of Tustin under its new name The Healing Word. Just as with the Crystal Cathedral, demographics also played a role in the fate of Melodyland.

Probably the most famous of Orange County's evangelical ministries is Saddleback Church in Lake Forest, founded by Pastor Rick Warren in 1980 and affiliated with the Southern Baptist Convention. Under Warren's skilled leadership, the church has grown rapidly with current weekly attendance at services of about twenty thousand. Since 1995, its home is a spacious campus that includes a thirty-five hundred–seat worship center, a bookstore, childcare facility, food outlet, and a permanent student ministry facility, the Refinery. There are now branch campuses in Irvine, San Clemente, Huntington Beach, San Juan Capistrano, and Anaheim; and international campuses in Manila, Hong Kong, Buenos Aires, and Berlin. Along with the immense success of his book, *The Purpose-Driven Life* (2002), Warren and his ministry received national attention by hosting in 2006 the Second Annual Global Summit on AIDS and the Church (which resulted in several parishioners traveling to Africa to assist AIDS sufferers), and the Civil Forum on the Presidency (see Chapter 1) in which President Obama and Senator John McCain (R-AZ) were each interviewed by Warren in a unique quasi-debate. Obama invited Warren to give the invocation at his first inauguration in January 2009.

Comparable in size and influence to Saddleback, Mariners Church—like some of the others just discussed—began with a small group of Christians meeting for Bible studies in private homes (in this case in the Newport Beach area) beginning in 1963. After hiring its first full-time pastor in 1967, the church built its first facility in Newport Beach and eventually relocated to an 18-acre site in Irvine. By 2008, the congregation had completed a worship center seating thirty-nine hundred, a bookstore, café, a large children's ministry building, and a student center. Following in the tradition of the other evangelical megachurches in Orange County, Mariners has added sites in Huntington Beach and San Juan Capistrano. There are, of course other smaller evangelical churches in the county, but these churches—with their traditional approach to issues such as abortion, gay marriage, evolution, and the like—have had a powerful influence on the politics of Orange County and, indirectly, the nation.

Despite the small percentage of African Americans residing in the county, the Rev. Mark Whitlock Jr. has been spearheading a remarkable growth in the black church there. Christ Our Redeemer African Methodist Episcopal Church began on the campus of UC Irvine in 1991 and was about to close in 1998 when presiding Bishop Witten Anderson appointed Whitlock to lead the struggling congregation. The church grew remarkably under Whitlock's leadership and took up residence in a 26,000-sq.-ft. building in Irvine in November 2014 to accommodate its growing congregation of 3,150 people. In 2001, the church founded the COR Community Development Corporation to raise funds for scholarships for students in OC colleges and universities. Over the years it has provided nearly $400,000 in college scholarships to 300 students.

And what would Orange County be without a large revival? For the past 26 years, Pastor Greg Laurie of Riverside has organized Harvest Crusade at Angel's Stadium in Anaheim. Occurring every August and drawing as many as one hundred thousand over three nights, the event resembles the format made famous by Billy Graham: music (in this case, very contemporary), a sermon by Laurie, and an altar call. In 2012, Laurie initiated "Harvest America," with people from across the nation watching the crusade via satellite TV or attending local crusades. Once again, Orange County evangelicalism has a national impact.

The county is also home to the Trinity Broadcasting Network (TBN), not only the largest evangelical television network in the world but the third largest over-the-air TV group. TBN's channels are aired on 70 satellites and over eighteen thousand television and cable affiliates. Paul and Jan Crouch founded the network in 1973 by renting time on a station in Ontario, California, but by 2005 TBN was available in 95 percent of American households. The network's headquarters are in Costa Mesa in a luxurious building with a lavish interior. TBN programming has included an impressive roster of evangelical preachers: Billy Graham, Kenneth Copeland, Bishop T. D. Jakes, Jack Hayford, Joel Osteen, John Hagee, Pat Robertson and the 700 Club, and Creflo Dollar. Paul Crouch died in 2013 and was succeeded by his son Matthew who appears to run the station jointly with his mother Jan. The Crouches were criticized over the years in the media for their lavish lifestyle, and there have been other controversies; but it is hard to underestimate how powerfully TBN has promoted evangelical Christianity worldwide.

Finally, in the vastly influential evangelical world of Orange County, the Traditional Values Coalition, the nation's largest nondenominational grassroots church lobby took root in 1980 under a former Presbyterian clergyman, Lou Sheldon. Its website claims to speak "on behalf of more than forty-three thousand allied churches and millions of like-minded patriots."[7] As its name implies, TVC promotes traditional family values, including being pro-life and very opposed to gay marriage and the gay lifestyle. Sheldon's daughter, Andrea Lafferty, is the organization's president and an effective Washington, DC, lobbyist.

Although attracting fewer adherents, liberal or so-called "mainline" Protestants also have a sizable footprint in the county. One of the most impressive churches in this tradition is St. Andrew's Presbyterian in Newport Beach headed for 31 years by nationally prominent pastor Dr. John A. Huffman Jr. until his retirement in 2000. However, though the Presbyterian Church USA tends to be more liberal in orientation, in Orange County it tacks mainly conservative in politics and values. Like Robert Schuller, Huffman was significantly influenced by Norman Vincent Peale and was also close to Billy Graham. Still, there is a cadre of liberal churches, such as Fairview Community Church in Costa Mesa whose Pastor Dr. Sarah

Halverson is a social justice liberal who has written on this topic in the Newport Beach–Costa Mesa *Daily Pilot.*

There are Lutherans in the county, too, with a strong core in the city of Orange and a prominent high school, Orange Lutheran, and a Missouri Synod University, Concordia Lutheran in Irvine. The Assemblies of God (Pentecostal) tradition has a significant presence in Orange County and California overall, and has attracted many Latinos in recent years. Vanguard University in Costa Mesa is the intellectual and spiritual core of the faith here.

CATHOLICISM IN THE OC AND ITS LATINO CORE

Roman Catholics comprise about 21 percent of the nation's population, but in Orange County that number is at least 35 percent. The percentage has risen sharply in the past 25 years along with the huge increase in immigrants—both documented and undocumented—from Mexico and other Latin American countries. Most of these new arrivals are still Catholic, though a sizable number have converted from the cultural Catholicism of their upbringing to Pentecostalism and other Protestant-based faiths. As mentioned in Chapter 4, the first language of 75 percent of Santa Ana's population is Spanish; and it has become a very Hispanic city, and very Catholic. There are also large Latino populations in Anaheim (53 percent), Costa Mesa (32 percent), and elsewhere. Still, about a third of Orange County's Catholics are white and generally affluent. Altogether there are 56 Catholic parishes in the county, 5 ethnic ministry centers, 44 parochial schools, 3 general hospitals, and a disabled center. Catholic Orange County will be crowned by Christ Cathedral when masses begin there in 2017.

The Catholic community went through a considerable crisis with the priestly pedophilia scandal that affected the entire nation, and the Archdiocese of Los Angeles in particular. But unlike LA, then–OC Bishop Todd Brown did a better job of handling it, including settling legal claims in a timely fashion.

THE OC'S OTHER FAITH TRADITIONS

Jews began moving to the county in the 1940s and 1950s from the Midwest and East Coast and from Los Angeles, so that today there is a growing Jewish community of about eighty thousand with 31 synagogues or temples in all the major branches of the faith. The Merage Jewish Community Center in Irvine, completed in 2004, has become the cultural center of

Jewish life with a parochial school, *Tarbut v'Torah*, recreational programs, sports facilities, and a social welfare system.

Muslims began arriving in the 1970s and 1980s with an estimated sixty thousand adherents who worship in ten or more mosques (Masjids) and are a growing presence in Buena Park, Anaheim, and elsewhere. The oldest mosque is the Islamic Society of Orange County in Garden Grove the founding Imam of which is Dr. Muzammil Siddiqi, a nationally recognized leader and former president of the Islamic Society of North America.

The Church of Jesus Christ of Latter-day Saints or Mormons also has a significant presence in the county with about sixty thousand adherents in 120 wards (comparable to parishes) and 16 stakes (group of wards) along with a LDS Temple in Newport Beach (open only to LDS members after its consecration in 2008). Mormons have a tradition not only of supporting their own when emergencies arise but also members of other ethnic and religious communities. In 2014, a fire at Temple Beth Sholom in Santa Ana rendered its sanctuary unusable, so the nearby Mormon stake in the City of Orange has been offering its facilities for worship services until repairs can be completed.

There is also a sizable Buddhist community in the county with about 45 temples, including Pao Fa in Irvine, one of the largest Buddhist monasteries and temples in the country, which attracts Chinese and Vietnamese adherents, and a Zen meditation center in Costa Mesa. There are about one hundred ninety thousand Vietnamese Americans in Orange County divided mainly between Buddhists and Catholics. A final Vietnamese import is the Cao Dai faith that combines elements from Buddhism, Confucianism, Taoism, and Catholicism. Its unique Garden Grove Temple is only one of four in the United States modeled after the home temple in Tay Ninh, Vietnam.

Soka University in Aliso Viejo, under the sponsorship of Soka Gakkai International, a Japanese Buddhist tradition, was founded in 1994 and moved to its current idyllic location in 2001. Humanistic Buddhism provides a backdrop to this small liberal arts institution that also sponsors classical and jazz music events for the community. In addition, there are large and impressive Sikh and Jain temples in Buena Park, a Zoroastrian Center in Westminster, and a small Hindu temple in Fullerton. Religion is clearly alive and variegated in the OC.

PIONEERING INTERFAITH WORK

In 1995, a visionary rabbi, the late Allen Krause, along with interfaith activist Kay Lindahl[8] and Prany Sananikone, director of diversity relations and educational programs at UC Irvine, conceived the idea for a countywide event to foster interfaith understanding—The Religious Diversity Fair (later renamed Forum). It was considered the first such event in the nation and inspired similar happenings around the country. Consisting of panel discussions and plenary addresses, the Forum drew several hundred participants in its early years, though attendance was more modest in the last four or five, and it was discontinued in 2013.

A valuable offshoot of the interfaith forums was the formation in 2008 of the Orange County Interfaith Network (OCIN) under the leadership of Rabbi Frank Stern and Mormon bishop Tom Thorkelson. For many years, 11 groups of clergy from different parts of the county and from many faith traditions had been holding monthly meetings to promote interfaith understanding and discuss common challenges, such as racism and bigotry. Stern and Thorkelson brought together the leaders of these councils and convinced them to form a Council of Religious Leaders that meets quarterly to review issues of community concern and promote interfaith understanding. It works cooperatively with the Human Relations Council of Orange County, the County Board of Supervisors, local police, and other agencies "to avoid interreligious and intercultural confrontation and enhance civility, tolerance and mutual understanding."[9] The OCIN also sponsors the Interfaith Youth Council of Orange County, which holds a youth forum each March where some two hundred high school students from diverse backgrounds meet to discuss a common issue, for example, religion and the environment. And each November near Thanksgiving, OCIN, along with other groups, sponsors a free concert, the Thanksgiving Music Festival where choirs from a variety of religious traditions share their music and spiritual values. Attendees are encouraged to bring packaged and canned foods for distribution to local food banks.

Finally, in Orange County's interfaith world, there is the work of Sande Hart and S.A.R.A.H. (Spiritual and Religious Alliance for Hope). This remarkable feminist group, founded by Ms. Hart after 9/11, seeks to promote a culture of peace by empowering women and the local community through interfaith dialogue, community service, and educational opportunities. She is also chair of the North American region of the United Religions Initiative, the world's largest network of interfaith grassroots organizations (see Chapter 12) and is chief compassion officer at Compassion California. This international organization stages the annual Compassion Games in which different cities compete in performing compassionate actions at the grassroots level.[10]

AN UNFORTUNATE IRONY

As mentioned in Chapter 1, there is what we consider an unfortunate irony in the remarkable interfaith work going on both in Orange County and around the country: Evangelical Christian leaders and most Orthodox Jewish rabbis, for different reasons, have chosen not to participate in interfaith councils. As explained in that chapter, most evangelical Christians, especially clergy, believe there is one way to eternal salvation—through the death and resurrection of Jesus Christ and a mature or born-again commitment to the Christian faith. They take very literally the words of Jesus, "I am the way, and the truth, and the life; no one comes to the father except through me" (John 14:6). Of course, Catholics and other more liberal Christians make that same commitment. But evangelicals see deficiencies of various kinds in these other types of Christianity. They believe they would be invalidating the fully authentic Christianity that only evangelicals possess by meeting with these Christians, and even more so Jews, Muslims, Buddhists, Hindus, and so on. What is perhaps even more ironic is that until the Second Vatican Council (1962–65) Catholic theology viewed other Christians in much the same way as evangelicals now do vis-à-vis the rest of the Christian world. Although official Catholic doctrine still teaches that Catholicism represents the fullness of the Christian faith and that Protestantism is lacking in certain respects, the bishops of the council decided, in effect, that Martin Buber[11] was right—the entire Christian family, as well as the family of world religions, must be "meeting," must be communicating, if a more just and peaceful world is to evolve.[12]

Religious life in Orange County is rich and diverse, and there is an impressive amount of interfaith dialogue and cooperation. In this respect, it mirrors California and the rest of the country. Yet, the great divide between evangelical Christians and the remainder of the Christian and non-Christian communities in the county—and the nation—is still significant. Not only do evangelicals have theological objections to interfaith dialogue, they also have values-based and political misgivings about their nonevangelical neighbors. Liberal views on abortion and gay marriage, coupled with acceptance of evolution, the existence of climate change, and other issues make evangelicals hesitant to enter into dialogue. Catholics also have problems with abortion and gay marriage, but have decided in the post–Vatican II world that those the council called "separated brethren" are still brethren (and sisters); and that the needs of a struggling planet make cooperation indispensable.

EXCURSUS: EVANGELICAL TRUTH AND TEA PARTY TRUTH

The Tea Party does not adhere to a theological platform in the way evangelical Christians do, but they have a similar mind-set. For their kind of Republicans, the Democrats and nonaffiliated progressives are simply lacking in truth. Liberal and progressive positions are false in being pro-choice, false in supporting gay marriage, false in accepting evolution, false in considering climate change a serious issue, false in wanting to liberalize immigration policy, and false in their support of the nation's social welfare agenda (Social Security, Medicare, and the Patient Protection and Affordable Care Act/Obamacare)—among other falsities. They also want God and religion to play a bigger role in national politics. As sociologists David E. Campbell and Robert D. Putnam write:

Tea Partiers . . . Seek deeply religious elected officials, approve of religious leaders' engaging in politics and want religion brought into political debates. The Tea Party's generals may say their overriding concern is a smaller government, but not their rank and file, who are more concerned about putting God in government.[13]

A 2014 Pew Forum poll validated this point of view in finding that nearly three quarters (72 percent) of respondents believe the influence of religion in society is waning, and most of them viewed that decline as negative. At the core of the group concerned about religion's perceived waning importance are white evangelicals, the kind of people who often identify with the Tea Party movement.

In short, Congress members strongly influenced by Tea Party politics find it difficult to achieve common ground with moderate Republicans and Democrats because Tea Partiers believe liberal policies are not simply wrong on the basis of reason and sound public policy, but on the basis of what is religiously true and what is false. And it is difficult to compromise with perceived falsehood.

In the end, Orange County is not a perfect microcosm of the country as a whole, but it is a fascinating mix of politics, culture, and religion that in many ways reflects the national mood.

NOTES

1. All seven members of the House of Representatives who represent all or part of the county are Republicans except Linda Sanchez in Santa Ana and Alan Lowenthal, most of whose district is in Long Beach in LA County.

2. KDOC in Anaheim and PBS-affiliate KOCE in Huntington Beach are the exceptions. Until 2010, LA's KCET was the PBS affiliate but dropped its connection in a financial dispute.

3. In 1942, Hoiles editorialized against the internment of one hundred ten thousand Japanese Americans, one of the few publishers in the country to speak out against this injustice.

4. "GOP Edge Shrinks," News, *Orange County Register*, June 1, 2014, p. 3.

5. Like many other municipalities, a city manager runs day-to-day operations in Costa Mesa.

6. www.latimes.com/local/orangecounty/la-me-costa-mesa-councilman -20141118-story.html.

7. www.traditionalvalues.org/content/about. Retrieved September 23, 2014.

8. See further discussion of Lindahl's work in Chapter 12.

9. http://ocin.weebly.com. September 27, 2014.

10. www.compassiongames.org/about-us/. Retrieved May 25, 2015.

11. See discussion of philosopher Buber in Chapter 4.

12. See *The Documents of Vatican II, Declaration of the Church to Non-Christian Religions,* Walter Abbott (ed.). New York: America Press, 1966, pp. 660–68.

13. www.nytimes.com/2011/08/17/opinion/crashing-the-tea-party.html.   See also Campbell and Putnam's *American Grace: How Religion Divides and Unites Us.* New York: Simon and Schuster, 2010.

Chapter 11

Besieged Media Go Polar

THE MEDIA CRAZY QUILT

The media, once a fairly recognizable entity of daily newspapers, legacy television outlets, news- or music-oriented radio stations, and national magazines such as *Time, Newsweek,* and *U.S. News & World Report,* is now a crazy quilt in which it is hard to know who really is a journalist in the traditional sense and who belongs to the ranks of so-called citizen journalists of varying skills. Over the past 15 to 20 years a host of online/.com news and opinion outlets have emerged: *Salon, Slate, Politico, Huffington Post, Truth Dig, Drudge Report, Redstate,* and so on, along with thousands of websites and blog sites from every news organization as well as from individuals seeking to get their point of view out there.

On the one hand, this is very enriching, as competition and varying interpretations of the news can be extremely valuable. On the other, we seem to be drowning in media with so many points of view that the average educated person sometimes feels like giving up. Further complicating this picture is the tendency of many media outlets to veer conservative or liberal with insufficient room for interpretations in the middle that strive to present a balanced, nonpartisan viewpoint on national and international issues. Talk radio is a prime example of right versus left, conservative versus liberal. There is very little room for talking about what people might agree on or whether differences are so stark that consensus or compromise on many issues becomes impossible. Consensus is certainly not the style of

Rush Limbaugh, Erick Erickson, or Glenn Beck. Dennis Prager, Michael Medved, and Hugh Hewitt are certainly fair and reasonable conservative commentators, but the left is their enemy and there's little room for "progressive" perspectives. Thom Hartmann on Sirius represents the liberal side of talk radio, and the *Daily Show with Jon Stewart*, and *The Colbert Report*—until their recent retirements—played a similar role on cable TV. *Real Time with Bill Maher* and *Last Week Tonight* with John Oliver still represent the left on that medium.

In some respects, CNN was the pioneer in this expanded media world. Its shaky start in 1980, when it was called the "Chicken Noodle Network," eventually led to vindication and credibility through its utilization of the 24-hour news format. It was able, for example, to scoop the major TV networks' coverage of the Challenger space shuttle disaster in 1985 and the Persian Gulf War in 1991. The CNN approach was later copied by the Fox News network and MSNBC, and—in some respects—by Rev. Pat Robertson's Christian Broadcasting Network (CBN).

Next was the emergence of the Internet via the National Science Foundation in the early 1980s, and by the mid-1990s the development of the World Wide Web that revolutionized and made possible the ".com" media world. Taken together, we have seen in the past 20 years a reinvention of the world of communications, such that better than 97 percent of all information is now communicated digitally.

So then, of what use are the news media in mediating or resolving our intractable differences? The answer is a complicated one. The potential is great given the promise of an independent press in a time-tested democracy enjoying constitutional protection. It is through the free flow of high-quality information that even a polarized society might expect to find tools for addressing varying points of view, determining what's true and what isn't, and finding some common ground. This is one of the reasons that community leaders have expressed profound distress at the prospect of important news organizations failing to survive; they recognize the connection between healthy media outlets and productive civic discourse. Yet the media are weighed down with existential problems of their own, distracted, searching for winning formulas in a time of technological and economic upheaval, and not exactly beloved by all. Thomas E. Patterson, professor of government and the press at Harvard's John F. Kennedy School of Government, suggests it's too much to expect perfection from journalists, but they matter a great deal because they "are our chief sense-makers." He cites a 2006 Carnegie Corporation report finding journalism quality wanting in the search for profits and entertainment value, and notes that a 2012 Gallup poll found that 60 percent of respondents had no confidence in the press, or very little.[1]

THE DIGITAL REVOLUTION

The digital revolution and economic forces are driving media to be more partisan and less able to broker resolutions between warring factions in American life. This is affecting all forms of news coverage, but it's not hard to see how it might inhibit profoundly the kind of deeper reporting on the normative attitudes and beliefs we've been talking about. The public's list of charges against the news media is long and familiar to even the most casual consumers. The low standing of the press in the estimation of the public is regularly chronicled in survey research. However, the press rises to the occasion on many important moments, and overall has to be credited with a heroic dedication to its higher mission in a time of convulsive change.

This is especially significant at a time when the very livelihoods of those putting themselves on the line in the interest of an informed democracy are in jeopardy. When the *New York Times* announced it was eliminating one hundred positions in the fall of 2014, it was the latest in a mind-numbing procession of industry cutbacks stretching back over a period of years as major news organizations sought to offset declining revenues, and reposition and rebuild their enterprises for the digital era. This process of urgent reinvention has been described across the industry as changing the oil in a car barreling down a freeway. Meanwhile, the economic challenges are wide and deep. The *New York Times'* announcement noted substantial cuts at both the *Wall Street Journal* and *USA Today* in recent months, and major job layoffs at Freedom Communications, parent of the *Orange County Register* and the *Press-Enterprise* in Riverside.[2]

In short, there are some things that the press can't do; there are others where it can do better; and there are others where it is simply bungling. Here we consider with no little dismay how traditional and emerging media have mishandled our polarization, the topic most before us in this book. They do this at a time when the news world itself has been turned on its ear in a relatively short period of time by profound changes. Some think traditional news forms such as newspapers are on borrowed time, and how and what journalism will be in the future is very much on the table in a state of uncertainty. It remains unclear what these old media might do differently in reporting both on concerns and potential solutions arising out of values-based conflicts, both religious and secular.

RELIGION AND VALUES COVERAGE

The new media's religion coverage is a slice of the big picture and has been hampered by a complex set of restrictive forces in play in all forms of news coverage. However, in fact, religion coverage has been much better in recent decades because of a better-educated and specializing class of journalists who acquired an understanding of religious concepts, or taught their editors to understand the importance of religion in the everyday lives of the consumers of news. For example, in the aftermath of the terrorist attacks of 9/11, newsrooms educated themselves on the varieties, accomplishments, and corruptions of Islam. In a lecture delivered at UC Irvine in 2008, Phil Bennett, former managing editor of the *Washington Post,* detailed the profound learning curve that an entire news organization embarked on to understand the importance of Islam, not only on the global stage but also in suburbs and neighborhoods inhabited with some of the newest Americans.[3] But even before this, newspapers were devoting special sections to religion coverage and developing a cadre of reporters with a really informed understanding of religion. This impressive progress from the days of the Saturday church supper listings of yore has in the past several years been hampered by budget cuts. At least now many websites and social media are in place, dedicated to the understanding of religion and values in the coverage of the day's news. This may not be ideal, but it is not by any means the case that religion is being ignored. One shining example is the PBS/WNET program *Religion and Ethics Newsweekly.* Launched in 1997 by veteran journalist Bob Abernethy, the half-hour show presents very professional news and analysis of key issues in the field of religion and ethics. Another gem is the Religion News Service,[4] a secular news agency founded in 1934 and owned since 2011 by the Religion Newswriters Association based at the University of Missouri. It is distributed to 170 leading secular and religious news outlets.

The problem in our great ongoing cultural and social war is that there are bigger dynamics at work than just covering religion as one beat among many others. We need the news media to help us understand these and other values-based perspectives that are competing for our attention, to sort fact from opinion, and to act as independent validators. Ideally there would be an understood assigned role of the news media as providers of information and, in some cases, on the opinion and commentary side, as mediators of conflict. They could do this based on credible news reports that serve as taking-off points for deeper analysis, supported by public confidence in the truth-telling mission. The problem, as Harvard's Patterson explains, is that consumers have gravitated to media outlets that confirm what they already believe. He writes: "Unlike during the broadcast era, when most Americans had a shared media reality, the Internet era is increasingly a time of separate realities—'cyber-ghettos,' in the words of the British scholar Peter Dahlgren."[5]

QUARANTINE BY CHOICE

In other words, the process of quarantine by choice that we see in other areas of the values battlefield extends prominently into the news media audience, and the suppliers of news are obliging. That means lost opportunity for seeking a middle ground. Some of the things that go to the root of our democratic experience, having to do with our beliefs and values, are left unexamined; or they are done inadequately while partisans in the media turn their formidable spotlight onto generating attention-getting controversy back on themselves and leave news consumers confused and disgusted.

There are a couple of key elements to break out here at the outset. One is the notion that reporting does not have to bend over backward just to present both sides, and that somehow it can take satisfaction in having done this. Climate change is a key issue in the illustration of this. (Yes, there are two sides to the global warming debate, but the pro side is better substantiated. See again discussion in Chapter 4.) The second is that the press has found it irresistible to indulge in identity-politics issues, and ends up becoming a scold. This threatens its independence and credibility, certainly with conservatives but especially with centrist thinkers in the country who might look to the press to provide independent and informed analysis that leads to reasonable conclusions.

DESCENT INTO PETTINESS

In this chapter, we'll talk about media performance in the current polarized national environment. Here we might turn on its head the slogan "an embarrassment of riches" and call it the reverse: "a riches of embarrassments." We begin with an anecdotal tour of media squabbles that are at best confusing and unflattering to the participants, and at worst inept. Why does this matter at the outset of a discussion of media's role in our national polarization? The media (now including online and social media) are everywhere and their gaffes and insider controversies are unavoidable. This inevitably can affect the public's impressions and overall assessments of press performance.

This is a multilayered problem, complicated by the changing nature of the field of journalism itself. The essence of the problem was captured succinctly in a *Fox News Insider* segment hosted by media critic Howard Kurtz in August of 2014.[6] Pollster Frank Luntz was shown interviewing a focus group of news consumers, in which there was uniform agreement that media bias was in play and skewing the presentation of the news made available to the public. In the discussion that followed, two media critics, David Zurawik of the *Baltimore Sun* and Joe Concha, media watchdog for the blog Mediaite.com, lamented a news media that has lost trust and confidence. Concha compared today's news organizations to a quarterback being rushed by the defense and forced to throw the ball before his receivers are in position. Similarly, the media rush stories into print or on air before they've been properly fact-checked. This results in errors that sometimes go uncorrected and increases the public's distrust. Concha believes, "We have never been more polarized than we are now. Audiences, therefore, are more polarized as well . . . The messenger, host, anchor is giving an opinion and half the audience may disagree with it, that's where the distrust comes in."

Zurawik, media critic for the *Baltimore Sun*, complained on the same show about uncorrected errors and said the press, battered by technology and economics, "has lost the sense of high purpose, of serving democracy."[7] All of this has the public caught in a perpetual sandstorm and contributes to confusion. The media beast is relentless and not all things are put properly in perspective in a way that might help news consumers understand what they are seeing and hearing. The media's embarrassments pile on top of existing questions. They contribute to the skepticism the public already has about a profession in turmoil and can undermine the good and difficult work being done by many dedicated journalists at a time of profound change. A June 2014 Gallup survey of institutions (presidency, Congress, business, education, etc.) found that only 22 percent of respondents had a great deal/quite a lot of confidence in newspapers, 43 percent some confidence, and 33 percent little or none. In a comparable May 1973 survey, 39 percent expressed a great deal or quite a lot of confidence in papers (a drop of 17 points) and only 18 percent little or no confidence. The same pattern existed for TV news with only 18 percent having a great deal/quite a lot of confidence in 2014, compared to 46 percent in 1993. Internet news didn't fare much better: 19 percent of respondents had a lot of confidence in it, 34 percent little or none (no comparable data available for earlier periods).[8] Note that this lack of confidence in media was comparable to a decrease in almost all of the other institutions in the survey.

The consuming public is generally wise to the gaming of the system, as the Luntz focus group made clear, and appears to grasp that media talking heads are playing deliberately to type in order to advance partisan positions, egg on controversial positions, and generally position their programs and networks as reliable reference points of view in an advantageous media slot. And yet, the public would be understandably aghast if it did not recoil at how really unqualified some of the so-called media experts paraded before the cameras are. The news media and commentator class are now spending an excessive amount of time in the apology business. The situation has become so bad that it is almost as if the offending parties can't help themselves. Yet, it doesn't take long for us to recognize how stupid something was that escaped the commentator's lips when the cameras and microphones were turned on. (Stewart of *The Daily Show* until retiring in 2015 provided side-splitting critiques to many of these gaffes.)

FRAUDULENT MEDIA EXPERTISE

We are living with a diverse galaxy of media actors, especially on the cable networks, in addition to the highly partisan world of talk radio. There is no shortage of fraudulent media expertise on display, along with the clever and better-informed hosts who anchor regular programming and understand that their role is to provide an edge to the news, so that it has the appearance of real reporting. The media beast, as it has been called, has an insatiable appetite, and the demands of programming for 24-hour news cycles mean we are stuck with some of these people, maybe because there aren't enough good ones to go around. The cost of producing real reporting does not line up favorably against the ease with which somebody— anybody—can be miked up and put on to give forth about anything and everything in the news.

The nation was taken up with some serious business as the Obama administration headed for its final turns before the 2016 election cycle fully captivated people's attention. Yet there is serious business confronting us, requiring serious media reporting and commentary. For example, the big debate over how best to combat ISIS/Islamic State, the ruthless self-proclaimed caliphate bent on terror and destruction in the aftermath of the Iraq disintegration, centered in part on the question of the nature of United States' involvement. Would it be solely air strikes and at least the appearance of backing from our allies, or supplemented with ground troops? Into the fray came the Fox News host Eric Bollings in a segment for which he later had to apologize for referring to a female pilot who led an attack on ISIS as "boobs on the ground." This prompted the *Daily Show*'s Stewart to lambaste Bollings for hypocrisy in view of the latter's previous attention given to a salute that a deplaning President Obama made with a cup of coffee in his hand. Stewart had more serious points to make about uneven criticisms of presidents who although of different parties both were seen as committing U.S. military forces to risky ventures without any comprehensive plan.[9] Bollings held an important time slot and yet his credentials for expertise traced to his view as a commodities trader, though he has done other work in business reporting for which he appears more qualified.

Other examples of a perpetual news cycle of tasteless or silly-season media bursts: Megyn Kelly of Fox News affirms that Santa Claus is white. *New York Post* puts a front-page picture, Sunday, September 28, 2014, of the delighted grandparent Clintons, with the headline announcing the arrival of "Another liberal crybaby for Dem Clintons: PARTY POOPER." The Fox News guest commentator Dr. Keith Ablow says that language changes in California state law could be broadened to allow people to marry a beloved dog.[10] Another Fox News contributor Erick Erickson concludes that "the homosexual movement is destroying America" after defending a Georgia Republican congressional candidate Jody Hice, who among other things said that gays were actively recruiting children and that being gay was equivalent to drug addiction or alcoholism.[11]

The media environment is so combustible that it's also easy to get caught up in these barbs. There isn't much of any effort in this wild media world of cable opinion-making, blogs, social media, and so on, to correct even ordinary mistakes when made, not to mention outrageous indictments of various groups of citizens. One of Zurawik's observations on the Kurtz program was that in the era when legacy print and broadcast media were dominant, erring reporters would be pressured by editors to set the record straight. Less so nowadays for certain, although the legacies—the big traditional surviving media in print and broadcast—have learned that their attention to accuracy bolsters their credibility and distinguishes them in the media landscape. For many outlets, the convenient way to address something outrageous is to ignore it, secure in the knowledge that some other incoming tide of nonsense cannot be far behind, or on the other side, simply to reply with something disparaging. While this is happening, the public is vulnerable to a general information deficiency, absent its own resolute effort and initiative to cull out the real news from the stream of media opinions.

The parent companies of two cable news networks had to call a truce in 2009 when the prime time combatants Bill O'Reilly and Keith Olbermann were having at each other across the airwaves. Both partisans are savvy observers of the news landscape and neither is in the know-nothing category of some of the offending parties above, although both provoke strong reactions and have strong detractors. More accurately, each at the time could be categorized as signature flagship voices of the conservative and liberal cable networks, respectively. Olbermann, who since has returned to sports work with ESPN, hosted an evening show on MSNBC that at the time was well back in the ratings pack. Through the vehicle of being an irreverent pest, it was attempting to chase off the leading show, *The O'Reilly Factor,* and irritate its host. Olbermann drew up a nickname for his nemesis, "Bill-o the Clown"; O'Reilly by that time wasn't even inclined to grant

Olbermann the courtesy of a call-out by name, opting instead for the all-purpose label, "vicious smear merchant." While this carping might confirm the views of some partisan viewers or even prove entertaining, there were two important takeaways from this tussle. The first is that the stakes are high enough in the cable battle of positioning for viewer loyalty and sentiment that executives of General Electric for MSNBC and News Corporation for Fox began to worry when it looked as if things were going too far. The second is that the egos of the media stars are sufficiently distracting that there is no argument to be made that the public gets any enlightenment out of something like this.[12]

The Salon editor-at-large Joan Walsh has had some important things to say about the role of race in politics but was compelled to answer a double standard claim when she accused the radio talk show host Rush Limbaugh of being a "racist troll."[13] The occasion had been an MSNBC *Politics Nation* segment in 2013 discussing Limbaugh's use of the term "Operation Shuck and Jive" to characterize President Obama's plans for U.S. action in Syria. It was pointed out that "shuck and jive," considered disparaging African American slang, had been used by Andrew Cuomo, a Democrat, and by Chris Matthews, a liberal commentator.[14] An unapologetic Walsh said others who had used the phrase had also been criticized regardless of political persuasion, but that her basic conclusion was justified, based on a long history of what Limbaugh had said on the air, and to black callers.

Just sorting all this intramedia sniping itself is extra work for news consumers, if they don't give up first and resort to the comfort of media opinions that conform to their own attitudes and beliefs. There is evidence we'll see that some of this, in fact, is happening. Perhaps the most important conclusion from these examples is that the media, in their quest to be provocative, are susceptible to a descent into petty squabbling, often among the partisans themselves, whose outsized visibility provides no safeguards from self-importance. This happens while the public scratches its collective head on the sidelines wondering what's going on. It sees the generally bad behavior as it channel surfs across waves of talking heads and has to decide whether to even bother figuring out for itself what is and isn't important.

RETREATING TO COMFORT ZONES

Very often, viewers retreat to their comfort zones and almost exclusively watch Fox News, MSNBC, or CNN, while a minority turn to the more professional but less sexy *PBS NewsHour*, and even a smaller minority to the primary texts offered by C-SPAN. The news divisions of CBS, NBC, and ABC and their Sunday morning talk shows have maintained greater fairness and balance but will always be seen by conservatives as part of the "liberal media." There is a degree of truth in this claim, but these legacy network TV organizations still maintain a higher degree of professionalism than do Fox News or MSNBC. Though CNN does a somewhat better job with balanced reporting than the latter two cable networks, its ratings have slipped and made it difficult for that channel to stay above the fray.

National Public Radio has also maintained a high level professionalism, although some conservatives see it as left-leaning and point to the controversial firing of Juan Williams as an example of this. Williams, now a Fox News commentator, is a distinguished journalist who spent 21 years with the *Washington Post* and more recently was a commentator on NPR. In addition, he occasionally appeared on Fox's *The O'Reilly Factor* where, during a discussion of Muslim extremism in fall 2010, he admitted that he worried when boarding an airplane and seeing someone wearing traditional Muslim garb. The Council on American Islamic Relations (CAIR) and the left-leaning journalism watchdog Media Matters criticized Williams who was almost immediately fired by NPR before being given an adequate chance, in his opinion, to defend himself.[15] One can certainly argue about whether Williams's choice of words on the subject were well chosen, but it appears to be another example of political correctness run amok and the way doctrinaire conservative or liberal codes have come to dominate the media atmosphere.

A more recent and more controversial example of the problems with political correctness was the response to a June 6, 2014, column by George Will in the *Washington Post* about sexual assault on college campuses. He notes the pressure put on college presidents by the Department of Justice to report cases of date rape and to take steps to prevent it, and states: "They [colleges and universities] are learning that when they say campus victimizations are ubiquitous ('micro aggressions,' often not discernible to the untutored eye, are everywhere), and that when they make victimhood a coveted status that confers privileges, victims proliferate."[16] Will cites the case of a Swarthmore coed who had been sleeping with a young man but claimed he had raped her on one occasion: yet, she didn't report the incident until six weeks later. He goes on to question statistics indicating that one in five women is sexually assaulted during their college years. Although arguably Will could have been more sensitive to the sexual assault issue, which is troubling no matter what the statistics, he received an avalanche of criticism leading to protests of his public appearances, the dropping of his column by the *St. Louis Post-Dispatch*, and his being disinvited to speak at Scripps College in Southern California. The capper was the announcement by the liberal watchdog Media Matters that Will had been named "Misinformer of the Year." However, a week after Will's column appeared,

Joan Vennochi wrote in the *Boston Globe* that he should not be fired for his admittedly controversial comments, because opinion writers have the de facto right to express . . . opinions. She then gets to the heart of the problem we are analyzing in this book and observes, "If everyone looks at the problem through a political prism, how can anyone objectively weigh the pros and cons of solutions? That's what bogs down Washington."[17] To some extent we all look at reality through our political lenses, but there is a need to acknowledge this, and then refocus and strive for different perspectives. This, we believe, is the essence of political wisdom.

"PSEUDO JOURNALISM"

In what may have been a stunning Snapchat moment in the twilight of newspapers, then–*Los Angeles Times* editor John Carroll gave a lecture at the University of Oregon in 2004 entitled, "The Wolf in Reporter's Clothing: The Rise of Pseudo-Journalism in America."[18] Carroll referred to hearing a rebroadcast while stuck in traffic on a Los Angeles freeway on Halloween of the famous Orson Welles "War of the Worlds" radio broadcast from 1938, during which a captivated nation was enthralled by an account of an invasion of Martians that sounded real. The editor drew a parallel to his own time and to talk shows and websites, especially Fox News, that have "the trappings of journalism." He elaborated: "Today, the credibility painstakingly earned by past journalists lends an unearned legitimacy to the new generation of talk show hosts. Cloaked deceptively in the mantle of journalism, today's opinion-brokers are playing a nasty Halloween prank on the public, and indeed on journalism itself."[19]

Carroll describes a difficult decision his newspaper had to make as a special election for governor in California in 2003 approached. Candidate Arnold Schwarzenegger had been accused of mistreating women, and so the question became whether to publish such an explosive story or not so close to an election. The newspaper ran the story knowing the timing would be controversial. It came under fire from O'Reilly, who accused it of liberal bias with a claim that the *Los Angeles Times* had ignored the story of alleged misconduct by Bill Clinton as Arkansas governor in the Troopergate scandal. This it had done, O'Reilly asserted, because the newspaper had a political agenda; namely, to go after Republicans and give Democrats a free ride. Carroll, who had not been editor at the time, recounts taking to his computer to check this out, and finding not only that the newspaper *had* sent top reporters to Arkansas to investigate the Clinton accusations, but that its stories led the field. Carroll disputed a second complaint made by a freelance writer that the paper deliberately held a completed story until just before the election in order to extract maximum political damage. And then Carroll summarizes his case as follows:

If pseudo-journalism is not journalism, what is it? Where did it come from? Will it last? Some view the difference between the talk shows and traditional journalism in political terms, as a simple quarrel between left and right, between liberal and conservative. Those differences exist, but they're not of great consequence. What we're seeing is a difference between journalism and pseudo-journalism, between journalism and propaganda. The former seeks earnestly to serve the public. The latter seeks to manipulate it.[20]

Carroll diverts ominously to the question of corrections, detailing the extent to which serious news organizations go to set the record straight in their databases, and to avoid repeat mistakes in the future. Not so with Fox News. Carroll waited and waited for somebody to set the record straight on what the *Los Angeles Times* had done on the Troopergate story. No correction was forthcoming. This, he concluded, was the essence of the talk show beast, a nonstop parade of assertions, charges, and countercharges with little concern or respect for truthful summing up. Co-author Steve Burgard, who had left the editorial board of the newspaper in 2002, became a minor actor as a journalism professor appearing on *The O'Reilly Factor* in the ongoing friction between O'Reilly and Carroll over bias and accuracy. When Carroll resigned in 2005 after bitter budgetary differences with the parent Tribune Co., the newspaper announced that thereafter the editorial page editor of the newspaper would no longer report to the editor, but instead to the publisher.[21] O'Reilly pounced on this as a singular example of reining in a wayward and politically biased editor at a major newspaper. As a guest on the show, Burgard explained that the *New York Times* in fact already had the same editorial page reporting arrangement as the one that the Los Angeles newspaper was adopting. So the arrangement was not unique; at this writing ten years later, Carroll is still waiting for a clarification.[22]

The question of where commentators are coming from on the cable news channels is in a constant state of change if not outright confusion. When she returned to the network after maternity leave in 2013, Fox News's Megyn Kelly asserted that her new show, *The Kelly File*, would be a news show, not opinion.[23] Kelly has shown flashes of independence in various interviews, but when Tea Party protests were held in 2009, Politico's media writer Michael Calderone took note of a prominent role that she and other Fox News correspondents played in coverage that flirted with advocacy. He said, "'On America's Newsroom' Wednesday morning, Fox News host Megyn Kelly declared that 'it's tea party time, from sea to shining sea.'" A short while later, "anti-tax tea parties" rose to the top of the network's "Hot List."[24] It is fair to ask whether a network's environment is so forceful that it affects the coverage offered even by its own reporters who may naturally lean either liberal or conservative. The "white Santa" discussion mentioned earlier suggests at least that Kelly is comfortable with the network's leaning on social and cultural issues. Her star-spangled characterization of the Tea Party protests could well have been the kind of promotional language that event organizers would wish they had penned themselves.

MEDIA BIAS: GOOD OR BAD?

The Project for Excellence in Journalism puts out yearly State of the News Media Reports that take a clear-eyed look at changes in the field year to year. These have become especially useful during the period of fast and convulsive change of recent years, because they constitute one of the best and most independent appraisals of what is happening both with the traditional, or "legacy," media and the new upstarts in the world of social media. Most important, the reports pinpoint changing media strategies brought on by economic demands resulting from declining advertising revenues, the splintering of audiences, and the search for relevance in the new online world. This is especially visible with the cable news networks, which, because of the way they are constituted, provide a window on the complicated journalism-wide question of media bias. We'll talk also about models for news and information as they have evolved in the early part of the twenty-first century and, in particular, the way in which the playing fields have changed.

First, some informative thoughts about media bias—the elephant in the room—from the Shorenstein Center on Media, Politics and Public Policy at Harvard. The Center publishes a "Journalist's Resource" website that includes an audio session with two experts in a discussion entitled, "Partisanship in the Non-Partisan Press: The Implications of Media Bias for Democracy," It featured Kathleen Hall Jamieson of the Annenberg School of Communication,[25] University of Pennsylvania; and Jesse Shapiro, an economist at Booth School of Business, University of Chicago. Shapiro makes some important points based on his research that may seem almost counterintuitive: not only that there is no such thing as unbiased reporting, but that we would not want it to be this way if we could have it. He says that consumers rely on their media of choice to filter information for them and tell them what's important. The flip-sided question, "What would unbiased reporting look like," has an unsatisfactory answer because to accomplish this would amount to putting everything out and leaving viewers and readers entirely on their own to make sense of it. This goes to the heart of what degree of truth there may be in journalism's mission of helping busy citizens become informed. For the discussion in this book, a key is the link between what the new media outlets aim to accomplish on behalf of consumers, what those consumers expect, and ultimately the things that people consider important at the level of core beliefs.

This was apparent in one of the early debates over the mission of journalism at the dawn of the Internet age that involved, of all people, the controversial blogger Matt Drudge, who was associated with the Monica Lewinsky scandal during Bill Clinton's presidency. Drudge, publisher of The Drudge Report, in a lively *Fox News Sunday* debate in 1998 with the veteran diplomatic correspondent Marvin Kalb, argued that the "put it all out there" model was the correct one for these times. Kalb, at the time director of the Shorenstein Center, vigorously disputed this role in favor of a more traditional one for journalism as intermediary and representative for the public in its task as filter of newsworthy information.[26]

There is, Shapiro says, evidence aplenty that news media cover the same news with a focus in content and headlines that their consumers actually expect. However, this is not to say that a selection of several accounts of the same event would turn up inaccuracies, only a difference in emphasis and approach to coverage that confirms the predispositions of the viewers and readers. This he concludes is not necessarily a bad thing; indeed, Shapiro advocates as much diversity in news selection as possible to spread around the credible sources of information across a vast landscape. If he is right, a loop connects media organizations and what their regulars saddling up daily to the news bar expect. But, ironically, it reinforces the "big sort" mentality of only watching the news that fits your comfort zone. One remedy is for viewers to take a cafeteria approach from time to time to get a reality check, a bigger picture than what a single news source provides.

Jamieson focuses on scientific reporting, but also is concerned with what matters most: what journalists aspire to accomplish in providing useful information in the larger policy conversation. She challenges them to be guarantors of information, which is actually a twenty-first century formulation of a traditional journalistic ambition of being stand-ins for the public in the policy conversation. One way is to escape the confines of an old reporting model that puts everybody who is interviewed or speaks out on equal qualifications footing in the interest of perceived "balance." She wants journalists to report if a scientific consensus has emerged on a particular topic that may be controversial in the policy realm, such as climate change. But she also prods journalists to go beneath the surface of claims made in scientific studies, to determine with confidence the level of validation within the scientific community itself. Her goal is to have the journalists serve in "the role of aspiring to traditional values," of getting at the truth as independent providers of information, to minimize the risk of having them get caught up as pawns in the policy storms that come out of scientific studies at the political level.[27]

The publication in early 2014 of a biography of Roger Ailes, chairman of Fox News Channel, was accompanied by attention to Fox and its influence in the news environment. The *New York Times'* advance noted that Ailes presided over a cable network that had more viewers than its two rivals MSNBC and CNN combined, and that he had told his own executives in 2012 that his ambition was nothing short of getting the next president elected.[28] The Pew Research Center looked into the influence and reach of Fox, and found no surprise: only 6 percent of the network's coverage of President Obama in the 2012 election was positive. This interestingly was higher than MSNBC's favorable coverage of the Republican candidate Mitt Romney at 3 percent, which suggests that the cable fragmentation of sympathetic coverage along political lines is not the exclusive domain of the conservative side of Fox.[29]

However, in all these discussions of bias, we come full circle to the expectations and attitudes of the news consumers, which is truly significant. The Pew study found that the Fox News viewers described themselves as conservative at a rate of 60 percent, almost twice as high as the degree to which viewers of CNN and MSNBC described themselves as either moderate or liberal. So as Shapiro suggested in his Shorenstein talk, the circle of confirmation matters between news source and consumers; it's one reason why media bias may not always be such a big deal. That is, provided that there are enough credible choices—with the emphasis on *credible*—for viewers and readers coming from many attitudes and political beliefs, some of them fixed. The emphasis and selection of story material in response to consumer wants lies at the root of the media-bias phenomenon and goes to the core of any meaningful understanding of strategic or market-positioning considerations. We also have to conclude that the societal advantage in this interpretation of media bias is fragile at best. We've already seen the gamble posed for media credibility by opting for partisan approaches as the race to feed the insatiable 24-hour news beast takes over. Any benefit can unravel if news crosses into propaganda, as Carroll warned in his speech, especially if there is reckless disregard for accuracy and setting the record straight.

Now to the question of the Project for Excellence in Journalism's state-of-media reports, and how the cable news channels provide a model for the deliberate positioning of news and opinion content along partisan lines. By the 2013 report, it was clear that for the cable news networks in prime time, having an opinion edge proved necessary to ratings. CNN, which alone strove for journalistic neutrality through a mix of reporting, opinion, and commentary, was lagging in the group of the three majors—itself, the front-running conservative Fox News, and the liberal MSNBC.[30] The most significant findings foreshadowing this trend occurred in the 2010 report. The report's essay on cable found it to be the one commercial sector not afflicted by declining revenues, and charted the advantages for ratings and in some cases profit to be found in opinion-driven content. It noted, for example, that partisan programming was a driver in building a 24- to 55-year-old audience for the liberal MSNBC and that this was coming at a cost in prime time audience for CNN. The report noted that the strongest growth was on the ideological programs as a result of focus on opinion, and concluded, "over all, these audience figures seemed to reward what had become a clear branding strategy at the channels."[31]

Under new leadership in subsequent years, CNN improved its ratings relative to MSNBC, even though overall viewership for CNN and other cables went down. This was attributable to an emphasis on breaking news and the development of new features (such as Anthony Bourdain's *Parts Unknown*) under the leadership of Jeff Zucker who, like other news executives, was trying to find a niche in the radically altered digital news environment.[32]

In its review of all news media for that 2010 year, the report raised the big questions about the news business that remain with us across all the media news platforms: "What are the prospects for alternative journalism organizations that are forming around the country? Will traditional media adapt and innovate amid continuing pressures to thin their ranks?"[33]

FAIRNESS OR PHONY BALANCE?

In the end, everything comes down to what the core values of journalistic enterprises are and will be in the changing media world. On the one hand, we have these commercial news ventures finding ways to give people the slant they want, even at the risk of breaking completely with conventional news standards. On the other, we find traditional media under assault for operating as if the ideological fix was not in. There is an inherent tension between the two visions today, especially as new media operate under fewer constraints.

In the standard journalistic model, the remedy to the perception of liberal bias in news coverage has been adherence to the overarching concept of "fairness." For years in newsrooms, this meant being sure that every source with a partisan interest in a policy debate had a chance to weigh in and get on the record. There are some experts on traditional and new media who think this was less about principle and more about marketing, an exercise designed to deliver mass audiences to advertisers by giving as little offense as possible. Building mass audiences is much more of a challenge today, because the new media environment turns the tables on legacy media dominance. It has them competing with anybody who owns a computer and enters the fray of information providers. With social media, blogs, and aspiring entrants into the journalistic arena like BuzzFeed, the playing field is much more lateral. It's less top-down as a communication model in the manner of the big networks and newspapers ruling the information roost.[34]

Despite these changes, the public generally has been served well by this approach during the years of dominance of the legacy media in newspapers and broadcast. The issue now is that the legacy media don't necessarily dominate the conversation. In fact, this significant change has not been lost within the walls of the traditional news giants. Robin Sproul, vice president of public affairs for ABC News, told students at Harvard's Kennedy School that her network was consciously reframing its relationship with consumers, mindful that visitors to its website were arriving on referral from many media sources. This has resulted in turning a big network into a kind of curator of news, rather than being an authority figure making pronouncements on what the important news of the day is. And it has meant a redefinition of competition, and even partnerships with other platforms. Sproul noted, "We're not just competing with NBC; we're competing with your friend's sunrise."[35]

Still, the traditional media also are wise to the degree that they recognize they are custodians of a tradition of news standards that have served the public well. That is, provided they don't succumb entirely to the siren call of news as entertainment, as Patterson has warned. If this function of setting standards for quality news reporting were to go away, it would at some point have to be reinvented as a way to restore order in a world of "truthiness" (Colbert) and flying factoids and listicles, a term used to describe the tendency of some social media to provide "ten best" lists.

The commitment to the news value of fairness is one way to ensure that a firewall is preserved between the opinion engines of the news organizations controlled by publishers and media owners, editorial writers, and columnists, and the mandate of producing an honest and complete report by open-minded journalists on the news-gathering side. Fairness, when all is said and done, is about credibility building. Carroll had this in mind when he wrote a memo to his *Los Angeles Times* staff in 2003 entitled, "Credibility/Abortion." The memo began:

I'm concerned about the perception—and the occasional reality—that *The Times* is a liberal, "politically correct" newspaper. Generally speaking, this is an inaccurate view, but occasionally we prove our critics right. We did so today with the front-page story on the bill in Texas that would require abortion doctors to counsel patients that they may be risking breast cancer.

The memo went on to criticize the account for failing to make any effort to explore a scientific or medical argument linking abortion to breast cancer, even though a strong case was made that no such link exists. Such attention to the tone and completeness of one story is ironic to say the least when one considers the accusation of liberal bias leveled by O'Reilly against this particular editor. There was, Carroll noted, a professor of biology and endocrinology quoted near the end of the story who might have refuted that link, but the newspaper didn't bother to explore any of that, and gave only his political views. Carroll wrote, "I want everyone to understand how serious I am about purging all political bias from our coverage. We may happen to live in a political atmosphere that is suffused with liberal values (and is unreflective of the nation as a whole), but we are not going to push a liberal agenda in the news pages of The Times."[36]

There is confirmation right off a news report of a commitment to making sure that the kind of reporting effort Jamieson was talking about is thorough before concluding that the evidence is irrefutable in a scientific or medical policy debate. The Texas abortion story illustrates the connection between perceived bias in a news organization and what happens in the actual act of daily reporting and editing. With all the fragmentation we have talked about, the mass media have been—through the massive body of work in countless stories about social and cultural controversies in the political sphere—one valuable provider of civic glue we have had in the post–World War II era.

And yet, the "balance" issue persists. The notion that balance in media has been a driver to fend off criticism of one-sidedness has been much in the discussion. Patterson suggests that there is more to it. Controversy to attract attention is also a powerful incentive for dispensers of news and commentary to set up a false dynamic in which opposing points of view are given an equal place at the table to set off sparks and attract attention. He suggests that journalists also find a too-comfortable haven in providing a semblance of balance, rather than doing the work to ferret out the truth of opinion leaders' claims, and perhaps risk irritating them. In an article excerpted from his book for *Salon*, he cited a number of occasions where this happened: in the John Kerry "Swift Boat" controversy during the 2004 presidential election, in the war in Iraq and concerns with terrorism, in the economic accounting of the Bush tax cuts, and in such euphemisms as "enhanced interrogation techniques" as an alternative to torture.[37]

The BBC became concerned enough about a false sense of balance in science reporting that it commissioned a study in 2011. It found areas where due consideration to scientific conclusions was given up in the interest of "impartiality" and proposed some remedies to improve what it called "editorial and organizational shortcomings."[38] *The Nation*'s Katrina vanden Heuvel made reference to this in a *Washington Post* article. She pointed to a 2012 Gallup poll that found 42 percent of Americans thought global warming was greatly exaggerated in the news, and she argued this is traceable to "the veil of false equivalence."[39]

Tom Rosenstiel, for nearly 12 years media critic for the *Los Angeles Times*, is now executive director of the American Press Institute. In 2011 he co-authored (with Bill Kovacs) *Blur: How to Know What's True in the Age of Information Overload*. They write eloquently, as discussed earlier in this chapter, that the news scene has changed tremendously. This produces a kind of "blur" where we get news from traditional sources as well as online, then function as our own editors and the creators of our particular news diet while we e-mail stories to one another. In an interview with CapitalNewYork.com,[40] Rosenstiel discusses "open journalism," a kind of mutual intelligence based on three forces: (1) the power of computers that provide reliable quantitative information, (2) the World Wide Web connecting news gatherers to audiences and communities with immense breadth, and (3) professional reporters and editors who have unique access to exceptional storytelling abilities and the discipline of open-minded and skeptical inquiry.

New York Times columnist David Carr elaborates on Rosenstiel's point that it is up to consumers to assemble a news diet of their own choice. He also observes that it is possible to be both journalist and activist, and cites the case of *The Guardian*'s Glenn Greenwald who served as a conduit for Edward Snowden's release of top-secret information about the National Security Agency. However, he adds the following caution: "That is not to say that Mr. Greenwald's work is suspect, only that the tendentiousness of ideology creates its own narrative. He has been everywhere on television taking on his critics, which seems more like a campaign than a discussion of the story covered."[41]

CONCLUSION: THE PRESS IS ALIVE AND REASONABLY WELL BUT LIVING IN A NEW DIGITAL WORLD

In his keynote speech at the Fifteenth International Symposium on Online Journalism, Martin Baron, executive editor of the *Washington Post*, said he remains optimistic about journalism's future despite the immense changes that have taken place. He points out that journalism has survived despite recent predictions of its demise; and that, while legacy media are spinning off journalists, these individuals are becoming entrepreneurial and finding work in the online world. Baron also thinks readers are now better able to digest more information than in the past and like the variety of platforms on which news and information is presented. He does worry about how journalism will be funded in the future and about the lack of journalists covering even the basics of politics at the local level.[42] And the authors of this study worry that the polarization in media will make it harder for those in the "endangered center" to make reasoned political and ethical judgments.

Still, in the end it is left to the news consumer to sort out the facts in this brave new media world, which probably is how we would want it to be in a functioning democracy with an independent press. What is essential, though, is that readers become more wide-ranging in their media choices—more willing, for instance, to read both the *New York Times* and the *Wall Street Journal*, both *The Nation* and *The National Review*; and more willing to watch both MSNBC and Fox News. Otherwise, we are left with dangerous polarization, with "the big sort" where citizens live in parallel political and media universes. As we discuss in Chapter 12 on civility, the nation's media consumers need to read and listen to divergent political and cultural viewpoints and respond critically but civilly. Professional journalists and commentators need to do the same: Stop "dissing" the competition and start looking instead for valuable insights from the other side that might promote democracy and "a more perfect union."

NOTES

1. Thomas E. Patterson, *Informing the News.* New York: Vintage, 2013, p. 5.

2. "*New York Times* Plans Cutbacks in Newsroom Staff," Ravi Somaiya, *New York Times*, October 1, 2014.

3. "Covering Islam: A Challenge for American Journalism," Phil Bennett, chancellor's lecture, UC Irvine, March 3, 2008.

4. www.religionnews.com

5. Patterson, op. cit., p. 13

6. "Americans Doubt That the News Is Being Delivered Straight," foxnewsinsider. com, August 31, 2014. Retrieved September 29, 2014.

7. Ibid.

8. www.Gallup.com/poll/1597/confidence-institutions.aspx

9. "The Way We War," Jon Stewart, *The Daily Show with Jon Stewart*, September 25, 2014.

10. "Fox News, the Network Where 'Spouse' Clearly Includes Your Dog," Mark Joseph Stern, slate.com, July 9, 2014. Retrieved September 29, 2014.

11. Hice's views and Erickson's celebratory tweet about him were contained in "11 Reasons Republican Jody Hice Will Likely Be the Most anti-Gay Member of Congress," Andrew Kacynski, BuzzFeedNews, posted July 23, 2014.

12. "Voices from above Silence a Cable TV Feud," Brian Stelter, *New York Times*, July 31, 2009.

13. "You Heard Me: Rush Limbaugh Is a 'Racist Troll,'" Joan Walsh, salon.com, September 10, 2013.

14. "Joan Walsh: Limbaugh a 'Racist Troll.'" Dylan Byers on Media, politico. com, September 9, 2013.

15. *Muzzled: The Assault on Honest Debate*. New York: Crown, 2011.

16. "Colleges Become the Victims of Progressivism," *Washington Post*, June 6, 2014.

17. www.BostonGlobe.com/opinion/2014/06/11/should-focus-gray-areas/.

18. "The Wolf in Reporter's Clothing: The Rise of Pseudo-Journalism in America," 2004 Ruhl Lecture, John Carroll, University of Oregon, School of Journalism and Communication, May 6, 2004. http://journalism.uoregon.edu/events/2004-ruhl-lecture-john-carroll/. Retrieved September 30, 2014.

19. Ibid.

20. Ibid.

21. "Editor at *Los Angeles Times* Stepping Down after 5 Years," Katharine Q. Seelye, *New York Times*, July 21, 2005.

22. *The O'Reilly Factor*, Fox News Channel, July 21, 2005.

23. Megyn Kelly: "I'm Not Going to Be the Female Bill [O'Reilly]," Alex Weprin, *TVNewser*, October 4, 2013.

24. "Fox Teas Up a Tempest," Michael Calderone, politico.com, April 15, 2009.

25. The Annenberg School maintains the highly respected and nonpartisan website www.Factcheck.org, which helps dispel rumors and inaccuracies in media.

26. *Fox News Sunday*, October 4, 1998.

27. "Partisanship in the non-Partisan Press: The Implications of Media Bias for Democracy," Shorenstein Center on Media, Politics and Public Policy, Journalist's Resource. http://journalistsresource.org/skills/research/media-bias-partisanship-what-it-means-democracy-chat-reading-list?utm_source=JR-email&utm_medium=email&utm_campaign=JR-email#. Retrieved October 1, 2014.

28. "Biography Casts Critical Light on Fox News Chief," Julie Bosman and Bill Carter, *New York Times*, January 7, 2014.

29. "5 Facts about Fox News," Jesse Holcom, Pew Research Center, January 14, 2014.

30. "Cable: Audience vs. Economics," Jesse Holcomb, Amy Mitchell, and Tom Rosenstiel, The State of the News Media 2011, Pew Research Center's Project for Excellence in Journalism. http://stateofthemedia.org/2011/cable-essay/. Retrieved October 2, 2014.

31. Ibid.

32. "How Jeff Zucker Is Reshaping CNN," Emily Steel, *New York Times*, October 4, 2014.

33. "Overview" State of the News Media 2010, The Pew Research Center's Project for Excellence in Journalism. http://stateofthemedia.org/2010/overview-3/. Retrieved October 2, 2014.

34. For a good discussion, listen to "The News about the News: Jay Rosen," Radio Open Source, Arts, Ideas and Politics with Christopher Lydon, March 28, 2008. http://radioopensource.org/the-news-about-the-news-jay-rosen/.

35. "Robin Sproul: Reporting the News in a Shifting Media Landscape," Speaker Series, Shorenstein Center, September 9, 2014.

36. "Memo on Abortion and Liberal Bias by *Los Angeles Times* Editor John Carroll," LA Observed, May 22, 2003.

37. "Phony Balance, Manufactured Conflict: The Media Just Confuses the Truth," Thomas E. Patterson, salon.com, October 5, 2013. Excerpted from *Informing the News*, op. cit.

38. "BBC Trust Review of Impartiality and Accuracy of the BBC's Coverage of Science," July 2011. http://downloads.bbc.co.uk/bbctrust/assets/files/pdf/our_work/science_impartiality/science_impartiality.pdf. Retrieved October 4, 2014.

39. "The Distorting Reality of 'False Balance' in the Media," Katrina vanden Heuvel, *Washington Post*, July 15, 2014.

40. www.capitalNewYork.com/article/media/2014/10/8555509/60-second-interview-Tom-Rosenstiel-executive-director-American-Press-Institute.

41. www.nytimes.com/2013/07/01/business/media/journalism-is-still-at-work-even-when-its-tilted/.

42. http://online.journalism.utexas.edu/detail.php?story=463&year=2014.

Chapter 12

Chivalry May Be Dead, but What about Civility?

A party of order for stability, and a party of progress for reform, are both necessary elements of a healthy state of political life. Each of these modes of thinking derives its utility from the deficiencies of the other; but it is in a great measure the opposition of the other that keeps each within the limits of reason and sanity. (John Stuart Mill)[1]

We're in this together because America is not defined by just red or the blue, but by the red, white, and blue. The obstacles we face are only surmountable if we continue to speak without listening. (Former Maine Senator Olympia Snowe)[2]

On a lazy campus day just before the start of fall classes, co-author Ben Hubbard was having lunch with a political science colleague and discussing the progress of this book. Ben and his liberal-leaning friend were agreeing on almost everything, as they bemoaned the current stalemate in Washington, DC, and Congress's inability to do the people's business. Then Ben mentioned the chapter dealing with gun control and the salience of John Lott's controversial theory (see Chapter 4) that the possession of guns by citizens might actually be reducing the rate of crime. At this juncture, Ben's colleague got a bit uncomfortable. We went on to other topics, but it was clear to Ben that his friend had experienced a negative-reflex response to the often-maligned Professor Lott. This was not surprising, because Ben himself had for many years held the same opinion of Lott. But researching this book had forced him to look again at an opposing viewpoint that he was also reflectively suspicious of when he first encountered it.

The moral of this anecdote is that, in simplest terms, human beings are genetically disposed to take a more conservative or liberal standpoint on a host of complex political, ethical, aesthetic, and religious issues. From an evolutionary standpoint, it is not surprising that some people are more cautious, some more daring, some more individualistic, some more communitarian. The human community, for its well-being, needs both conservatives and liberals, Republicans and Democrats, red states and blue states. Evolution would not have it otherwise.

Ben illustrates this point in some of his classes with a parable:

Somewhere in Africa 30,000 years ago, a tribe was experiencing a severe drought. Yet they were aware that in a valley on the other side of a mountain pass there had been rainfall, bringing an abundance of fruits and grasses to sustain life. However, the tribe on that side was known to be fiercely territorial and might very likely kill anyone who crossed over to their side. So the elders of the drought-suffering tribe held many council meetings trying to decide whether crossing the pass was worth the risk: Stay where they were and face starvation, cross the mountain pass and risk annihilation. There were passionate voices on each side of the debate and it seemed for a time nothing would be decided. Finally, however, the elders agreed to send a delegation of volunteers who would risk their lives but might be able to explain their plight to the tribe on the verdant side of the mountain.

Was it worth the risk? We will let our readers write their own ending to the story. But one thing is clear: Inaction meant death, action meant the possibility of survival. And only in the give and take of debate did a consensus emerge. Conservatives and liberals desperately need each other; for no individual, no political party, no philosophy, and—dare we say—no religion possesses all wisdom.

THE VIEW FROM RECENT SCHOLARSHIP

In his book *The Righteous Mind—Why Good People Are Divided by Politics and Religion*,[3] social psychologist Jonathan Haidt provides a highly enlightening analysis of why it is inevitable that in any democratic society some people will be conservatives, others liberals. (He also explains that libertarians are actually liberals who love liberty and free markets, and lack bleeding hearts!) First, there is a genetic predisposition to one or the other of these tendencies, both of which are indispensable. According to Haidt, our genetic endowment accounts for between a third and half of the variability among humans on their political (and, we would add) religious attitudes; being raised in a liberal or conservative household accounts for considerably less.[4] But, while genes make brains (nature), traits guide children along different paths. That is, children grow up in different kinds of home settings (nurture) and they will have a variety of experiences that will provide "life narratives" to influence and inform their conduct in society. Those who have lived in a politically repressive society, for instance, will crave liberty more intensely than those who took freedom for granted.

Haidt then discusses the shortcomings of both a liberal and a conservative political philosophy. The left tends to overlook "moral capital," the absolute need for the kind of Bill-of-Rights safeguards that keep a society from becoming despotic and totalitarian. Yet, the right fails to be sufficiently compassionate toward the needs of what the Gospel of Matthew (25:40)[5] calls "the least of these," individuals whose physical, intellectual, economic, and societal circumstances put them at a de facto disadvantage from the start. He sums it up this way:

Liberalism—which has done so much to bring about freedom and equal opportunity—is not sufficient as a governing philosophy. It tends to overreach, change too many things too quickly, and reduce the stock of moral capital inadvertently. Conversely, while conservatives do a better job of preserving moral capital, they often fail to notice certain classes of victims, fail to limit the predations of certain powerful interests, and fail to see the need to change or update institutions as times change.[6]

Haidt concludes his discussion by describing how American political culture, both in Congress and many state capitals, has become black and white. He compares this to the Manichaean philosophy of the early Christian centuries in which the world was seen as a battleground of forces, good and evil. Today, the battleground is starkly political. Starting when President Lyndon Johnson signed the Civil Rights Act of 1964, there has been a geographical realignment of political parties, making the South and plains states generally Republican, and the Far West, upper Midwest, and Northeast Democratic. This process was really catalyzed when Newt Gingrich, speaker of the House of Representatives in 1995, began to encourage Republican Congress members and their families to stay in home districts rather than moving to Washington. Prior to this, many of them lived in the DC area, socialized on weekends, saw their children playing on the same sports teams, and got to know one another. Today most legislators in Washington arrive on Monday night, do legislative battle for the next three days and fly home on Thursday night. Hence, a good-guys-versus-bad-guys Manichaean worldview begins to dominate and civil dialogue becomes more difficult. To go back to the quotation from Martin Buber in Chapter 4, "All real living is meeting." You cannot live a life of political dialogue in Congress unless you're able to meet the political other in a nonconflictual setting. Haidt believes that our politics will only become more civil when we can find ways to change the mechanisms for electing politicians, and the institutions and environments in which they interact (see suggestions from Olympia Snowe, below).

Haidt concludes his remarkable book with this sentence: "We're all stuck here for a while, so let's try to work it out."[7] It reminds one of Rodney King's[8] statement, "Can't we all just get along?" There are elements of profundity and banality in both. We hope that the succeeding discussion of civility will demonstrate that some common-sense suggestions (discussed below) might make at least a modest difference in moving the business of government forward.

Center-left columnist and political historian, E. J. Dionne, presents an incisive analysis of the current political malaise in *Our Divided Political Heart*.[9] Dionne contends that, *"Americans disagree about who we are because we can't agree about who we've been."*[10] He believes we have lost our gift for reasoning together and must recover our respect for balance, remembering its central role in our history. We are, he contends, a nation of individualists who care passionately about community. The book is an attempt to document historically his thesis about the indispensability both of individualism and communitarianism. It looks in particular at the "long consensus" that existed during the American century, beginning with Teddy Roosevelt in 1901 and persisting through the twentieth century. (It is our contention, incidentally, that the American century ended in 2003 with the invasion of Iraq. Dionne believes the country is in the moment of "asymmetric polarization." Democrats hold faith both in government and the capitalist marketplace, while Republicans oppose compromise in the belief that it will set back their larger agenda of limited government and the demise of the welfare state. He notes how very differently the Tea Party interprets our history and pushes the logic of a particular kind of American conservatism to its limits. It thus deserves credit for framing the debate very sharply.

Dionne draws on the insights of Bill Bishop in *The Big Sort*[11] who describes how Americans are "forming tribes," not just in neighborhoods and churches but volunteer groups as well (and, we would add, media neighborhoods as well—MSNBC versus Fox, *New York Times* versus *Wall Street Journal*, Jon Stewart versus Rush Limbaugh, etc.). (Haidt makes a parallel observation about "landslide counties" that voted either Democratic or Republican by a margin of 20 percent or more. In 1976, only 27 percent of Americans lived in such counties; by 2008, the number—aided by gerrymandering—had risen to 48 percent.)[12] Dionne's concluding hope is that conservatism might rediscover its moderate and communitarian side. The authors of this book agree with that wish, but also hope that progressives might rediscover the power of individual initiative and the need to keep the federal government within reasonable limits. Is our "political heart" so divided that a new consensus remains out of reach, or might bypass surgery put us on the road to recovering "a more perfect union"?

In *Religion, Politics, and Polarization* by William D'Antonio et al.,[13] we get a careful statistical analysis of how religion factors into the current political divide we have been discussing. Ironically, it seems that political party affiliation by members of Congress is the primary determinant of their voting patterns rather than membership in a particular religious community. On such key issues as abortion, taxes, defense, and welfare, legislators appeared to vote more along party lines than religion ones. For example, most Catholic Democrats supported a pro-choice position, while most Protestant Republicans were solidly pro-life. However, a deeper analysis indicates that it was shifts in the American religious landscape that led to these voting patterns. Liberal Catholics generally considered termination of pregnancy to be a moral choice in at least some instances. Conservative-evangelical Protestants are now the majority among non-Catholic Christians, and this is reflected in their preponderance in the ranks of Republican Congress members. In short, religious affiliations have contributed to the polarization in Congress, albeit indirectly.

One of the finest recent studies of civility is Stephen L. Carter's *Civility—Manners, Morals, and the Etiquette of Democracy.*[14] Carter notes that there never was a golden age of political politeness in America. Nonetheless, in a book written 17 years ago, Carter sensed that political discourse was unraveling. Recalling the civility and courage of the civil rights marchers in the 1960s, he notes that civility is a precondition of democratic dialogue. He states five reasons for democracy to value this kind of generous civility:

1. It encourages us to view those with whom we disagree as full equals before God (one might substitute "before our common human Nature") so that respectful dialogue becomes possible.
2. It reminds us that in a democracy all our actions must pass the test of morality, and that our ability to discipline ourselves to do so is what distinguishes us from animals.
3. Self-discipline, in turn, helps us resist the urge to keep politics and the market from dominating all social life.
4. Our adherence to standards of civil behavior provides a "letter of introduction" to our fellow citizens, thereby assisting us in building community.
5. By treating each other with the respectful civility that our common humanity requires, we help make more tolerable the many slights and frictions of everyday life.[15]

Then Carter turns to incivility, in particular the strategy of political campaigns to diminish the reputation of the other side. Politics will always use this tactic, but Carter believes such political battles must take place against the background of a shared understanding of what we as a nation stand for. Moreover, struggles for political power must represent only a modest part of the nation's life and must be balanced by institutions—religious, humanistic, and cultural—that serve to keep political nastiness in check. He concludes his study with an "etiquette of democracy," a set of summary rules for civil conduct both in politics and life in general.

- Being civil toward others does not depend on whether we like them or not.
- Civility has two components: generosity, even when it is costly, and trust, even when there is risk.
- Civility requires that we come into the presence of our fellow human beings with a sense of awe and gratitude.
- Civility assumes that we will disagree, but it requires us not to hide our differences but to resolve them respectfully. Criticism of others is permissible, and sometimes even required, but must remain civil.
- Civility requires that we listen to others with the realization they might be right and we wrong.
- Teaching civility is an obligation of the family and not primarily of the state.
- Religions do their greatest service to civility by preaching not just love of neighbor but resistance to evil. [16]

One of the wisest recent books on the topic of civility and dialogue is *The Dignity of Difference—How to Avoid the Clash of Civilizations*[17] by Rabbi Jonathan Sacks, former chief rabbi of the United Kingdom. Sacks says, in effect, that no religious or philosophical tradition encompasses all wisdom. He quotes the Talmud: "Who is wise? One who learns from all men." The truly wise person knows that all persons possess some share of wisdom, and he or she is willing to learn from all of them. In our global age, Sacks stresses, we need to understand that, just as the natural environment depends on biodiversity, so the human one depends on cultural diversity, "because no one civilization encompasses all the spiritual, ethical and artistic expressions of mankind."[18] This mind-set might help both politicians and preachers from very different backgrounds at least entertain the possibility that they have something to learn from another political philosophy or religious tradition.

LISTENING AS AN ART FORM

Carter's stress on the importance of listening segues into the work of Kay Lindahl, a prominent interfaith activist in Southern California and founder of the Listening Center. Through her interfaith work, Kay (a personal friend of co-author Ben Hubbard) developed techniques for listening with care and attentiveness to persons from religious and spiritual traditions quite different from her own. In fact, she cofounded with the late Rabbi Allen Krause what was perhaps the first Religious Diversity Fair (later Forum) in the nation in 1994 that continued in various formats until 2013. The premise of her work is that listening is a creative force that can transform relationships. She considers listening a sacred art, a way of being fully present to the other and of deeply hearing them as they listen to you. Such listening requires three qualities: silence, or contemplative listening to God or one's spiritual Source; reflection, which means listening to yourself and getting to know the voice of your soul; presence, which involves "heart listening"—listening with care and taking the time to connect with others heart to heart. Although Kay developed her approach to the art of listening to promote dialogue between people with different belief systems, the technique could also be very valuable tool in the political sphere. She presents ten listening practices:

1. Stop talking and allow one person at a time to speak. Interrupting someone is very irritating.
2. Pause before speaking to allow the other person to complete their thought. Or simply ask, "Is there anything else?"
3. Listen to your inner voice so that you will better know what needs to be said next.
4. Listen for understanding, even though you may not agree with, or even believe, what the other person is saying.
5. Ask for a clarification if you don't understand what someone is saying.
6. Let the speaker know you have heard them with body language—nodding, facial expressions, and the like.
7. Be patient and present, because listening well takes time and your active presence.
8. Listen with an open mind by appreciating what you are hearing and reaching out for new ideas.
9. Enhance the environment for listening by stopping what you're doing (making dinner, gazing at your computer, or whatever), or perhaps moving to a quiet room or clearing off your desk.
10. Listen with empathy and compassion. Put your own agenda aside for the moment and place yourself in the shoes of the other.[19]

In sum, one can use these techniques to become a "listening presence," someone open to the views of those from diverse cultures, religions—and, yes, political parties. The sacred art of listening is about being a presence for understanding rather than for judging; about being open, curious, and attentive to others so they can fully express themselves and feel more alive. Dare we say that Lindahl ought to conduct seminars on listening for members of state legislatures and for members of Congress.

Similar themes are expressed by Senator Snowe in *Fighting for Common Ground*. The moderate Republican represented Maine in Congress for 34 years, including three terms as a senator. Prior to that, she spent six years in the Maine legislature. She allows that there have been even darker days of incivility in Congress. For example, in 1858, during a debate on Kansas's pro-slavery constitution, 50 congressmen brawled on the house floor as the speaker desperately tried to restore order. Today there are rules for decorum in both the House and Senate that are generally followed. However, a principal reason for her decision not to seek reelection was the growing incivility she was experiencing in Congress. Harking back to Lindahl's insights, Snowe writes:

It's obvious there is no shortage of people inside and outside the Beltway who are talking; it's less apparent in recent times that much listening is occurring. Even when we were able to remain polite and observe the niceties of the process, the 112th was the least productive Congress since 1947. I believe we are afflicted with what Shakespeare in *Henry IV, Part II* called "the disease of not listening."[20]

(The 114th Congress may yet top that dismal record.) Civility in Congress ought to be about being willing to compromise and to accept in advance that seeking common ground on important issues is positive and beneficial. So, if you are member of the U.S. Congress, elected to solve the nation's pressing problems, how do you meaningfully reconcile your differences? If a legislator's chief objective is to position him or herself in the next election so as to defeat the other side, the results will surely be the politics of failure. Snowe compares the growing lack of political comity to the increasing "narrowcasting" occurring in the media where an appeal is made to one ideological standpoint or another along with harsh criticisms of the other side. Finally, she notes that the vast majority of political commercials are attack ads that take the place of debate but are no substitute for it. If most of a candidate's time and money is spent trying to diminish the opponent, he or she can avoid having to articulate their own position. In 1990, total spending on the presidential election was $7.2 million; in 2012 it was $524 million—most of it spent on negative advertising.

Author Ben Hubbard interviewed two members of the House of Representatives about the problems of our dysfunctional polity. Democratic Congressman Adam Schiff of northern LA County thinks the degree of polarization in Congress is "getting worse every year." He attributes the situation, first, to the *Citizens United* Supreme Court decision discussed earlier which has brought with it a massive increase in campaign spending and made members of Congress more and more beholden to special interests and their lobbyists (gun lobby, anti-immigrant lobby, etc.). Second, he cites changes in the nature of public affairs media (see Chapter 11). "It's not entertainment if there's not a brawl . . . leaving a very narrow space for moderation." Schiff did note that congressional orientations for new members and fact-finding trips can bring members of both parties together. For instance, he has formed a close bond with Texas Republican Congressman John Culbertson. Both Schiff and his legislative assistant Ann Peifer mentioned the increase in Internet and even telephone vitriol as a symptom of a far-from-ideal political climate.[21] Republican Congressman Dana Rohrabacher of Orange County, by contrast, does not see polarization as that much of a problem and, in fact, thinks it is healthy up to a point. He does, however, feel that the de facto three-day workweek, now the rule in Congress, is undesirable. He agrees with Schiff that getting to know members of the other party is not easy when only half the week is spent in Washington.[22] Without doubt, social interaction builds friendships and makes cooperation on complex legislative action easier. Congress needs to find ways to increase interparty encounters.

David Bornstein in his essay, "The Questions We Share,"[23] reports on "Ask Big Questions," a movement cofounded by Hillel Rabbi Josh Feigelson and students from Northwestern University after an incident involving humiliation of African American students. A big problem in achieving reconciliation, after a painful happening like this, is that a campus forum on such an emotional issue turns into a debate rather than a discussion. That is, people begin discussing *hard* questions rather than *big* ones. The former requires special knowledge to answer, which only some participants may possess, and produces results only if the participants in the discussion share some amount of trust or rapport. In contrast, the big question is one that matters to everyone and that all can answer; for example, "For whom are we responsible?" "How does technology change us?" "When do you conform?" or "When do you take a stand?" By contrast, if you start a student discussion with a question such as, "How can we bring peace in the Middle East?" a few very informed, but very opinionated, individuals will duke it out while most of the others may feel they have nothing to contribute. However, a big question opens a forum in which many people can contribute by speaking from experience and without feeling pressured to win a debate or show loyalty to a particular point of view. Big questions build trust and empathy, which might, at a later point, provide the foundation for asking hard questions in the right setting. For example, one method for building toward a discussion of campus sexual assault is to frame a conversation on the question: "When have you been witness?" rather than, "When does a date become date rape?" Making this exercise work demands listening, and 80 percent of participants reported that the experience transformed the way they listen to others. Over the past four years, Ask Big Questions has taken its model to 47 college campuses and trained hundreds of fellows (students, faculty, and staff) who have in turn facilitated over two thousand conversations involving tens of thousands of students from across religious, racial, ethnic, and LGBT groups. So here is Kay Lindahl's approach transformed from the realm of interfaith dialogue to that of campus conversations. Might not members of Congress or state legislatures become more effective lawmakers if they took the time for a bipartisan retreat at the beginning of the legislative session and used the big-question methodology as an entrée into dealing eventually with hard legislative matters? That question might sound quixotic, but the absence of dialogue, cooperation, and the current inability even to pass legislation makes it appear relevant and necessary.

ELECTIONEERING GONE VIRAL

Senator Snowe concludes her book with a number of wise suggestions on how to make Congress a more effective institution. Although it is not within the scope of this book to summarize all of her suggestions, a few seem indispensable to a life of civility, and very much relate to the prior discussion about listening and dialogue both in the political and religious realms:

1. *Establish a bipartisan leadership committee.* At present, engagement between and among party leaders takes place mainly on an ad hoc basis. Members of the Senate sit separately on committees and on the Senate floor, and have separate weekly policy luncheons and other separate discussion groups. Not much chance for listening under this arrangement. The bipartisan group No Labels (see below) has proposed that congressional party leaders form a bipartisan congressional leadership committee to discuss legislative agendas and seek substantive solutions. Snowe suggests the committee should meet at least monthly with the president. It would include the president pro tem of the Senate (that is, the vice president), the speaker of

the House, and the Senate and House majority and minority leaders, and, according to No Labels, four open slots for two members of
the Senate and House to be determined on a rotating basis in each
Congress. (Snowe, however, believes the four additional slots should
be occupied by the other four official members of the congressional
leadership: the majority and minority whips in the two houses.) It is
amazing, she opines, "the positive things that can happen when you
get people talking in a room together!"[24]

2. *Abolish leadership political action committees (PACs).* Leadership
PACs are separate committees that can be established by Senate and
House members in addition to their regular reelection committees,
regardless of whether they are running for, or serving in, a position of leadership in Congress. The PACs permit more money to be
raised than would otherwise be allowed to support other candidates
or causes. Snowe believes these political action committees ought to
be banned at least for those in Congress not actually in official positions of leadership. The relentless scramble for money contributes to
a significant reduction in the number of days spent actually legislat-
ing and puts congressional scheduling at the mercy of fund-raising
events. One Democratic congressman was told by his leadership to
plan on spending 30 hours per week in fund-raising calls![25]

3. *Establish campaign finance reform.* The Supreme Court's 5–4 decision in *Citizens United v. Federal Elections Committee* (2010) was
arguably the most momentous and controversial ever in the area of
campaign fund-raising. Prior to this, corporations or unions could
make direct contributions to candidates. If they wished to fund
advertising for or against a candidate, they could do so only through
individual contributions from their employees, or their members, to
PACs. Because of restrictions on how much an individual can contribute to a PAC, there are de facto limits on how much a PAC can
raise and how much can be contributed to a particular candidate.
Because the contributions and expenditures of PACs were subject
to disclosure requirements, the public could see who was making
the contributions. After *Citizens United*, these limitations and disclosure requirements no longer controlled electioneering advertising
and independent expenditures, and an avalanche of dollars broke
loose to create essentially unrestricted campaign activity. Hence,
billionaires such as the Koch brothers, Sheldon Adelson, or George
Soros have become paymasters who can massively influence election results all over the country. *Citizens United* came ten years after
the Bipartisan Campaign Reform Act cosponsored by Senator John
McCain (R-AZ) and former Senator Russ Feingold (D-WI) had

required candidates to disclose their major funders and to utilize only voluntary individual donations through PACs rather than corporate or union treasury money. It's a new ballgame now. Although a movement is under way in Congress to repeal *Citizens United* via a constitutional amendment, the current makeup of Congress makes the amendment seem like a very long shot.

To add to the campaign finance problems created by *Citizens United*, the Supreme Court in 2014 (after Snowe's book was published) in *McCutcheon v. Federal Election Commission* overturned, by another 5–4 decision, a section of the Federal Election Campaign Act. It had imposed a biennial combined limit on contributions by individuals and national party federal candidate committees. While the decision kept in place the $2,600 limit on how much an individual could give to any one candidate in an election cycle, it meant that this amount could be contributed to virtually an unlimited number of candidates. The floodgates of political giving were now almost completely open. Politicians and those seeking office are now engaged in a race to raise money that became even more frenetic during the fall 2014 election season while this book was being written. Like many Americans on the right and the left, the authors of this book could barely keep up with the daily volume of e-mails and letters beseeching us to give, give, really give.

PROPHETIC POLITICS

One of the really prophetic voices in the campaign to find religious and political commonalities—the moral center in American life—is Jim Wallis, president and CEO of Sojourners and editor-in-chief of *Sojourners Magazine*. He is an evangelical Christian and public theologian, but he confounds both conservatives and liberals with his reconciling approach. In *On God's Side*,[26] he analyzes the civility issue and comments that the 24/7 news coverage on radio, cable TV, and the Internet blogosphere "doesn't really 'cover' the news but rather fuels the audience's already-held prejudices about what is happening." He stresses that the nation is overlooking genuinely important ideas from both conservative and liberal ideologies that are often lost on the media battlefield. The "best big conservative idea," in his opinion, is personal responsibility. Individuals who make good, ethical, virtuous, noble, and courageous personal choices are indispensable to the common good. For example, the most serious personal choice any parent will make is the decision to make one's children an absolute priority in life. Moreover, programs for social betterment, without the ethic of personal responsibility, often fail and can turn into situations and cycles of dependence. The language of individual responsibility and family values is not often articulated in liberal circles, but in a society adrift in self-gratification and moral relativism it should be. For Wallis, the "best liberal idea" is social responsibility. Strong and responsible families are essential, but so is the health and well-being of "*the commons* in our society"—the places where we come together as neighbors and citizens to share the public square. Good health care and education are crucial not just for one's own children and grandchildren but for all the kids in our society.[27] We are, of course, our brothers' and sisters' keepers.

Wallis also has important ideas on government's role—that it should be a "servant government" where what is important is not so much the size of government but its effectiveness. He asks rhetorically whether anyone really thinks it isn't necessary for the government to make sure our food is kept sanitary, waterways unpolluted, and air fit to breathe. Antigovernment forces, for example the Tea Party, don't believe in a sinless government (nor does Wallis), but these critics should also not believe in sinless markets. Government must be able to "punish the evil" or "reward the good"[28] when it comes to the behavior of huge corporations and banks; because, if it does not do so, who will? We certainly saw the consequences of "sinful" markets that caused the Great Recession of 2008. In conclusion, what is most valuable in Wallis's approach to civility in government is his remarkable evenhandedness and biblically inspired wisdom. We could use more such wise voices in the halls of Congress and state legislatures, and in the nation's newsrooms.

CIVILITY ON THE GROUND: NO LABELS

Ostensibly one of the more encouraging new movements for civility and cooperation in government is the nonpartisan, nonprofit organization No Labels (see earlier discussion in Chapter 8). It was founded in 2010 by long-time Democratic fund-raiser Nancy Jacobson, Republican political strategist Mark McKinnon, and former U.S. Comptroller David Walker with the aim of moving from the old politics of point scoring toward a new one of problem solving. It hopes to do this by getting politicians from across the political spectrum to work together to solve common problems (for example, the gargantuan national debt). On December 13, 2011, No Labels issued an action plan, "Make Congress Work," that included such items as automatic pay-docking for Congress if the federal budget is not passed on time, an up-or-down vote on all presidential appointments within 90 days of their nomination, five-day workweeks for Congress, and a bipartisan leadership council similar to the one proposed by Senator Snowe (above). The following year, No Labels offered suggestions for making the presidency work better, for example, by instituting a question time between Congress and the president similar to what happens in parliamentary systems. As mentioned earlier, the organization is now cochaired by former Utah governor and 2012 Republican presidential candidate Jon Huntsman and Senator Joe Manchin (D-WV), and it published an e-book restating the movement's goals in 2014, *No Labels: A Shared Vision for a Stronger America*.[29] The group can claim one legislative victory: "No Budget, No Pay," directing both the House and Senate to adopt a budget for fiscal 2014 but not requiring a budget conference, became law in February 2013.

VOTE SMART: A PROMISING NEW TOOL FOR DEMOCRACY

A potentially powerful tool for voter literacy, Vote Smart, was launched in 1992 and presents an encyclopedic listing of the voting record of every member of Congress and of the legislators of the 50 states. The organization was founded by a group of luminaries that included former presidents Jimmy Carter and Gerald Ford; former Senators Barry Goldwater, William Proxmire, and George McGovern; and former Massachusetts governor and presidential candidate Michael Dukakis. It bills itself as "perhaps the only positive, uplifting and hopeful story in politics today." The organization is nonpartisan, receiving no financial support from political parties. Author Ben Hubbard toured its impressive website (www.votesmart.org) by typing in the name of his member of Congress, Republican Dana Rohrabacher. There you can find a brief biography of the lawmaker, his voting record listed by category (climate change, gun rights, defense, etc.), endorsements by public organizations, published articles, and additional valuable information. On the "Vote Easy" tab, you can "find your political soul mate" by entering your own position on a dozen of the most pressing issues facing our nation and then watch as this particular politician's yard sign either moves toward you or away from you based on his or her public record.[30] Vote Smart has received endorsements from across the political and media spectrum. If potential voters took the time to compare candidates in both national and statewide races—and then if they actually went out and voted—democracy would be significantly served. Back to civility: If you know what a politician's voting record actually is, you can still disagree with your contemporaries about whom to vote for, but do so with facts and not simply feelings.

CODA: DISRESPECT FOR PRESIDENTS AS A SYMPTOM OF PROFOUND INCIVILITY

Every president, from Washington to Obama, has felt the sting of political opponents. Lincoln, Garfield, McKinley, and Kennedy were assassinated; and attempts were made on the lives of 14 others, including Truman, Ford and Reagan. President George W. Bush was pilloried for his supposed lack of intellectual heft and called a "village idiot." Just before President Obama took the oath of office in 2009, Bush was booed by some of those attending the inauguration. But one could make the case that the level of opprobrium against Obama is about as bad as that ever experienced by a president; and that it not only distracts Congress from fulfilling the people's business but leads to an international sense that the United States has lost some of its exceptionalism. There is no doubt that Obama's missteps—exacerbated by his inexperience, his perceived aloofness, and his political miscalculations—have fueled dislike and disrespect for him among Republicans. But the ad hominem nature of the attacks against him have been really vile. A few examples:

- Congressman Joe Wilson (R-SC) shouting out, "You lie," at his first State of the Union address in 2009.
- Former Alaska governor and Republican vice presidential candidate Sarah Palin describing his response to the murder of Libyan ambassador Chris Stevens as "shucking and jiving."
- Former Arizona Republican governor Jan Brewer publicly shaking her finger at President Obama on the tarmac when his plane arrived in that state in January 2012.
- Rock musician Ted Nugent, in February 2014, deploring the election of a "communist-raised, communist-educated subhuman mongrel like the ACORN community organizer-gangster, Barack Hussein Obama." (Nugent offered a begrudging apology a few days later.)
- The chronic "birther" controversy in which the likes of Donald Trump and a chorus of acolytes tried proving that Mr. Obama was born in Kenya, not Hawaii.
- The signage and conduct of some members of the Tea Party. For example, Obama is a "destructive, unpatriotic black Muslim;" "The zoo has an African, and the White House has a lyin' African" (accompanied by a photo of a lion); an image of the president dressed like an African medicine man and accompanied by the words, "Obamacare = Obamafascism" with a Soviet Union hammer-and-sickle symbol in the center of the quote.

It is also no coincidence that, since the election of Obama, the number of hate groups identified by the Southern Poverty Law Center has grown from 150 to more than a thousand. The so-called "Patriot" or militia movement, which crested between 1994 and 2000 (the Clinton era), tapered off during George W. Bush's presidency, and resurged after Obama's election is, in fact, hyper-unpatriotic. For example, on April 12, 2014, a confrontation took place between the Bureau of Land Management (BLM), accompanied by law enforcement personnel, and militia movement leader Cliven Bundy over his longtime illegal use of federal lands for cattle grazing. Fearing bloodshed, the BLM personnel backed down and called off the roundup of Bundy's cattle that sparked the standoff.

CONCLUSION

It might seem quixotic that the concepts of civility—including politeness, courtesy, active listening, and sincere respect for the views of other politicians and activists—might change the atmosphere in the nation's capital and in state capitals. But these are the virtues that Confucius enunciated to overcome the chaos he experienced in sixth-century BC China, that enabled those 55 members of the Constitutional Convention in Philadelphia in the humid summer of 1787 to compose one of history's finest political documents, and that enabled Mr. Lincoln (granted, with a civility that could be hard edged) to steer the nation through the crisis of the Civil War and the emancipating of tens of thousands of enslaved human beings. And, we should add, a civility that has enabled the people's business to be more or less successfully transacted for the past 227 years since the first Congress convened in 1788. The task of forming "a more perfect Union" will move forward more expeditiously, we believe, if the civic virtues discussed in this chapter are taken seriously by politicians, the media, and the general public.

NOTES

1. *On Liberty*. New Haven, CT: 1859/2003, p. 113.
2. *Fighting for Common Ground—How We Can Fix the Stalemate in Congress.* New York: Weinstein Books, 2013, p. 245.
3. New York: Vintage Books, 2013.
4. Ibid., p. 324.
5. Scriptural citation from authors, not Professor Haidt.
6. Ibid., p. 343.
7. Ibid., p. 371.

8. The late Mr. King is the African American severely beaten by Los Angeles police after a high-speed chase. The subsequent acquittal of police officers accused of using excessive force triggered the 1992 civil disturbances in LA.

9. *Our Divided Political Heart—The Battle for the American Idea in an Age of Discontent.* New York: Bloomsbury, 2012.

10. Ibid., p. 4. Italics by author.

11. *The Big Sort: Why the Clustering of Like-Minded Americans Is Tearing Us Apart.* Boston: Houghton Mifflin Harcourt, 2009.

12. Haidt, op. cit., p. 364.

13. William V. D'Antonio, Steven A. Tuch, and Josiah R. Baker. *Religion, Politics, and Polarization—How Religiopolitical Conflict Is Changing Congress and American Democracy.* Lanham, MD: Rowan and Littlefield, 2013.

14. New York: Basic Books, 1998.

15. Ibid., p. 111.

16. Ibid., pp. 279–85.

17. New York: Continuum, 2002.

18. Ibid., pp. 62–65.

19. www.sacred listening.com/tlc_listening101.htm. Retrieved August 22, 2014.

20. Op. cit., pp. 239–40.

21. Interview with Congressman Schiff on March 10, 2015.

22. Interview with Congressman Rohrabacher on April 24, 2015.

23. http://opiniator.blogs.nytimes.com/2014/08/07/the-questons-we-share/.

24. Op. cit., p. 256.

25. Ibid., p. 257.

26. *On God's Side—What Religion Forgets and Politics Hasn't Learned about Serving the Common Good.* Grand Rapids, MI: Brazos Press, 2013.

27. Ibid., pp. 160–64.

28. Wallis makes frequent reference to the Bible in his analysis, in particular, Paul's Letter to the Romans, Chapter 13.

29. Edited by Governor Huntsman. New York: Diversion Books, 2014.

30. From pamphlet, "Vote Smart—Just the Facts."

Chapter 13

Conclusion—Still Embattled, Still Endangered, but Still Hopeful

By the time this book appears, Congress will undoubtedly still be polarized on many issues, and conservatives and liberals will be duking it out on presidential and congressional electoral podiums, in the press, on television, on the Web, and even sometimes around dinner tables. But our hope is that a softening of positions will begin to occur both because this is an exceptional and centrist nation that always comes to its senses and rises to the occasion when the "general Welfare" is at stake, and because we continue to face stark realities. These include the continuing rise of the Islamic State/ISIS and the lengthy struggle with extremist Islam we will inevitably be facing; the fact of climate change (whatever its causes) and its consequences; and the consensus of the American people that we must do better for our children, for the homeless and hungry in our midst, and for our responsibilities to the global community as the still-exceptional nation.

We began this study by examining the extent to which religion in its many manifestations has always been a factor to be reckoned with in American civic life. It has been a source both of inspiration and of strife, of immense philanthropy and narrow-minded hypocrisy. But the failure to take the religious dimension into account both in national politics and international affairs has led to many missteps: witness the incessant wrangling over the birth control provisions in the Affordable Care Act and the diplomatic blunders during the conduct of the Iraq War.

In Chapter 2 we looked more directly at the religion factor in terms of what people actually believe and how it affects their politics. We then described the very deep rift in our current political landscape that keeps so many people in separate camps and leaves the center dangling. We went on in the next chapter to analyze the philosophical standpoints that have come to frame the religious and secular outlooks that are both now prominent nationally. Does God "await our discovery" or is God unprovable and unnecessary? Are feelings of transcendence simply part of the human condition irrespective of a personal deity? Debate will continue, but religious convictions have the potential to intensify our cultural divide or to do some healing. It may depend on whether conservative and liberal religionists can bridge their considerable divide and jointly seek justice and the common good. We need a big, binding narrative for democracy, but right now there are competing narratives—especially in the media—which are divisive and keep the people's business from getting done.

In Chapter 4, we described the "great debates" over the high-voltage issues of immigration, gun rights, and climate change. Our aim was to look as fair mindedly and empathetically as possible at the stances taken by conservatives and liberals on these issues. We concluded that "true believers need to talk" and that it's really unfortunate how little dialogue is going on between partisans.

Chapter 5 began with an in-depth analysis of how American religiosity has evolved since colonial times and how much it has shaped the American character. This led into a discussion of American foreign policy since the end of World War II and the extent to which religious and ethical considerations have shaped that policy. We looked in particular at our nation's impact on the human rights dimensions of the United Nations Charter and its ongoing activities, on our special relationship with the state of Israel—and the extent to which religious considerations have shaped this bond—and then at our complicated relationship with the Muslim world, especially in light of President Obama's idealistic efforts to heal old wounds between the West and Islam.

The three subsequent chapters (6, 7, and 8) were a kind of workbook exercise in which we attempted to look with sensitivity and fairness at those issues of public policy that mattered most to the right (repealing Obamacare, for example), to the left (such as getting shameful amounts of money out of politics), and to the center—a de facto common ground for everyone—such as balancing the federal budget on a fixed schedule and addressing a torrent of social ills (homelessness, substance abuse, gang violence, etc.) We concluded Chapter 8 by lamenting the loss of pragmatism in the conduct of our national affairs.

We took up the theme of pragmatism again in Chapter 9 to ask whether the "new centrists," with their practical orientation could rescue our endangered democracy from its polarization, cynicism, and disillusionment. We analyzed low voter turnout as a symptom of this malaise, and the rise of independent voters as a consequence of frustration with polarized politics. We also discussed the significant growth over many years in the number of Americans with no religious affiliation, the so-called nones, and theorized a connection between them and political nones or independent voters. In both universes, there is a sense of disillusionment and frustration either with organized religion or the government in their respective failures to reach out and cooperate with those in the opposite camp.

Chapter 10 was an exercise in examining local politics and religion through the lens of a distinctive and prominent region, Orange County, California, with a long-standing conservative reputation but an evolving movement to the center of American politics that reflects the national mood in several respects. In an excursus, we lamented the unwillingness of evangelical Christians and Orthodox Jews to enter into dialogue and cooperation with their liberal counterparts and compared it to the way the Tea Party considers the political left in some sense beyond redemption (at least in this world). This is the case despite the fact that conservative religionists have high moral standards and do much good in their communities, both religious and secular.

We then turned to an examination of the health of the media in an era when cable television, the proliferation of Internet news sites, and the struggle of traditional newspapers to survive have all added to the polarization in society we've been discussing. The television news giants of the twentieth century, CBS, NBC, and ABC, may have tilted liberal but they excelled in professionalism. The same is certainly not true with Fox News, which has become the media arm of the Republican Party in its quest for the presidency. Conversely, there are liberal slants at MSNBC and, to a lesser extent, CNN in their quest for ratings, so that people now choose their TV-news comfort zone and seldom leave it. Result: more polarization. Legacy newspapers such as the *New York Times, Wall Street Journal, Washington Post,* and *Los Angeles Times* still do exceptionally good work, but their desire for balance and fairness sometimes produces false equivalencies, for example, about the climate change debate where both sides often get equal time, even though the preponderance of scientific evidence documents a warming planet.

Finally, in Chapter 12, we examined the civic virtues that might make the business of governing more successful. We reviewed recent scholarship indicating that people are—by genetic predispositions, upbringing, and pivotal life experiences—destined to be more or less conservative or liberal in their standpoints on politics, culture, and morality. This is as it should be, because only the clash of ideas and the back-and-forth of argumentation produce good legislation as well as effective cooperation in all spheres of life. The problem has always been, especially in the current atmosphere in Washington, that civility is profoundly lacking. In particular the careful and respectful listening that produces worthwhile debates over public policy, rather than name-calling and sniping, has been in short supply. Constructive social interaction between members of the two parties in Congress happens less now than in the past. In the body politic, the "big sort" produces classes of people who read and listen to the same media, associate almost exclusively with their ideological kinfolk, and even live in the same neighborhoods as those with similar views.

We're not looking for "kumbaya" moments but for candid ones, moments of political courage when politicians, the media, or a public citizen state their positions with respect and fairness, and a willingness to accept the consequences. We are convinced that such candor and courage would produce a better-functioning government and increase civility and respectfulness in all levels of government and across backyard fences. And we think that conservative and liberal religious organizations could be harbingers of better communication by reaching out to the other side to confront the sea of societal issues facing America from crime to poverty to drug addiction to school dropouts.

In the end, this book is a cry for rationality, dialogue, and cooperation in the world of politics and, indirectly, in the nation as a whole. We all know there is a sickness in the way that politics is being conducted, and we are struggling to find a cure. Our hope is that the publication of this volume will prove to be a modest step in the direction of greater political and cultural health for our nation as it continues striving "to form a more perfect Union."[1]

NOTE

1. From the Preamble to the U.S. Constitution.

Bibliography

Abbott, Walter (ed.). *The Documents of Vatican II*. New York: America Press, 1966.

Albright, Madeline. *The Mighty and the Almighty—Reflections on America, God, and World Affairs*. New York: HarperCollins, 2006.

Balmer, Randall. *God in the White House—A History*. New York: HarperCollins, 2008.

Berlinerblau, Jacques. *Thumpin' It—The Use and Abuse of the Bible in Today's Presidential Politics*. Louisville: Westminster John Knox Press, 2008.

Bishop, Bill. *The Big Sort: Why the Clustering of Like-Minded Americans Is Tearing Us Apart*. Boston: Houghton Mifflin Harcourt, 2009.

Brown, Lester, Janet Larsen, J. Matthew Roney, and Emily Adams. *The Great Transition—Shifting from Fossil Fuels to Solar and Wind Energy*. Washington, DC: Earth Policy Institute, 2015.

Buber, Martin. *I and Thou*. Walter Kaufmann (trans.). New York: Charles Scribner's Sons, 1958.

Burgard, Stephen (ed.). *Faith, Politics and Media in Our Perilous Times*. Dubuque, IA: Kendall Hunt, 2nd rev. ed., 2013.

Burgard, Stephen. *Hallowed Ground—Rediscovering Our Spiritual Roots*. New York: Insight Books, 1997.

Carter, Stephen L. *Civility—Manners, Morals, and the Etiquette of Democracy*. New York: Basic Books, 1998.

D'Antonio, William V., Steven A. Tuch, and Josiah R. Baker. *Religion, Politics, and Polarization—How Religiopolitical Conflict Is Changing Congress and American Democracy*. Lanham, MD: Rowan and Littlefield, 2013.

Dionne, E. J., Jr. *Our Divided Political Heart—The Battle for the American Idea in an Age of Discontent*. New York: Bloomsbury, 2012.

Drinan, Robert F. *Can God and Caesar Coexist? Balancing Religious Freedom and International Law*. New Haven: Yale University Press, 2004.

Gaddy, C. Welton and Barry W. Lynn. *First Freedom First—A Citizens' Guide to Protecting Religious Liberty and the Separation of Church and State*. Boston: Beacon Press, 2008.

Galbraith, Peter. *Unintended Consequences: How War in Iraq Strengthened America's Enemies*. New York: Simon and Schuster, 2008

Haidt, Jonathan. *The Righteous Mind—Why Good People Are Divided by Politics and Religion*. New York: Vintage Books, 2012.

Haynes, Charles and Oliver Thomas. *Finding Common Ground (A First Amendment Guide to Religion and Public Schools)*. Nashville: First Amendment Center, 2007.

Kruse, Kevin M. *One Nation under God—How Corporate America Invented Christian America*. New York: Basic Books, 2015.

Langerak, Edward. *Civil Disagreement—Personal Integrity in a Pluralistic Society*. Washington, DC: Georgetown University Press, 2014.

Lott, John. *More Guns, Less Crime—Understanding Crime and Gun Control Laws*. Chicago: University of Chicago Press, 1998.

Marty, Martian and R. Scott Appleby. *Fundamentalism Observed*. Chicago: University of Chicago Press, 1991.

Matthews, Chris. *Tip and The Gipper: When Politics Worked*. New York: Simon and Schuster, 2013.

Meeks, Wayne A. (gen. ed.). *The HarperCollins Study Bible (New Revised Standard Version)*. New York: HarperCollins, 1993.

Newport, Frank. *God Is Alive and Well—The Future of Religion in America*. New York: Gallup, 2012.

Noonan, John T., Jr. *The Lustre of Our Country: The American Experience of Religious Freedom*. Berkeley: University of California press, 1998.

Patterson, Thomas E. *Informing the News*. New York: Vintage Press, 2013.

Putnam, Robert D. and David E. Campbell. *American Grace—How Religion Divides and Unites Us*. New York: Simon and Schuster, 2010.

Sacks, Jonathan. *The Dignity of Difference—How to Avoid the Clash of Civilizations*. London: Continuum, 2002.

Snowe, Olympia. *Fighting for Common Ground—How We Can Fix the Stalemate in Congress*. New York: Weinstein Books, 2013.

Tocqueville, Alexis de. *Democracy in America*. Harvey C. Mansfield and Delba Winthrop (trans. and ed.). Chicago: University of Chicago Press, 2000.

Wald, Kenneth D. and Allison Calhoun-Brown. *Religion and Politics in the United States* (7th ed.). New York: Rowman & Littlefield, 2014.

Wallis, Jim. *On God's Side—What Religion Forgets and Politics Hasn't Learned about Serving the Common Good*. Grand Rapids, MI: Brazos Press, 2013.

Williams, Juan. *Muzzled: The Assault on Honest Debate*. New York: Crown Publishers, 2011.

Wolfe, Alan. *Does American Democracy Still Work?* New Haven: Yale University Press, 2006.

Index

Abernethy, Bob, 180
Abingdon v. Schempp, 19
Ablow, Keith, 184
abortion, 5, 10–13, 122, 148, 155, 174; Catholic church view of, 11, 13; legalization of, 82; the moral middle's views on, 156; opposition to, 11; and the Texas breast cancer story, 194. *See also Roe v. Wade*
absentee balloting, 154
Abu Ghraib prison, 85
ACA (Patient Protection and Affordable Care Act; "Obamacare"), 9–10, 40, 102, 116–17, 148, 175, 217
ACLU (American Civil Liberties Union), 8, 19, 123
Adelson, Sheldon, 118, 209
Affordable Care Act (Patient Protection and Affordable Care Act; "Obamacare"), 9–10, 40, 102, 116–17, 148, 175, 217
Afghanistan: U.S. aid to, 95; U.S. invasion of, 89; U.S. war in, 95
Africa, Christian-Muslim warfare in, 24
African Americans: abortion rate among, 13; hate crimes against, 136;

in Orange County, 163, 169; voting rights of, 121
African Methodist Episcopal Church, 169
agendas: centrist, 127–44; common, 111–2; conservative (right), 99–109; liberal (left), 112–24
agnostics, 32, 35, 47, 48, 49, 51, 147, 154
Ailes, Roger, 191
Al Qaeda, 21, 95, 112, 139
alcohol addiction, 134–5, 149
Alcoholics Anonymous, 134
Alfred P. Murrah Building bombing, 140
Ali, Ayaan Hirsi, 106
America (film), 56
American Atheists, 7
American Baptist church, 15
American Civil Liberties Union (ACLU), 8, 19, 123
American dream, 83
American exceptionalism, 83–4
American Family Association (AFA), 106
American Family Radio, 106
American Freedom Defense Initiative, 21

American Friends Service Committee (Quakers), 7, 25

American Jewish World Service, 25

American Meteorological Society, 74

American Press Institute, 195

American Psychiatric Association (APA), 13

American Society for the Prevention of Cruelty to Animals (ASPCA), 116

"Americans College Promise" program, 117

Americans for Peace Now, 93

Americans for Tax Reform (ATR), 100

Americans United for Separation of Church and State, 8, 19, 20

Anaheim Christian Junior College, 168

Anderson, Witten, 169

Anglican Church, 26, 80

animal rights, 115–16

antidiscrimination issues, 38

anti-Semitism, 82, 90, 92, 108, 112, 137–8

apocalyptic thought, 2–4, 6

Arab Spring, 21

Arab states, U.S. relationship with, 95. *See also* Iran; Iraq

Arabs, hate crimes against, 20

Armageddon, 6. *See also* apocalyptic thought

Armenian genocide, 87

Asian Americans, in Orange County, 163–4

Ask Big Questions, 207–8

Assemblies of God, 171

Association of Vineyard Churches, 168

atheists, 7, 47, 48, 51, 52, 81, 106, 154

Augustine of Hippo (saint), 12

Barbour, Haley, 56

Baron, Martin, 195

BBC, 195

Beck, Glenn, 36, 178

beliefs: political, 45–58; religious, 31–43; religious vs. secular, 45–7; tied to identity, 56–7

Bellah, Robert, 82

Ben-Gurion, David, 92

Bennett, Phil, 180

Bhagwati, Jagdish, 64

Bible: inerrancy of 22–3, 81; reading in schools, 18–19

Biden, Joe, 5

The Big Sort (Bishop), 202

Bill of Rights, 83, 86. *See also* First Amendment; Second Amendment

Biola Seminary, 23

Bipartisan Campaign Reform Act, 118, 209

birth control, 4, 9–10, 28n12, 40–41, 217

Bishop, Bill, 202

BJP Hindu nationalist party, 24

Bloomberg, Michael, 21

Blue Dog Democrats, 142, 212

Blur: How to Know What's True in the Age of Information Overload (Rosenstiel and Kovacs), 195

Bob Jones University, 23

Boehner, John, 5, 105, 144

Boies, David, 15–16

Boko Haram, 21, 139

Bollings, Eric, 183

Border Patrol, 64

Bornstein, David, 207

Bosnia-Herzegovina, genocide in, 87

Boston Marathon bombing, 140

Bourdain, Anthony, 192

Boycott-Divestment-Sanctions (BDS), 94

Brady, Jim, 68

Brady Act (Brady Handgun Violence Prevention Act), 68–70

Brady Campaign to Prevent Gun Violence, 69

Bramananda, Swami, 48

Brandeis University, 107

Bread for the World, 7

Brewer, Jan, 213

Brooks, David, 57, 58

Brown, Sherrod, 124

Brown, Todd, 171

Bruni, Frank, 48, 50–2
Buber, Martin, 76, 174, 201
Buddhists, 172
bullying, prevention of, 112, 132–3
Bump, Philip, 119
Bundy, Cliven, 214
Bunning, David, 122
Buono, Frank, 6
Bureau of Indian Affairs, 84
Bureau of Land Management (BLM), 214
Burgard, Steve, 147, 167, 188
Burwell v. Hobby Lobby Stores, Inc., 10, 40
Bush, George H.W., 100
Bush, George W., 2, 7–9, 46, 89, 91, 103, 104, 143, 148, 213, 214
Bush, Jeb, 5, 132, 165
Bush v. Gore, 15
Byrd, James, Jr., 136

Calderone, Michael, 188
California State University, Fullerton, 162
Calvary Chapel, 168
Calvert, Cecil, 80
Calvert, George, 80
Calvert, Leonard, 80
Cambodian genocide, 87
Camp David Peace Accords, 6
Camp Pendleton Marine Corps Base Camp, 162
campaign finance reform, 118–19, 124, 209
Campbell, David E., 175
Cao Dai faith, 172
capitalism, 57
Caritas International, 25
Carr, David, 195
Carroll, John, 187–8, 193
Carter, James "Jimmy", 5, 212
Carter, Stephen L., 203–4, 205
Catholic Charities USA, 7, 25
Catholic Church: on abortion, 11, 13; and birth control, 9–10,

28n12, 41; Catholic candidates, 4, 5; child abuse scandals in, 154, 171; in colonial America, 80; on gay marriage, 15, 174; and homosexuality, 14; on immigration issues, 65; interfaith participation of, 174; in Orange County, 167, 171
Catholic schools, 103
Central African Republic, religious violence in, 24, 88
Central America, immigrant children from, 35–6, 63–4
centrist agenda: addressing alcohol and drug addiction, 134–5; addressing religious persecution, 137–9; alleviating poverty and homelessness, 133–4; balancing the federal budget, 127–8; blunting appeal and violence of hate groups, 136; combatting human trafficking, 136–7; confronting terrorism, 139–40; Congressional reform, 129–30; dealing with inner-city gangs, 135–6; education improvement, 131–2; ending elephant and rhinoceros slaughter, 140; energy security, 128–9; hookup culture, 140; infrastructure repair, 131; job creation, 128; Medicare reform, 130; mental illness treatment 140; preventing bullying and cyberbullying, 132–3; prison reform, 140; reflections on issues that matter, 140–1; sexually transmitted diseases (STDs), 140; Social Security reform, 130; suicide prevention, 140
Chancey, Mark, 19
Chapman University, 162
character education, 20
Charlie Hebdo terrorist attack, 21, 38
Chemerinsky, Erwin, 10
Chesterton, G. K. 84
China: abuse of religious freedom in, 90; U.S. relations with, 144

Christ Our Redeemer African Methodist Episcopal Church, 169
Christian Broadcasting Network (CBN), 178
Christian denominations: African Methodist Episcopal Church, 169; American Baptist Church, 15; Anglican Church, 26, 80; Assemblies of God, 171; Churches of Christ, 25; Church of Jesus Christ of Latter-day Saints (Mormons), 5, 11, 14, 172; Coptic Christians, 24, 90, 139; Dutch Reformed Church, 80; Episcopal Church, 15, 26; Evangelical Lutheran Church in America, 15; Lutheran Church, 80, 171; Mennonites, 25; Methodist Church, 15, 80; Missouri Synod Lutheran Church, 23, 171; Presbyterians, 80, 107, 170; Puritans, 79–80; Quakers (Society of Friends), 7, 25; Reformed Church in America, 167; Southern Baptists, 12, 23, 168; Unitarian Universalists, 15; United Church of Christ, 15. See also Catholic Church
Christianity: in America, 83–4; apocalyptic themes in, 2–3; cross as symbol of, 6–7; and divine grace, 48; governmental endorsement of, 9; and the presidency, 4–6. See also Christian denominations; Christians
Christians: decline in share of U.S. population, 154; fundamental, 22–3; global attacks on, 90; on homosexuality, 14; Islamist persecution of, 138–9; persecution of in the Middle East, 112; in Syria, 90. See also Christian denominations; Christianity; Christians, conservative; Christians, evangelical; Christians, protestant
Christians, conservative, 54; on homosexuality, 13; and the teaching of evolution in schools, 16
Christians, evangelical, 2, 3, 22–3, 26–7, 81, 155, 167, 210; on abortion, 11–13; abstaining from interfaith activity, 173–4, 219; on homosexuality, 14; on immigration issues, 65; support for Israel by, 93, 108
Christians, Protestant, 19, 22, 81; on abortion, 11–12; evangelical, 81; on homosexuality, 14; on immigration issues, 65; liberal, 81
Christians United for Israel, 108
Christmas, defense of, 105
Church of Jesus Christ of Latter-day Saints (Mormons), 5, 11, 14, 172
Church World Service, 25
Citizens United, 118–19, 124, 207, 209–10
citizenship, habits of, 46–7
civil rights, 84, 87, 106, 148, 203
Civil Rights Act (1964), 123, 201
Civil Rights Congress, 87
civility: and disrespect for presidents, 213–14; listening as art form, 205–8; need for, 199–200; and the No Labels movement, 211–12; and prophetic politics, 210–11; recent scholarship, 200–4; and viral electioneering, 208–10; and the Vote Smart tool, 212
Civility—Manners, Morals, and the Etiquette of Democracy (Carter), 203–4, 205
Clark, Tom, 19
Clifford, Clark, 92
climate change, 5, 56, 91–2, 115, 217, 218, 219; media coverage of, 181; moral middle's views on, 157; proposed measures to address, 75; scientific consensus on, 72–3; the skeptical view of, 73–5. See also global warming
Clinton, William "Bill," 19, 87, 144, 151, 187, 190
clothing trade, and animal welfare, 116

CNN, 66, 152, 178, 185–6, 191–2, 219

Cohen, Roger, 94

Cohn, Nate, 46, 53

The Colbert Report, 178, 193

Cold War, end of, 144

Collins, Gail, 40

Collins, Susan, 142

Columbian Exposition (Chicago 1893), 25–6

common agenda: addressing anti-Semitism, 112; addressing drug addiction, 112; addressing religious persecution, 112; addressing underemployment, 111; alleviating homelessness, 112; alleviating poverty, 112; balancing the federal budget, 111; combatting sex slavery, 112; combatting terrorism, 112; Congressional reform, 111; education improvement, 112; energy security, 111; job creation, 111; lowering the unemployment rate, 111; Medicare reform, 111; preventing bullying in schools, 112; prison reform, 112; Social Security reform, 111; suicide prevention, 112; support for Israel, 112; weakening street gangs, 112

communism, Soviet, 25

compassion, 27, 55, 65, 81, 148, 155, 173, 201

Compassion California, 173

Comprehensive Addiction and Recovery Act (CARA), 135

Concha, Joe, 182

Concord Coalition, 128

Concordia Lutheran University, 171

Conestoga Wood Specialties Corp., 9

Conestoga Wood Specialties Corp. v. Burwell, 10

conflicts: public nature of, 34–5; in religion, 33; in values, 33

Congressional reform, 111, 129–30; abolition of PACs, 209; bipartisan leadership committee in, 208–9;

civility in, 206–8; suggestions for, 208–10

conservative agenda: countering the attack on conservative religious values, 105–7; deficit reduction, 101; issues common with the left, 111–12; less environmental regulation, 104; lower taxes, 100–1; opposition to immigration reform, 104–5; opposition to labor unions, 108–9; overturning *Roe v. Wade,* 101–2; public school prayer, intelligent design, and vouchers, 102–4; repealing Obamacare, 102; shortcomings of, 201; smaller government, 100–1; support for Israel, 107–8

Constitution: and American exceptionalism, 83; interpretation of, 54

Constitutional Amendments: Second, 66–7; Fifteenth, 121; Eighteenth, 134; Nineteenth, 121; Twenty-First, 134; Twenty-Fourth, 121; Twenty-Sixth, 121. *See also* First Amendment

contraception. *See* birth control

Convention on the Prevention and Punishment of the Crime of Genocide, 86–8

Coptic Christians, 24, 90, 139

Cornerstone Church, 108

Correa, Lou, 164

Costa Mesa, California, 165–66

Council of Religious Leaders, 173

Council on American Islamic Relations (CAIR), 107, 186

court cases: *Abingdon v. Schempp,* 19; *Burwell v. Hobby Lobby Stores, Inc.,* 10, 35, 40–3; *Bush v. Gore,* 15; *Citizens United,* 118–19, 124, 207, 209–10; *Conestoga Wood Specialties Corp. v. Burwell,* 10; *District of Columbia v. Heller,* 67; *Edwards v. Aguillard,* 16; *Engle v. Vitale,* 19;

court cases (*Continued*)
  Hein v. Freedom from Religion Foundation, 8; *Hollingsworth v. Perry*, 15; *King v. Burwell*, 102, 117; *Kitzmiller v. Dover Area School District*, 17; *McCollum v. Board of Education*, 18; *McCutcheon v. Federal Election Commission*, 118–19, 124, 210; *McDonald v. Chicago*, 67; *Murray v. Curlett*, 19; *Obergefell v. Hodges*, 16; *Planned Parenthood v. Casey*, 11; *Prosecutor v. Dominic Ongwen*, 88; *Prosecutor v. Joseph Coney, Vincent Oti, and Okot Odhiambo*, 88; *Roe v. Wade*, 10, 12–13, 82, 101–2; *Salazar v. Buono*, 6; *Shelby v. Holder*, 121; *Town of Greece v. Galloway*, 8; *United States v. Windsor*, 15; *Wallace v. Joffrey*, 19; *Zelman v. Simmons-Harris*, 103; *Zorach v. Clauson*, 18
creation science, 16–18
creationism, 16–18, 168
criminal justice reform, 112, 140
Croatians, killing of, 87
cross, as Christian symbol, 6–7
Crouch, Jan, 170
Crouch, Matthew, 170
Crouch, Paul, 170
Cruz, Ted, 5, 129
Crystal Cathedral, 166, 167
C-SPAN, 185
Culbertson, John, 207
Cuomo, Andrew, 185
cyberbullying, prevention of, 132–3
cybercrime, 137

Dahlgren, Peter, 180
Daily Show with Jon Stewart, 178, 183
D'Antonio, William, 203
Darfur, violence in, 88
date rape, 186
Davis, Kim, 122
dealignment, 143
Declaration of Independence, 86

defense budget. *See also* military spending
Defense of Marriage Act, 14, 37
Deferred Action for Childhood Arrivals (DACA), 62, 105, 151
Deferred Action for Parents of Americans and Lawful Permanent Residents (DAPA), 63, 104, 151–2
democracy, 57; etiquette of, 204; inclusive aspects of, 31–2; need for civility in, 203
Democracy for All Amendment, 119
Democratic Republic of Congo, violence in, 88
Department of Health and Human Services, 64
Dewey, John, 143
dialogue, value of, 71, 76
digital revolution, 179
Dignity of Difference—How to Avoid the Clash of Civilizations (Sacks), 204
Dimel, Rob, 166
Dionne, E. J., 36, 148, 202
Discovery Institute, 17
The Dish (blog), 38
Disneyland, 162, 168
dissent, crushing of, 106–7
District of Columbia, gun laws in, 67
District of Columbia v. Heller, 67
Do, Andrew, 164
Dobson, James, 82
"Documented: A Film by an Undocumented American," 66
Dodd-Frank Banking Act, 115
domestic spending, 101
Dornan, Bob, 164
DREAM Act (Development, Relief, and Education for Alien Minors), 63, 66
Driessen, Paul, 73
Drudge, Matt, 190
drug addiction, 112, 134–5, 149
D'Souza, Dinesh, 56
Du Bois, W. E. B., 87

Duck Dynasty, 56
Dukakis, Michael, 212
Dutch Reformed Church, 80

Easterbrook, Don, 73
e-commerce, illicit, 137
economic fairness, 54
economic stagnation, 31
Edsall, Thomas B., 58
education: higher education costs,
    117–18, 132; improvement of, 112,
    131–2, 149. *See also* public school
    issues
Edwards v. Aguillard, 16
Egypt, religious violence in, 24, 90
Eich, Brendan, 38–9, 106
Eighteenth Amendment, 134
Eisenhower, Dwight D., 55, 81, 144
Eisner, Michael, 106
El Toro Marine Air Station, 162
Elazabawy, Mostafa (Sheikh), 22
electoral politics, patterns of, 53–5
electric vehicles, 129
elephant slaughter, 140
Ellzey, Michael, 162
energy security, 111, 128–9, 141, 148
Engle v. Vitale, 19
entertainment industry, and animal
    welfare, 116
environmental issues, 54
environmental legislation, 73, 104
Environmental Protection Agency, 72,
    144
Environmental Protection Agency
    Science Advisory Board, 104
Episcopal Church, 15, 26
Equal Employment Opportunity
    Commission, 123
Erickson, Erick, 178, 184
eugenics, 18
Europe, attacks on Jews in, 138
Evangelical Lutheran Church in
    America, 15
evolution vs. creation science, 16–18, 155
exceptionalism, American, 83–4

factory farming, and animal welfare,
    116
Fairview Community Church, 170
Falwell, Jerry, 12
Family Research Council (FRC), 133
farm subsidies, 115
federal budget, 101, 111; balancing of,
    127–8, 141, 144, 148
federal debt, 101, 128
Federal Election Campaign Act, 118,
    210
Federal Republic of Yugoslavia, 87
Feigelson, Josh, 207
Feingold, Russ, 118, 209
felon disenfranchisement, 153
feminism, 173
Ferarra, Peter, 73
Fifteenth Amendment, 121
A Fighting Chance (Warren), 113
Fighting for Common Ground (Snowe),
    206
filibuster, 129–30
Findings on the Worst Forms of Child
    Labor Report, 90
First Amendment: on establishment of
    religion, 80, 83–4, 103, 105–6; free
    exercise clause in, 41; litigation, 6–7,
    9, 10, 19, 20, 40
"First Budget", 128
"A Flock of Dodos: The Evolution-
    Intelligent Design Circus"
    (documentary), 17
Foley, Katrina, 166
Ford, Gerald, 212–13
Foreign Assistance Act (1961), 89
foreign policy: American philanthropy,
    95–6; and the Convention on the
    Prevention and Punishment of the
    Crime of Genocide, 86–8; and the
    faith factor, 2; and the formation
    of the United Nations, 85; and
    the International Criminal Court,
    88–9; and the Kyoto protocol, 91–2;
    Obama's outreach to Muslims 94–5;
    relationship with Israel, 92–4; and

foreign policy (*Continued*)
  the Universal Declaration of
  Human Rights, 85-6; and the
  yearly U.S. reports on human rights
  practices and religious freedom,
  89-90
Fox News, 105, 152, 178, 181-8, 190-2,
  196, 202, 219
fracking, 104, 129
Francis (pope), 120
Franklin, Benjamin, 80
Freedom Communications, 179
Freedom from Religion Foundation,
  19
Freedom Partners, 119
Frey, William, 117
Fukuyama, Francis, 58
Fuller Theological Seminary, 23
Fund, John, 56
fundamentalism: Christian, 22-3;
  Islamic, 24; non-Christian, 23-5
Fundamentalism Observed, 23-4
Fundamentalism Project, 23

Galbraith, Peter W., 2
Galloway, Susan, 9
gangs, inner-city, 112, 135-6, 149
Garden Grove Temple (Orange County),
  172
Gardner, Cory, 142, 212
Garfield, James A., 213
gay marriage, 5, 13-16, 82, 101-2;
  churches opposing, 15, 174;
  churches sanctioning, 15; court
  clerk's refusal to issue licenses,
  122; moral middle's views on, 157;
  opposition to, 38; support for, 37;
  wedding cakes for, 38
gay rights, 13-16, 155
genocide, 18, 86-8; Armenian, 87; in
  Rwanda, 87, 88; in Yugoslavia, 87,
  88
G. I. Bill, 143
Gingrich, Newt, 144
Ginsburg, Ruth Bader, 10, 40

global warming, 17, 91-2. *See also*
  climate change
globalization, 31
God, invisibility of, 49-53
Goldberg, Jeffrey, 138
Goldwater, Barry, 212
Gorbachev, Mikhail, 144
Gore, Al, 15
Graham, Billy, 81, 82, 167, 170
Great Awakening, 80
Great Depression, 143
Great Recession, 114, 115, 128, 211
Green, David (Hobby Lobby), and
  bible study in schools, 19-20
greenhouse gas emissions, 91, 104
Greenpeace, 116
Greenwald, Glenn, 195
Gross, Dan, 71
Groundswell, 65
Guantánamo Bay military prison
  (Gitmo), 120-1
Guantánamo Diary (Slahi), 120
Gulf War, 2
gun control, 67, 115; the Brady Act,
  68-70; the moral middle's views on,
  156
Gun Owners of America, 70
gun rights, 66-72, 218; and American
  culture, 66; concealed carry permits,
  69, 70; emotional debate, 67-8;
  and the NRA, 70-2; and the NRA
  weapons training program, 70-1;
  and the Second Amendment, 66-7;
  and self-defense, 67, 70
Gutting, Gary, 50

Habitat for Humanity, 7
Hagee, John, 4, 108
Haidt, Jonathan, 200-2
Halpern, Diane, 58
Halverson, Sarah, 170-1
Hamas, 94, 139
Hanen, Andrew S., 105
Haredi, 24
Harris, Sam, 48, 50-1

Hart, Sande, 173
Hartmann, Thom, 178
Harvest Crusade, 169–70
hate crimes: against African Americans, 136; against Jews, 136; against Muslims and Sikhs, 20; against racial minorities, 136
hate groups, 136, 140, 149, 214
Hawking, Stephen, 50, 129
The Healing Word, 168
Heartland Institute, 73
hedonism, 4
Hein v. Freedom from Religion Foundation, 8
Hewitt, Hugh, 178
Hezbollah, 94, 139
Hice, Jody, 184
higher education costs, 117–18, 132
Hinduism, 24, 48, 172
Hobby Lobby Stores, Inc., 9
Hobby Lobby Supreme Court Case, 10, 35, 40–3
Hoffman, James, 17
Hoiles, Raymond C, 163
Hollingsworth v. Perry, 15
Hollywood entertainment industry, 162
Holocaust, 4, 25, 87, 92, 108, 137–8; denial of, 136
homelessness alleviation, 112, 133–4, 137, 149
homosexuality, 13–14, 82. *See also* gay marriage; gay rights; LGBT community
hookup culture, 140
Hour of Power (TV program), 167
Hubbard, Ben, 1, 25, 62, 82, 87, 123, 134, 139, 147, 166, 199, 205, 212
Huckabee, Mike, 5, 122
Huffman, John A., Jr., 170
Hughes, John, 103
human cloning, 17
Humane Society, 116
Human Relations Council of Orange County, 173

human rights: advocacy for, 35; yearly report on, 89–90
human trafficking, 136–7, 149
humanitarian assistance, 95–6
Humphrey, Jay, 166
Huntsman, Jon, 142, 212
hybrid vehicles, 129
hydraulic fracturing, 104, 129

I Am Cait (TV show), 123
identity politics, 181
ideological silo, 149
immigrants: Central American children, 35–6, 63–4; Muslim, 80
Immigration and Naturalization Service, 64
immigration issues, 5, 35–6, 54, 55, 61–6, 218; compromise on, 64–6; deportation hearings, 64; religious response to, 65; Senate immigration bill, 62–3
immigration reform, 148; opposition to, 104–5; supporters of, 64–5
Immigration Works USA, 105
income gap, 113, 114; in Orange County, 163
independent voters, 142–3, 151–2
Indiana Senate Enrolled Act 101, 14
individual rights, 54
infrastructure repair, 131
Inhofe, James, 115
"In Our Era" (Second Vatican Council document), 138
Institute for Historical Review, 136
Institute for Legislative Action, 70
intelligent design, 16–18, 102
interfaith movements, 25–7, 82, 155; denominations abstaining from, 173–4, 219; in Orange County, 167, 172–3
Interfaith Youth Council of Orange County, 173
International Criminal Court, 88–9
International Religious Freedom Report, 90

International Symposium on Online Journalism, 195

Iran, nuclear agreement with, 95

Iranian Revolution, 23

Iraq: Muslims in, 2; U.S. war with, 85, 95, 217

ISIS (Islamic State in Iraq and Syria), 2, 21, 85, 95, 112, 123, 139, 148, 217

Islam: apocalyptic themes in, 2–4; conservative view of, 129; fundamental, 24; at ground zero, 21–2; radical, 2, 95, 112, 139, 186; Shiite, 2, 24; Sunni, 24. *See also* Islamism; Muslims

Islamic Society of Orange County, 172

Islamic State in Iraq and Syria (ISIS), 2, 21, 85, 95, 112, 123, 139, 148, 217

Islamism, 20–1, 140. *See also* Islam, radical

Islamist extremism. *See* Islam, radical; Islamism

Israel: as apartheid state, 94; creation of, 92; settlements in West Bank and Gaza, 93, 94, 107; support for, 107–8, 112; U.S. relationship with, 2, 3, 92–4

issues of concern, 111–12

ivory trade, 140

Jacobson, Edward, 92

Jacobson, Nancy, 141, 211

Jacoby, Tamar, 105

Jain temple, 172

James, William, 51, 143

Jamieson, Kathleen Hall, 189, 190

Jefferson, Thomas, 80, 81, 83

Jenner, Bruce/Caitlyn, 123

Jesus movement, 168

Jewish Anti-Defamation League, 7

Jewish War Veterans Association, 7

Jews: on abortion, 11–12; attacks against, 21; in colonial America, 80; fundamental, 24; on gay rights, 15; hate crimes against, 136; on homosexuality, 14; on immigration issues, 65; in Orange County, 171. *See also* anti-Semitism; Judaism

jihadism, 20

Jilani, Zaie, 58

Jim Crow era, 84, 87

job creation, 111, 128, 141

job migration, 31

John Birch Society, 161, 167

John M. McKay Scholarship program for Students with Disabilities, 103

John Wayne Airport, 162

Johnson, Lyndon, 93, 201

Jones, Jeffrey, 151

Jordan, Jim, 124

journalism: future of, 195–6; open, 195; pseudo- 187–8. *See also* media

J Street, 93

Judaism: apocalyptic themes in, 2–3; Orthodox, 24, 28n16, 90, 92, 93, 155, 173–4, 219; Reform, 15, 24, 92. *See also* anti-Semitism; Jews

Justice for Victims of Trafficking Act, 137

Kalb, Marvin, 190

Kelly, Megyn, 184, 188

The Kelly File (TV show), 188

Kennedy, Anthony, 9, 41, 122

Kennedy, John F., 5, 213

Kerry, John, 46, 194

Khamenei, Ayatollah Ali, 2, 95

Khmer Rouge, 87

Khomeini, Ayatollah, 2, 95

King, Rodney, 202

King v. Burwell, 102, 117

Kitzmiller v. Dover Area School District, 17

Koch, Charles, 73, 118, 119, 209

Koch, David, 73, 118, 119, 209

Kohut, Andrew, 150

Korean War memorial, 7

Kovacs, Bill, 195

Krause, Allen, 172, 205

Ku Klux Klan, 163

Kurtz, Howard, 181
Kushner, Aaron, 163
Kushner, Tony, 107
Kyoto Protocols, 91–2, 104

Labor-Management Relations Act, 109
Labor Relations (Wagner) Act, 109
labor unions, opposition to, 108–9
Lafferty, Andrea, 170
Lanzillo, Chris, 165–6
La Pierre, Wayne, 71
Last Week Tonight (TV show), 178
Latinos, in Orange County, 163–5,
    167, 171
Laurie, Greg, 169
Left Behind series, 3
leftism, 56–7
Lemkin, Raphael, 87
Lewinsky, Monica, 190
LGBT community, 13–16, 106;
    acceptance of, 133; bullying directed
    at, 133; hate crimes against, 136;
    rights of 101–2, 122–3
liberal agenda: animal rights, 115–16;
    climate change, 115; decreasing
    military spending, 123–4; defending
    LBGT rights, 122–3; distribution of
    wealth, 112–15; gun control, 115;
    issues common with the right, 111–
    12; overturning Citizens United,
    118–19; protecting reproductive
    rights, 122; protecting voting
    rights, 121; reducing cost of higher
    education, 117–18; shortcomings
    of, 201; shutting down "Gitmo",
    120–1; social safety net, 116–17
libertarianism, 57, 200
Libya, violence in, 88
Limbaugh, Rush, 152, 178, 185, 202
Lincoln, Abraham, 84, 213
Lindahl, Kay, 172, 205, 206, 208
Lipstadt, Deborah, 138
listening: importance of, 205–8;
    practices for, 205
Listening Center, 205

Little Sisters of the Poor, 41
lobbying, 113, 207
Long Consensus, 148
Los Angeles Times, 195, 219
Lott, John, 69, 70, 199
Louisiana Science Education Act, 17
Loy, David, 7
The Lustre of Our Country: The
    American Experience of Religious
    Freedom (Noonan), 9
Lutheran Church, 171; in colonial
    America, 80; Evangelical, 15;
    Missouri Synod, 23, 171
Lutheran World Service, 25
Lynch, Loretta, 137

Madison, James, 67, 80, 81, 83
Maher, Bill, 107, 152, 178
"Make Congress Work" plan, 141,
    211
Mali, violence in, 88
Manchin, Joe, 142, 212
manifest destiny, 83
Mann, Charles, 74–5
Maoism, 25
Mariners Church, 169
marriage: nature of, 16. See also gay
    marriage
Marshall, George C., 92
Marshall Plan, 85, 143
Marty, Martin, 23
Marxism, 25
Matthew Shepard and James Byrd Jr.
    Hate Crime Prevention Act, 136
Matthews, Chris, 185
McCain, John, 4, 108, 118, 120, 169, 209
McCollum v. Board of Education, 18
McConnell, Mitch, 137
McCutcheon v. Federal Election
    Commission, 118–19, 124, 210
McDonald v. Chicago, 67
McGovern, George, 212
McKinley, William, 213
McKinnon, Mark, 141, 211
McVeigh, Timothy, 140

media: bias in, 189–92, 219; in
   the digital world, 179, 195–6;
   fairness vs. phony balance, 192–5;
   fraudulent expertise in 183–5;
   narrowcasting by, 206; pettiness
   in, 181–3; print, 177; proliferation
   of, 177–9; pseudo-journalism in,
   187–9; quarantine by choice in, 181;
   religion and values coverage by,
   179–80; scientific reporting in, 190;
   use of fraudulent experts by, 183–5;
   viewers' comfort zones, 185–7. *See
   also* journalism
Media Matters, 186
Medicaid, 101
medical marijuana, 134
Medicare, 101; reform of, 111, 130,
   141, 149
Medved, Michael, 178
megachurches, nondenominational,
   167–71
Melodyland Christian Center, 168
Mennonite Central Committee, 25
Mensinger, Steve, 165–6
mental health issues, 140; and gun
   violence, 71
Merage Jewish Community Center,
   171
Methodist Church, 15, 80
middle, political and moral, 155–7
middle class, shrinking, 113–14
Middle East: persecution of Christians
   in, 138–9; religious turmoil in,
   20–1
Miles, Jack, 2
military spending, 101, 123; reducing,
   123–4
military-industrial complex, 123–4,
   144
militia movement, 214
Miller, William, 3
Mills, James, 6
minimum wage, 114
Mojave Land Reserve, 6
Monahan, Gary, 165

Monkey Trial, 16
Mooney, Chris, 74
Moore, Stephen, 102
moral capital, 201
Moral Majority, 12, 82
moral middle: on abortion, 156;
   on climate change, 157; on gay
   marriage, 157; on gun control, 156
*More Guns, Less Crime—
   Understanding Crime and Gun
   Control Laws* (Lott), 70
Mount Soledad, 6–7
Mount Soledad Memorial Association,
   7
Moynihan, Daniel Patrick, 94
Mozilla controversy, 38–9, 106
MSNBC, 152, 178, 184–6, 191–2, 196,
   202, 219
Murray v. Curlett, 19
Museum of the Bible, 20
Muslims: in colonial America, 80;
   hate crimes against, 20; killing of
   in Bosnia, 87; Obama's outreach
   to, 94–5, 218; in Orange County,
   172; persecution of, 139; Shia 2, 90;
   Sunni, 2, 90, 139; U.S. relationship
   with, 218; as victims of religious
   violence, 21. *See also* Islam

Naphtali, Timothy, 161
narrowcasting, 206
NASA, 115
National Crime Prevention Council,
   133
National Center on Family
   Homelessness, 133
National Council for Community and
   Justice, 82
National Council of Christians and
   Jews, 82
National Council of Churches of
   Christ, 25
National Defense Authorization Bill, 7
National Highway Traffic Safety
   Administration, 131

National Instant Criminal Background Check System, 68

National Oceanic and Atmospheric Administration (NOAA), 72, 74, 115

National Park Service, 104

National Public Radio, 186

National Rifle Association (NRA), 68, 69, 70-2, 115

National Science Foundation, 178

National September 11 Memorial and Museum, 7, 21

National Youth Gang Survey, 135

Native Americans, 80, 83, 84; use of peyote by, 41

natural selection, 18

Nazism, 82

neo-secessionism, 58

Netanyahu, Benjamin, 2

New Deal, 53

new nationalism, 43n1

news outlets, online, 177

Newtown massacre, 67, 71

New York Times, 179, 202, 219

Nguyen, Bao, 164

Nguyen, Janet, 164

Nigeria, religious violence in, 21, 24

9/11 site, memorial cross at, 7

9/11 terrorist attacks, 89, 140

Nineteenth Amendment, 121

Nixon, Richard, 94, 104, 134, 144

Nixon Presidential Library and Museum, 161-2

No Labels movement, 125n1, 141-2, 149, 211-12

No Labels: A Shared Vision for a Stronger America (e-book), 142, 212

nones (religiously unaffiliated Americans), 34, 48, 49, 52, 154-5, 219; political, 154-5, 219

Noonan, John T., Jr., 9

Norquist, Grover, 100-1

North Atlantic Treaty Organization (NATO), 87

Northern Ireland, peace initiative in, 144

NRA. *See* National Rifle Association (NRA)

nuclear power plants, 129

Nugent, Ted, 213

NumbersUSA, 64

Nyhan, Brendan, 57

Obama, Barack: and the "Americas College Promise" proposal, 117; association with Jeremiah Wright, 4; call for impeachment of, 36; on campaign finance reform, 119; contact with Billy Graham, 81; executive orders by, 55, 62-3, 104-5, 151; and faith-based initiatives, 8; on gay marriage, 16; and Gitmo, 120-1; and gun control, 71; on human trafficking, 137; and the ICC, 89; lack of pragmatism or compromise, 144, 150; lack of respect for, 213-14; and the media, 183, 185, 191; Muslim roots of, 5; outreach to Muslims 94-5; participation in Faith Forum, 4; policy on Israel, 2, 3, 93; reproductive rights, 122; Rick Warren interview, 169; on sick leave, 114; on student aid, 132; on the union slowdown, 108; voter support for, 53-4. *See also* "Obamacare"

"Obamacare" (Patient Protection and Affordable Care Act; ACA), 9-10, 40, 102, 116-17, 148, 217

Obergefell v. Hodges, 16

Occupy Wall Street (OWS) movement, 114

Odierno, Ray, 124

oil dependency, 128-9. *See also* energy security

Oklahoma City bombing, 140

Olbermann, Keith, 184-5

Oliver, John, 178

Olson, Theodore, 15-16

O'Neill, Tip, 144

On God's Side, 210
Open Door USA, 138
open journalism, 195
Operation Rescue, 10
Operation Save America, 10
Orange County, California, 219;
    abstentions from interfaith councils,
    173–4; and the battle for Costa
    Mesa, 165–6; Catholicism in, 171;
    ethnic mix in, 163–5; interfaith
    work in, 172–3; nondenominational
    megachurches in, 167–71;
    other faith traditions in, 171–2;
    polarization in, 165–6; political
    evolution of, 161–3; religion in,
    166–7; California, sports and
    entertainment in, 162; Tea Party in,
    174–5
Orange County Interfaith Network
    (OCIN), 173
Orange County Register (newspaper),
    163, 179
O'Reilly, Bill, 184, 187, 188, 194
The O'Reilly Factor (TV show), 184,
    186, 188
Organisation for Economic
    Co-operation and Development
    (OECD), 152
Our Divided Political Heart (Dionne),
    202
*Our Kids: The American Dream in
    Crisis* (Putnam), 132
OxyContin, 135

PACs (political action committees),
    118, 143, 209
Paine, Thomas, 80
Pakistan: attacks on Christians in, 90;
    drone strikes in, 95
Palestine, 92, 94. *See also* Israel
Palestinian Authority, 89, 107
Palin, Sarah, 36, 213
Parliament of Religions, 26
partisanship, 42–3
Parts Unknown (news program), 192

Patient Protection and Affordable Care
    Act (ACA; "Obamacare"), 9–10, 40,
    102, 116–17, 148, 175, 217
Patriot Act (2001), 148
"Patriot" movement, 214
Patterson, Thomas E., 178, 180
Paul of Tarsus (saint), 13
Paul VI (pope), 9
PBS NewsHour, 185
Peace Corps, 143
Peale, Norman Vincent, 167, 170
Pearl Harbor attack, 140
Peifer, Ann, 207
Peirce, Charles S., 143
Pence, Mike, 14
Penn, William, 80
People for the Ethical Treatment of
    Animals (PETA), 116
People's Climate March, 75
Perez, Thomas, 109
personal responsibility, 210–11
personhood, meaning of, 16
peyote, use by Native Americans, 41
philanthropy: American, 95–6; by
    religious groups, 25
Planned Parenthood v. Casey, 11
Planned Parenthood, 13
polarization: media role in, 181–3;
    political, 34–5, 42–3, 55–8, 99–100,
    149–51
Political Action Committees (PACs),
    118, 143, 209
political beliefs, 45–58
political diversity, and genetics, 200
Politics Nation (MSNBC), 185
politics: identity, 181; prophetic,
    210–11
poll tax, 121
Portman, Rob, 124, 135
poverty, 112, 133–4, 137, 149
Prager, Dennis, 56, 82, 106, 107, 115,
    178
pragmatism, 218; loss of, 143–4
prayer in public schools, 18–20, 82,
    102–3

Presbyterian Church, 170; in colonial America, 80
Presbyterian Church USA, criticism of Israel by, 107
prescription drug abuse, 135
presidents: assassination attempts on, 213; assassination of, 213; disrespect for, 213–14; religion of, 4–6
Press-Enterprise (Riverside), 179
prison reform, 112, 140
privacy rights, 54
Project for Excellence in Journalism, 189, 191
Project Reason, 51
Proposition 8 (California), 15, 38–9, 106
Prosecutor v. Dominic Ongwen, 88
Prosecutor v. Joseph Coney, Vincent Oti, and Okot Odhiambo, 88
Proxmire, William, 212
pseudo-journalism, 187–8
public safety, 54
public school issues: bullying, 112; character education, 20; evolution vs. intelligent design, 16–18, 102; moment of silence, 19; school prayer, 18–20, 82, 102–3; vouchers, 103–4. *See also* education
Puritans, 79–80
The Purpose-Driven Life (Warren), 169
Putnam, Robert D., 132, 175

Quakers (Society of Friends), 7, 25
"The Questions We Share" (Bornstein), 207

Reagan, Ronald, 6, 12, 56, 68, 82, 100, 103, 144, 213
Real Time with Bill Maher, 178. *See also* Maher, Bill
Reformed Church in America, 167
Reich, Robert, 113, 114
religion(s): in American compared to Europe, 84; as cause of war, 25; civil, 82–3; in the colonial era,

79–80; cooperation among, 25–7; criticism of, 32–3; cynicism about, 155; and foreign policy, 2; impact of, 1; inclusive aspects of, 31; influence of, 217; need for a morality of accommodation in, 27; and the nondenominational megachurches, 167–71; and political polarization, 203; in the presidency, 5–6; in presidential politics, 4–5; press coverage of, 179–80; and school prayer, 18–20. *See also* Christianity; Islam; Judaism
Religion and Ethics Newsweekly (PBS), 52, 180
Religion News Service, 180
Religion Newswriters Association, 180
Religion, Politics, and Polarization (D'Antonio), 203
religiosity: American, 79–82; and American exceptionalism, 83–4; and American foreign policy, 85–96; evolution of, 218; Judeo-Christian vs. civil religion, 82–3
religious absolutism, 148
religious beliefs, 31–43; vs. public policy, 56
Religious Diversity Fair (Forum), 172–3, 205
religious freedom, 10, 38; yearly report on, 89–90
Religious Freedom Restoration Act (1993), 10, 14, 41
religious persecution, 112, 137–9, 149
religious right, vs. secular left, 33
religious symbols, 6–7
reproductive rights, 40, 54, 122
Republican National Committee, 119
research laboratories, and animal welfare, 116
rhinoceros slaughter, 140
Richardson, Heather Cox, 55
Righeimer, Jim, 165–6

The Righteous Mind—Why Good People Are Divided by Politics and Religion (Haidt), 200–1
right-to-work states, 109, 166
Riley, Thomas F., 162
"Rise of Al Qaeda" (film), 21–2
Rivea-Batiz, Francisco, 64
Robertson, James, 120
Robertson, Pat, 82, 178
Robertson, Phil, 56
Robeson, Paul, 87
Roe v. Wade, 10, 12–13, 82, 101–2
Rohingya, persecution of, 24
Rohrabacher, Dana, 115, 207, 212
Roman Catholic Church. *See* Catholic Church
Rome Statute, 88
Romney, Mitt, 5, 191
Roosevelt, Franklin D., 53
Roosevelt, Theodore, 104, 148, 202
Rosenstiel, Tom, 195
Rubio, Marco, 165
Rwanda, genocide in, 87

Sacks, Jonathan, 204
Saddleback Church, 155, 168–9
Salaam-Shalom groups, 139
Salafism, 24, 29n35
Salazar v. Buono, 6
Salvation Army, 7
same-sex marriage. *See* gay marriage
Sananikone, Prany, 172
Sanchez, Loretta, 164
Sanctuary Movement, 65
Sanders, Bernie, 113, 114
Santorum, Rick, 4, 5
Scalia, Antonin, 67
Schiff, Adam, 207
schools. *See* Catholic schools; public school issues
school vouchers, 103–4
Schroer, Diane, 123
Schuller, Robert, 167–8, 170
Schwarzenegger, Arnold, 187
Science Education Act (Louisiana), 17

Scopes, John, 16
Sebelius, Katherine, 9
Second Amendment, 66–7
Second Vatican Council, 138, 174
Segerstrom Center for the Arts, 162
self-defense, 67, 70
service organizations, religious, 25
sex slavery, 112
sex trafficking, 136–7, 149
sexual conduct, illicit, 137
sexually transmitted diseases (STDs), 140
shale oil, 129
Shapiro, Jesse, 189, 190
Shelby v. Holder, 121
Sheldon, Lou, 170
Shepard, Matthew, 136
sick leave, 114
Siddiqi, Muzzammil, 172
Sikhs, 20, 172
Sirota, David, 58
Six-Day War (Israel), 92
Slahi, Mohammedou Ould, 120
slavery, 84
Smith, Chuck, 168
Snowden, Edward, 195
Snowe, Olympia, 141, 202, 206, 208, 212
Social Gospel movement, 81
social issues, 54
social justice, 81, 171
social responsibility, 211
social safety net, 116–17
Social Security, 101, 116–17, 144; establishment of, 143; reform of, 111, 130, 141, 149
Society of Friends (Quakers), 15, 80
Sojourners, 210
Sojourners Magazine, 210
Soka Gakkai International, 172
Soka University, 172
Solario, José, 164
Soros, George, 118, 209
South Coast Plaza, 162

Southern Baptist Convention, 12, 23, 168

Southern Poverty Law Center (SPLC), 106, 133, 136, 214

Soviet communism, 25

special interest lobbies, 207

Spiritual and Religious Alliance for Hope (S.A.R.A.H.), 173

spirituality, vs. religiosity, 52

Sproul, Robin, 193

St. Andrew's Presbyterian Church (Newport Beach), 170

Stephens, Linda, 9

Stern, Frank, 173

Stevens, Chris, 213

Stewart, Jon, 178, 183, 202

Stewart, Lyman, 22, 23

Stewart, Milton, 22

Steyer, Tom, 118

street gangs, 112, 135–6, 149

Student Aid Bill of Rights, 132

student debt, 117–18

Stuyvesant, Peter, 80

suicide prevention, 112, 140

Sullivan, Andrew, 37–9

Sunrise Rock, 6

"Swift Boat" controversy, 194

Swing, William, 26

Syria, persecution of Christians in, 90

Taft-Hartley Act, 109

Taliban, 89

talk radio, 177–8

taxation 100–1

tax exemptions, 114–15

Taxpayer Protection Pledge, 101

tax reform, 144

Taylor, James, 74

Teaching Tolerance (magazine), 133

Tea Party, 55, 63, 65, 104, 148, 174–5, 188–9, 202, 211, 213, 219

terrorism, 21, 112, 139–40, 149

Texas Freedom Network, 19

Thomas Aquinas (saint), 12

Thorkelson, Tom, 173

ticket-splitting, 143

Tiller, George, 24

Timlin, Robert, 6

Tocqueville, Alexis de, 1, 47

Tomasky, Michael, 58

totalitarian ideologies, 25

Town of Greece v. Galloway, 8

Traditional Values Coalition, 170

Trafficking in Persons Report, 90

Trafficking Victims Protection Reauthorization Act, 137

Tran, Van, 164

transgender individuals, 122–3

Trinity Broadcasting Network (TBN), 170

Truman, Harry, 92, 213

Trump, Donald, 213

Tuesday Group (moderate Republicans), 142, 212

Tutsis, killing by Hutus, 87

Tuttle, Robert, 40

Twenty-First Amendment, 134

Twenty-Fourth Amendment, 121

Twenty-Sixth Amendment, 121

Udall, Mark, 142, 212

Uganda, violence in, 88

Undercover Boss (TV show), 114

underemployment, 111

unemployment, 111, 148

Unintended Consequences: How War in Iraq Strengthened America's Enemies (Galbraith), 2

Unitarian Universalists, 15

United Church of Christ, 15

United Nations: and the Convention on the Prevention and Punishment of the Crime of Genocide, 86–8; discussion on climate change, 75; formation of, 85; and the International Criminal Court, 88–9; and the Universal Declaration of Human Rights, 85–6; as world government, 3

United Nations Intergovernmental
    Panel on Climate Change (IPCC), 73
United Religions Initiative, 26, 173
United States: colonial era, 79–80;
    international influence of,
    85; involvement in wars, 66;
    relationship with Arab states,
    95; relationship with China, 144;
    relationship with Israel, 2, 3, 92–4;
    reports on human rights practices
    and religious freedom, 89–90;
    welfare state in, 96
United States v. Windsor, 15
Universal Declaration of Human
    Rights, 85–6
University of California, Irvine (UCI),
    162, 164
urban gangs, 112, 135–6, 149
U.S. Climate Reference Network, 74
USA Freedom Act, 148
USA Today, 179

values, press coverage of, 179–80
vanden Heuvel, Katrina, 195
Vanguard University, 171
Van Hollen, Christopher, 115
Vargas, José Antonio, 66
Vedic scripture, 48
Vennochi, Joan, 187
veterans, suicide prevention initiatives
    for, 112
Veterans of Foreign Wars, 6
Vietnam War, 87
Vietnamese Americans, 164, 172
violence: in Africa, 88; anti-Semitic,
    137–8; in Egypt, 24, 90; and gun
    ownership, 66–72; of hate groups,
    136; religious, 20–1, 24–5, 88; and
    street gangs, 136
Vivekananda, Swami, 26
Von Drehle, David, 122
voting: absentee balloting,
    154; patterns of, 53–5; voter
    identification laws, 121; voter
    registration, 153; voter turnout,
    152–4, 219; voting rights, 121

voters, independent, 142–3, 151–2
Voting Rights Act (VRA), 121

Wahhabism, 29n35
Walker, David, 141, 211
Walker, Scott, 5, 109, 166
Wallace v. Joffrey, 19
Wallis, Jim, 210–11
Wall Street Journal, 179, 196, 202,
    219
Walsh, Joan, 185
Warner, Mark, 55
War of Independence (Israel), 92, 93
war on drugs, 134
Warren, Elizabeth, 113, 114, 117
Warren, Rick, 4, 155, 168
Washington Post, 195, 219
wealth, distribution of, 112–15
welfare reform, 144
Wellford, Charlds F., 69
whaling industry, 116
"What ISIS Really Wants and How to
    Stop It" (Wood), 4
Whitefield, George, 80
Whitehouse, Sheldon, 135
White House Office of Faith-Based
    and Community Initiatives, 8
White House Office of Faith-Based
    and Neighborhood Partnerships, 8
Whitlock, Mark, Jr., 169
Wildmon, Donald, 106
Wilkerson, Ralph, 168
Will, George, 186
Williams, Juan, 186
Williams, Roger, 79–80
Wills, Gary, 57
Wilson, Joe, 213
Wimber, John, 168
wind farms, 129
Winthrop, John, 83
women: marginalization of, 24;
    ordination of, 155; treatment
    of by Islam, 106–7; voting rights of,
    121
Women, Infants and Children (WIC)
    program, 116

Wood, Graeme, 4

Work Projects Administration (WPA), 143

World Trade Center attack (1993), 140. *See also* 9/11 terrorist attacks

World War I memorial, 6

World Watch List (Open Door USA), 138

Wright, Jeremiah, 4

Yemen, drone strikes in, 95

Yugoslavia, genocide in, 87, 88

Zelman v. Simmons-Harris, 103

Zionism, 92, 93–4

Zorach v. Clauson, 18

Zoroastrian Center, in Orange County, 172

Zucker, Jeff, 192

Zurawik, David, 182, 184

About the Authors

STEPHEN D. BURGARD was for 12 years a professor and director of the School of Journalism at Northeastern University in Boston until his untimely death in October 2014. Prior to entering the academic world, he was a distinguished journalist for 26 years, including 12 years on the editorial board of the *Los Angeles Times* where he won several awards. His published work includes *Hallowed Ground: Rediscovering Our Spiritual Roots* and *Faith, Politics and Media in Our Perilous Times*.

BENJAMIN J. HUBBARD is professor emeritus of comparative religion at California State University, Fullerton, where he has taught for the past 31 years, 15 years as department chair. Prior to that he taught at Marquette University and St. Jerome's University (affiliated with the University of Waterloo in Ontario, Canada). His books (all coauthored) include *Reporting Religion: Facts and Faith*; *The Abraham Connection: A Jew, Christian, and Muslim in Dialogue*; and *An Educator's Classroom Guide to America's Religious Beliefs and Practices*. He was for several years a columnist for the Orange County edition of the *Los Angeles Times*.